Expanding Human Rights

ELGAR STUDIES IN HUMAN RIGHTS

Discourse on human rights has grown ever more visible and essential, with human rights principles being discussed and scrutinized on both the international and national stage. This series brings together high-quality works of scholarship in the field of human rights, primarily in law, but particularly those with a critical or analytical edge, or those taking innovative and interdisciplinary approaches. Books in the series also address concerns at the intersection of human rights and other fields such as trade, the environment, international investment and religion, thus contributing to the depth and breadth of scholarship so vital to understanding the complicated matters at stake.

Titles in the series include:

Refugees, Regionalism and Responsibility
Penelope Mathew and Tristan Harley

Expanding Human Rights
21st Century Norms and Governance
Edited by Alison Brysk and Michael Stohl

Expanding Human Rights

21st Century Norms and Governance

Edited by

Alison Brysk

Mellichamp Chair of Global Governance, University of California Santa Barbara, USA

Michael Stohl

Professor of Communication, Political Science and Global Studies and Director of the Orfalea Center for Global and International Studies, University of California Santa Barbara, USA

ELGAR STUDIES IN HUMAN RIGHTS

Edward Elgar
PUBLISHING

Cheltenham, UK • Northampton, MA, USA

Published by
Edward Elgar Publishing Limited
The Lypiatts
15 Lansdown Road
Cheltenham
Glos GL50 2JA
UK

Edward Elgar Publishing, Inc.
William Pratt House
9 Dewey Court
Northampton
Massachusetts 01060
USA

A catalogue record for this book
is available from the British Library

Library of Congress Control Number: 2016953930

This book is available electronically in the **Elgar**online
Social and Political Science subject collection
DOI 10.4337/9781785368844

Printed on elemental chlorine free (ECF)
recycled paper containing 30% Post-Consumer Waste

ISBN 978 1 78536 883 7 (cased)
ISBN 978 1 78536 884 4 (eBook)

Typeset by Servis Filmsetting Ltd, Stockport, Cheshire
Printed and bound in the USA

Contents

Figures

Tables

Contributors

Joshua Alley, Doctoral Student, Political Science, Texas A & M University

Clair Apodaca, Associate Professor of Political Science, Virginia Tech

Phillip M. Ayoub, Assistant Professor of Political Science, Drexel University

Madeline Baer, Assistant Professor of Political Science, San Diego State University

Alison Brysk, Mellichamp Chair of Global Governance, University of California Santa Barbara

Felipe Gómez Isa, Professor of Public International Law, Deusto University (Spain)

Shareen Hertel, Associate Professor of Political Science and Human Rights, University of Connecticut

Rhoda E. Howard-Hassmann, Canada Research Chair in International Human Rights 2003–2016, Wilfrid Laurier University (Canada)

Valerie M. Hudson, Bush Chair in Government, Texas A & M University

Hyeran Jo, Assistant Professor of Political Science, Texas A & M University

Wayne Sandholtz, John A. McCone Chair in International Relations, University of Southern California

Cynthia Stohl, Professor of Communication and Director of the Center for Information Technology and Society, University of California Santa Barbara

Michael Stohl, Professor of Communication and Director of the Orfalea Center of Global and International Studies, University of California Santa Barbara

Kiyoteru Tsutsui, Associate Professor of Sociology, University of Michigan

Acknowledgements

This volume draws in part on papers presented at the workshop, Expanding Human Rights: 21st Century Norms and Governance, hosted by the Global Studies conference at the Orfalea Center at the University of California Santa Barbara, 25–27 February 2016. We would like to thank all of the participants in the workshop for their contributions to the discussion, as well as the conference and Center staff. We appreciate the skillful logistical and research assistance for the project by UCSB student Bayanne Alrawi. Funding for the workshop was provided by the Duncan and Suzanne Mellichamp Chair in Global Governance and the Orfalea Center, and we are very grateful for their ongoing support of scholarship and academic exchange at UCSB.

PART I

Introduction

1. Expanding human rights

Alison Brysk

In the 21st century, the human rights repertoire established during the post-war years is necessary but not sufficient for global governance of an expanding range of abuses. In the second generation, human rights is caught between realist, structural and multicultural critiques that rights are not enough. On the one hand, critics contend that the classic corpus of rights does not attend to the most vulnerable populations and emerging forms of exploitation – and conversely, that even conventional rights cannot be enforced or fulfilled. To meet these challenges, this project analyses dynamic expansions of the norms and mechanisms of human rights that have emerged in practice. We will chronicle the mobilization of new actors, new rights claims, new institutions and channels of leverage, and new modes of accountability.

We respond to the challengers with affirmative evidence of new mechanisms for enforcing existing rights and new strategies for claiming rights for new populations and processes. As we examine the potential and limitations of these expansions of the horizon of human rights, we will assess how an expanded notion of human rights can lead to new possibilities for reform – and where it still falls short. Our analysis is multi-disciplinary, multi-method, with balanced attention to civil-political and social-economic rights, and draws from a full range of global experience, including cases from Asia, Europe, Africa, and Latin America.

WHAT'S WRONG WITH RIGHTS?

After decades of development, the international human rights regime is under siege in theory and practice. The human rights regime consists of a set of interlocking claims, practices, and institutions that seek freedom, equality, and human dignity, codified in a set of core treaties that establish a normative consensus on minimal standards. In the generation since the 1994 Vienna Conference concluded that human rights are "universal, indivisible, and interdependent," human rights standards, movements, and mechanisms have been extended to embrace a majority of the world's population and almost every aspect of the human condition – at least in theory. The power of human rights has been associated with the democratization of dozens of states, the rescue of many thousands of political prisoners and refugees, and the protection and empowerment of millions of members of vulnerable groups.

But these gains have been uneven, and rights have stumbled on sovereignty, statelessness, and structural oppression. The age of rights has not forestalled genocide, war crimes, forced displacement, resurgent authoritarianism, contemporary slavery within and across borders, deprivation of basic needs, or gender-based violence. Critics of theory and history trace these shortfalls in rights to their basis in Enlightenment liberalism, state-centric enforcement, disregard of economic structures, and alleged Western bias. Thus, there are challenges to the historical exclusions of human rights (Charlesworth, 2005), human rights dependence on international law (Posner, 2014), the relationship between rights promotion and humanitarian intervention (Barnett, 2011; DeWaal, 1997), cultural constructions and projections of rights norms (Goodale, 2009; Stern and Straus, 2013), the bureaucratic politics of human rights organizations (Hopgood, 2013), appropriations of human rights discourse by neo-liberal and security states to subvert empowerment (Postero, 2007; Tate, 2007), distortions of transitional justice (Meister, 2012), and systematic political barriers to implementation (Ignatieff, 2001).

However, a more revisionist sociological approach sees rights as sound in theory but rather skewed in practice, and focuses on restructuring incentives and institutions to close the compliance gap and extend the reach of rights to the full range of violators (Risse, Ropp, and Sikkink, 2013). Rather than critiquing rights as problematic natural law, we see rights as a political construction: a contested and evolving basis for mobilization and empowerment with the capacity for counter-hegemony in a liberal world order (Beitz, 2009; Goodhart, 2012; Hiskes, 2014; Nussbaum, 2000).

In that tradition, in this project we seek to analyse and extend the range and reach of rights. Rights must expand above and below the state to the power relations of globalization and "private wrongs" of non-state actors, and widen the community of rights-bearers from dominant citizens to include all subjects of power. This means that our best strategy for expanding rights is to build upon the dynamic practice of the global community, which continues to transcend the limitations of rights by crafting new norms, campaigns, and enforcement strategies.

Our analysis thus extends human rights scholarship that moves beyond law as the foundation of the regime to a more multi-faceted complex of foreign policy, campaigns, and other forms of global governance. Across this project, we take law as a possible means to the realization of rights, not an end or sufficient goal. Overall, our project builds the case for a sociological and strategic analysis of law and the shifting relationship between international norms, transnational mechanisms, and state implementation (Brysk, 2013b). The path from norms to fulfillment may involve some combination of domestic implementation, civil society empowerment, transnational socialization, and global accountability.

CONSTRUCTING RIGHTS

All human rights campaigns must work to establish standards of violation, legitimate bearers of rights, responsibility to address human rights claims, and implementation mechanisms. But beyond the established human rights model, for "private wrongs" committed by non-state actors and transnational forces, rights campaigns must work to identify new rights standards, find new leverage points, and establish new responsibilities for states and global governance. As a social imaginary, a political doctrine of human rights must answer three questions (Brysk, 2005): Who is human? What is right? And who is responsible?

The history of human rights is an expansion of rights-bearers from white male Christian property-owning citizens towards universalism, progressively incorporating slaves, women, refugees, workers, ethnic, religious, and sexual minorities. But rights still struggle to incorporate "people out of place" who stand outside the citizenship order or those who demand protection and empowerment from non-state actors (Brysk and Shafir, 2007). In the 21st century, some of these populations have gained greater capacity to mobilize for rights, notably indigenous peoples, sexual minorities, and global workers. The passage of new United Nations and regional instruments and resolutions for indigenous rights, economic migrants, domestic workers, and LGBT non-discrimination testify to both the expansion of rights subjects and the incorporation of new sectors of global civil society. The chapters by Felipe Gómez Isa, Kiyoteru Tsutsui, and Phillip M. Ayoub discuss the construction and recognition by global governance of new movements for indigenous peoples, descent-based discrimination, and sexual minorities.

Meanwhile, the broadening domain of power relations in a globalized world demands and inspires new claims for rights and governance. Patterns of development in the 21st century highlight the salience of access to basic resources such as food and water to fulfill long-recognized economic and social rights to life and health. Growing recognition of gender violence in wartime, urban streets, and families highlights the gap between women's rights and physical security in public, private and cross-border spaces. Madeline Baer's treatment of water suggests conversely that globalization is the predominant challenge to realization of the right to water. Alison Brysk's discussion of expanding claims for women's security from sexual violence highlights a gendered gap in core physical integrity rights in the international regime and the interdependence of security with the most fragile reproductive rights. Michael and Cynthia Stohl profile the development of corporate social responsibility as an economic and social rights norm, accountability regime, and response to global civil society campaigns.

Even as global governance grapples with enforcement mechanisms for both established and emerging rights through international law, diplomacy, and transnational action networks, the human rights regime has also expanded its reach. New and strengthening remedies for human rights include regional institutions, new pathways of domestic and grassroots appeals, and rights-based foreign policy promotion. On the affirmative side of foreign policy promotion, Valerie M. Hudson outlines the emergence of feminist foreign policy as a rights-based bilateral strategy for empowerment. At the multilateral level, Wayne Sandholtz considers the value added by regional organizations to extend the reach of rights, deepen horizontal accountability, and transcend cultural claims against universalism. At the domestic level, Shareen Hertel shows horizontal expansion of food rights claims that circumvents weak international mechanisms and reinforces citizenship.

Finally, we must consider who is responsible for fulfilling new rights claims and enforcing rights in ungoverned domains of power relations. Beyond the state, new addressees for global governance and rights violations include transnational corporations, sub-national rebel groups, and international organizations themselves. In the absence of true global government, international institutions may still exercise authority as peacekeepers, aid providers, economic managers, or even transitional governments in post-conflict states – and with such power comes the potential for abuse. At a more structural economic level, Claire Apodaca considers how and when human rights standards extend further to international organizations' economic programs that affect basic rights of children's survival. On the war crimes side of the rights agenda, Hyeran Jo and Joshua Alley show the expansion of human rights accountability to non-state militaries that exercise authority in conflict zones. Meanwhile, Rhoda E. Howard-Hassmann's contribution shows how state sovereignty remains a barrier to the right to food highlighting the limits to expanding responsibility in an inter-state system.

These pathways to constructing rights through norms, claims, mechanisms, and responsibilities are interdependent in practice and reveal common themes for analysis. Baer's exploration of water involves new norms, actors, and responsibilities at the same time – yet she shows that norm promotion and mobilization for water as a human right are a necessary condition for proposing new responsibilities for non-state actors to provide access to water. The new role of meso-level regional institutions cuts across Sandholtz's discussion of domestic incorporation of human rights law, inter-American norms for marginalized groups discussed by Brysk and Gómez Isa, and Ayoub's chronicle of European Union norms as mobilizing opportunities for LGBT movements in recalcitrant states. Thus, we must consider the regional venue of global governance as a source of new claims, empowerment of actors marginalized in their own states, and enforcement mechanisms at the same time – and assess the panoply of regional organizations for their ability to play this range of roles. Moreover, in most of our cases, there is an interplay between identities and institutions: for Ayoub, Hertel, Tsutsui, Gómez Isa, Brysk, Hudson, and sometimes Jo, a mobilization based on a marginalized identity requires new forms of access, accountability, and enforcement.

EXPANDING RIGHTS

What then can we learn from our survey of new pathways for expanding rights that can inform human rights scholarship and practice? First, we see that our chronicle of new claims and mechanisms must engage and extend the existing literatures on the struggle for new rights norms (Brysk, Baer, Hertel), global civil society (Ayoub, Tsutsui), and compliance (Gómez Isa, Sandholtz, Jo). In each case, we add new dynamics to the relevant literature. For new norms, Brysk and Baer suggest that movement framing now includes crafting new frames, Baer and Hertel show that advocates may not be traditional human rights groups and can transcend traditional gatekeepers, and Hertel shows vernacular alternatives to norm diffusion. On global civil society, Ayoub and Tsutsui depict horizontal transnational networks and multi-level appeals that go beyond the boomerang effect of pressure from above and below the state. In terms of compliance, Gómez Isa and Sandholtz add to the repertoire of enforcement the adoption of international legal norms as "benchmark" or reference points, while these authors along with Stohl and Stohl and Jo add to the fulfillment pathway the power of recognizing new stakeholders or new standing.

Next, several of our authors expand the conventional picture and counter the critique of human rights as a hegemonic or Northern agenda.

Hertel, Baer, and Tsutsui depict the creation of new norms from below, while Sandholtz and Stohl and Stohl consider alternatives to US power for enforcement. The interdependence of civil-political and bodily integrity rights with social-economic rights theorized by Howard-Hassmann is also central to the analysis of Baer, Hertel, Apodaca, and Gómez Isa. Our assessment of the potential for these new forms of the power of human rights beyond the conventional agenda ranges from Hertel's positive innovation to Howard-Hassman's pessimistic evaluation of nationalist manipulation in the global South.

To account for these variations, our investigations deepen the conventional wisdom and push beyond. In our cases, the type or status of rights matters for new claims: Are the rights claimed individual or collective? Derogable or absolute? Historic or innovative? This is true across Sandholtz's cases of regional jurisprudence, Tsutsui's Japanese ethnic mobilizations, and Brysk's reproductive rights gap alike. In general, more collective, derogable and innovative rights are most resistant to expansion.

Another consideration that helps to advance our analysis is comparative context. In many cases, rights are not the only kind of claims, and rights compete with or borrow from alternate frames of security, development, corporate responsibility, humanitarian, and national identity norms. This is characteristic of problems for Hudson, Baer, Stohl and Stohl, Hertel, and Apodaca. But in each of these cases, a broader repertoire of claims seems to facilitate broader initiatives and coalitions.

Most rights struggles occur at multiple levels. Even as the chapters stress less studied meso or local levels of analysis, we frequently find that state sovereignty remains an impediment or at least a filter for expanding rights. At the state level, rights claims are enabled, blocked, complemented, or in some way transformed by citizenship for Howard-Hassmann, Hertel, and Ayoub.

Overall, we witness more expansion of claims and pathways than responsibilities. A dearth of duty-bearers, distorted incentives for compliance, and blocked pathways to fulfillment are the limiting factors in most of our cases. We will see this limitation grow in the course of the volume, as the emergence of new actors and frames often founders on old governance dilemmas.

In most cases, rights expansion encounters backlash, resistance, counter-frames, or silences, and this is a critical determinant of the success of new campaigns and mechanisms. Baer, Tsutsui, Ayoub, Gómez Isa, Brysk, Howard-Hassmann, Hudson, and Sandholtz all report important levels of challenge and even counter-mobilization to rights initiatives. In all of these cases, as emphasized by Hudson and Sandholtz, the political process of rights initiatives becomes a significant resource or impediment – above and beyond the content and subjects of rights.

This leads to our key conclusion: process matters. Even as we expand rights, we must continue to defend and deepen rights won in a previous era, and new claims and responsibilities depend on older forms of empowerment and accountability: from citizenship to anti-discrimination norms. Moving forward, our contributors will evaluate the potential of evolving processes by asking:

- Does the process empower new or different actors?
- Are new norms sustainable and resilient to challenges and competition?
- Do new processes cumulate, complement or compete with prior practices?
- How do new forms of leverage and accountability address the shifting power relations of globalization?

If we can chart the potential, limitations, and implications of these unexpected expansions of rights, this project may provide a resource for the next wave of the process by the next generation of human rights activists. To begin, we unfurl a fresh map to chart our explorations of the new frontiers of the quest for human dignity.

REFERENCES

Barnett, Michael (2011). *The Empire of Humanity: A History of Humanitarianism*. Ithaca, NY: Cornell University Press.
Beitz, Charles (2009). *The Idea of Human Rights*. Oxford: Oxford University Press.
Brysk, Alison (2005). *Human Rights and Private Wrongs: Constructing Global Civil Society*. New York: Routledge.
Brysk, Alison (2013a). *Speaking Rights to Power: Constructing Political Will*. New York: Oxford University Press.
Brysk, Alison (ed.) (2013b). *The Politics of the Globalization of Law: Getting from Rights to Justice*. New York: Routledge.
Brysk, Alison and Gershon Shafir (eds) (2007). *People Out of Place*. Berkeley, CA: Routledge.
Charlesworth, Hilary (2005). "Feminist Ambivalence About International Law," *International Legal Theory* **11**: 1–8.
DeWaal, Alex (1997). *Famine Crimes: Politics and the Disaster Relief Industry*. London: Oxford University Press.
Goodale, Mark (2009). *Surrendering to Utopia*. Stanford, CA: Stanford University Press.
Goodhart, Michael (2012). "Human Rights and the Politics of Contestation," in Mark Goodale (ed.), *Human Rights at the Crossroads*. Oxford: Oxford University Press, pp. 347–62.
Hiskes, Richard (2014). "A Very Promising Species: From Hobbes to the

Human Right to Water," in Steve J. Stern and Scott Straus (eds), *The Human Rights Paradox: Universality and Its Discontents*. Madison, WI: University of Wisconsin Press, pp. 224–46.
Hopgood, Stephen (2013). *The Endtimes of Human Rights*. Ithaca, NY: Cornell University Press.
Ignatieff, Michael (2001). *Human Rights as Politics and Idolatry*. Princeton, NJ: Princeton University Press.
Meister, Robert (2012). *After Evil: A Politics of Human Rights*. New York: Columbia University Press.
Nussbaum, Martha (2000). *Women and Human Development: The Capabilities Approach*. New York: Cambridge University Press.
Posner, Eric (2014). *The Twilight of Human Rights Law*. New York: Oxford University Press.
Postero, Nancy (2007). *Now We Are Citizens*. Stanford, CA: Stanford University Press.
Risse, Thomas, Steve Ropp, and Kathryn Sikkink (eds) (2013). *The Persistent Power of Human Rights: From Commitment to Compliance*. New York: Cambridge University Press.
Stern, Steve J. and Scott Straus (eds) (2013). *The Human Rights Paradox: Universality and Its Discontents*. Madison, WI: University of Wisconsin Press.
Tate, Winifred (2007). *Counting the Dead: The Culture and Politics of Human Rights Activism in Colombia*. Berkeley, CA: University of California Press.

PART II

Expanding actors

2. A struggle for recognition and rights: expanding LGBT activism

Phillip M. Ayoub

This chapter offers an account of movement mobilization surrounding LGBT (lesbian, gay, bisexual, and trans) activism.[1] For a movement that has emerged with speed and suddenness on the global stage of 21st century human rights activism, it sheds light on the transnational dynamics of mobilizing new actors and new identities across borders, as well as extending rights to "new" populations. It thus builds on earlier conceptions of national political opportunity structures for mobilization in order to look at the emergence of new activism and rights in world politics more broadly (see also Tsutsui and Gómez Isa, this volume). I ask: What types of new actors comprise LGBT movements, and how do they organize across borders? In doing so, I explore the roles of transnational identities and public spheres in shaping the claims of recognition on behalf of new norm entrepreneurs in human rights politics.[2] I argue that the use of available transnational identities and resources – social spaces, organizational capacity and personal networks – drives a process that has brought together otherwise disparate groups of activists, shaping the transnational mobilization around sexual minority issues. These cross-border opportunities among states – in interaction with meso-level institutions – serve as mobilizing structures that bring together distinct and ever-changing

[1] The chapter focuses primarily on activism by lesbian and gay activists. I use the acronym LGBT because, while the chapter does not explore bisexual and trans* activism specifically, these activists and their goals have been part of the broader movement – though often made invisible – and are increasingly part of the rhetoric for advancing the rights of people with sexual orientations and gender identities that fall outside the hetero-norm.

[2] Norm entrepreneurs are actors who try to "'mobilize popular opinion and political support both within their host country and abroad,' 'stimulate and assist in the creation of likeminded organizations in other countries,' and 'play a significant role in elevating their objectives beyond its identification with the national interests of their government'" (Nadelmann, 1990, p. 482; cited in Acharya, 2004, p. 248).

constellations of transnational actors. In this chapter I chart the mobilization of new norm entrepreneurs in human rights politics as well as their innovative transnational strategies for human rights promotion, thus addressing two core themes of the volume.

I use the case of Europe, a region at the forefront of human rights activism surrounding sexual minorities, to illustrate these transnational dynamics. The fall of the Berlin Wall resulted in the unprecedented exposure of former Communist Bloc states to Western European norms and institutions. Especially in new member states, Europe's enduring network of transnational advocacy and the European Union's (EU) rules and regulations serve as a case for understanding the introduction and construction of prominent 21st century human rights discourses. This is due to variation in the presence of LGBT people in both popular discourse and legal standing across countries, with comparatively less recognition east of the former Iron Curtain. While discussing the contemporary European movement in general, the analysis will also focus on a case study of LGBT activists in Germany and Poland, making explicit the multi-level connections between the transnational, the national and the local by illustrating how Polish and German activists used resources available in Berlin to pressure the Polish society and state. The involvement of groups across the Oder-Neisse border is representative of a type of activism that Imig and Tarrow call "cooperative transnationalism" (2001, p. 17). The concept, which I argue is an increasingly common form of human rights activism used by sexual minorities, describes a process in which the actors involved are transnational but the foreign target of contention is domestic. The research methods employed for this chapter include expert interviews, archival research and participant observation.[3]

This chapter proceeds in five sections. First, I sketch the history of the transnational nature of the movement, which leads up to an overview of the current state of LGBT activism in Europe. Second, I present 21st century LGBT activism in Poland as an example for thinking through

---

[3] Much of the data is drawn from an organizational survey (described below) and 82 semi-structured interviews I conducted for a larger project on LGBT activism in the EU (Ayoub, 2016). The interviews were primarily with activists and politicians who were asked about their motivations and the strategies behind their mobilization, as well as their perception of the outcomes of that mobilization. Archival research uncovered organizational documents, mission statements, grant applications and press releases relating to transnational activism in Poland. Finally, participant observation at various LGBT marches, prides, street fairs and strategic activist meetings in Poland and Germany since 2005 also informed this analysis.

opportunities for mobilization beyond the arena of the nation state. Third, I discuss the varying contextual settings of German and Polish gay life in urban areas – focusing on Berlin and Warsaw – and how the resources and networks in Berlin were used to support the recognition of sexual minorities in Poland. Fourth, I present the set of new transnational actors involved in Polish LGBT activism and how their identities brought them together transnationally, concentrating on German-Polish cooperation. I close by reflecting on the strengths and limitations of such processes, as well as implications for future research, which needs to explore the effects of anti-gay transnational activism – acknowledging that human rights standards of appropriate behavior concerning sexual minorities smack of outside imposition to some and welcome modernity to others. Indeed, the chapter focuses primarily on the expansion of human rights politics to include LGBT people. It has less room to chart the dynamics of resistance and backlash to such rights, which are often portrayed as external and incompatible with local national tradition (see Ayoub, 2014; also see Baer and Tsutsui, this volume).

A LONG HISTORY OF "NEW" TRANSNATIONAL ACTIVISM

On a spring day in 1933, the renowned German sexologist Magnus Hirschfeld packed his bags and embarked on a world tour, never to return to the city that he helped make known for its revolutionary thought on sexualities (Beachy, 2014). While temperatures may have been warm on that May day in Berlin, the political climate was icy cold for early movements by sexual minorities – small movements that had made notable advances in Germany during the four decades preceding Hirschfield's departure. The leaders of those early movements saw the situation for homosexuals as at least partially shared across borders – an idea that still resonates with many of their contemporary counterparts. With letters pouring in from across the continent by individuals describing similar desires and predispositions, the writings and activism of Hirschfeld, and Karl Heinrich Ulrichs before him, would mobilize an identity group that referred to themselves as homosexuals (or *urnings* in Ulrichs's time) – and later as gays and lesbians. The movement's early epicenter was in Berlin, but its reach was far. Hirschfeld's Wissenschaftlich-humanitäre-Komitee (Scientific Humanitarian Committee), Institut für Sexualwissenschaft (Institute for Sexual Sciences) and the Weltliga für Sexualreform (World League for Sexual Reform) – founded in 1897, 1919 and 1928, respectively – were the earliest precursors to modern LGBT organizations (Kollman and Waites,

2009, p. 3). Among their active research on sexuality and gender identity – including the theorization of the "third sex" – these groups petitioned against the draconian Paragraph 175, which criminalized homosexual relations. Reflective of their international orientation, research studies were organized in collaboration with new groups in other German cities, the Netherlands and the United Kingdom. Additionally, a Hirschfeld protégé, Henry Gerber, would help found an early organization in Chicago in 1924 (Dececco and Bullough, 2002, p. 25).

When the national socialists burned Hirschfeld's research in 1933, it would symbolically foreshadow the extinguishing of the emerging movement in Europe (neutral Switzerland's *Der Kreis* remained the only exception). That said, the movement's transnational fervor remained intact. With the founding of Amsterdam's Cultuur en Ontspanningscentrum (Center for Culture and Leisure) in 1946, the center of the movement shifted to the Netherlands during its post-war homophile period (Rupp, 2011).[4] While it did not encompass them directly, the universal human rights rhetoric of the post-war years greatly resonated with sexual minorities. They often employed this rhetoric, and continue to employ it, in their movement claims. Homophile groups also had a strong transnational character, which manifested itself in a new organization, the International Committee for Sexual Equality (ICSE), founded in Amsterdam in 1951. The initial meeting was comprised of activists from several European countries, including Denmark, Germany, Great Britain, Italy, the Netherlands and Switzerland (Beachy, 2014).

It was later, with increasing international ties among states, that the movement saw the possibility to effectively place political pressure on states from the outside by seeking out the support of international organizations (IOs) and other states (Ayoub and Paternotte, 2014a). The politics of the post-Stonewall Gay Liberation Movement reverberated across borders, and various enduring international non-governmental organizations (INGOs) emerged. In Europe, the International Gay Association (later the International Lesbian, Gay, Bisexual, Trans and Intersex Association, ILGA) first convened in 1978. Its European regional branch (founded in 1996) would form a close relationship with the European Union (EU) institutions they lobbied. More recently, trans organizing has also emerged centrally in European human rights activism, and with its umbrella organization, Transgender Europe, it has also adopted a strong transnational orientation (Balzer and Hutta, 2014). Similarly, US-based Outright lobbies the United Nations (UN) in hopes of attracting

[4] Homophile organizations often use inconspicuous names, like the COC.

international attention on human rights violations against LGBTIQ (Intersex and Queer) people (Thoreson, 2014). While umbrella organizations like these have had a complicated historical relationship with the UN, they have played an important gatekeeper role in bringing the issue to the fore of human rights discourses internationally.[5]

In all of these international examples, a felt identification – such as the experience of "coming out" to family, for many – with other sexual minorities was paramount to mobilization (Adam, Duyvendak and Krouwel, 1998; Tremblay, Paternotte and Johnson, 2011). Indeed, some commentators have argued that LGBT rights are particularly well suited to universal human rights norms because the people they represent "are uniquely dispersed in all cultures, states, economic levels, ethnicities and religions" (Kneefel, 2016). A strong understanding of such transnational LGBT identity is described by Allen (1996):

> Gay men the world over live similar lives and dream similar dreams. The poet WH Auden invented a word for this international homo-culture, "homintern", meaning the life experiences and innate personality traits that connect gays more closely with gays from other countries than with the heterosexual citizens or their own country, or even their own family. I know I often feel closer to a gay foreigner I've known for five minutes than to heterosexual relations I have known all my life. (cited in Binnie, 2004, p. 37)

This phenomenon of awaking transnational dimensions of group identity has been a driver in transnational LGBT human rights activism, at times transcending other components of individual identity to connect potential actors across states.

As the above history suggests, it is thus with some caution that I speak of the "new" transnational activism surrounding LGBT rights, and instead address the "expanding" construction of such rights as part of human rights, as well as the expanded forms of activism and alliances that it fosters. Indeed, for the better part of the 20th century, sexual minorities had cultivated transnational dimensions to their identities and mobilizations in all of the distinct periods of their activism. The term "expanding" is appropriate for this volume because movements by

---

[5] ILGA was the first international advocacy group to attain consultative status at the UN in 1993, but it lost it the following year – finally attaining it again in 2012. Other UN consultative members include: LBL in Denmark, COC in the Netherlands, FELGT in Spain, LSVD in Germany, ABGLT in Brazil, IGLHRC in the USA (see http://ilga.org/ecosoc-lgbt-voices-at-the-united-nations-ecosoc-council-vote-grants-consultative-status-to-ilga/ for more history, accessed 20 January 2016).

sexual minorities have found a far more prominent role within the human rights discourse of the 21st century – a core factor that makes them look quite different today. A 2011 speech by United States Secretary of State Hillary Clinton in Geneva illustrates the emerging and (in the view of some onlookers) unambiguous place of LGBT people among other groups in human rights discourse (see also Hudson, this volume):

> Like being a woman, like being a racial, religious, tribal, or ethnic minority, being LGBT does not make you less human. And that is why gay rights are human rights, and human rights are gay rights.[6]

While Clinton's speech in Geneva is just one example of human rights discourse including LGBT people, it is symbolic of a changed normative context for the global LGBT movement – a context activists have carefully crafted for over a century of movement struggle. The newfound global visibility of LGBT people has changed much about the actors, claims and strategies of the contemporary movement. It has also led to intensified transnational ties among its members.

Europe is exemplary of such new transnational LGBT activism. LGBT rights as human rights are increasingly codified as a European value in the rhetoric of European IOs, and we can chart intensified cross-border transactions between LGBT advocates. Across the 47 Council of Europe member states, the ILGA-Europe network included 291 member organizations in 2010, and that number has risen considerably in recent years. An organizational survey of that group, which yielded a 62 percent response rate, provided descriptive statistics of the transnational network. Table 2.1 demonstrates that the average organization relies heavily on volunteer work, and the majority function on relatively low financial resources. Furthermore, the data also show that these resources are not always procured within the domestic sphere. Especially for states east of the former Iron Curtain, they relied on foreign resources for much of their funding. As I will demonstrate with the ethnographic case study, these resources (both human and material) are often the result of cooperative transnationalism. Cooperative practices between Polish and German organizations provide an illustration, demonstrating the discrepancies between countries in terms of LGBT people being conceived of as having human rights, and how new actors and activism are fueled by transnational cooperation.

---

6 http://photos.state.gov/libraries/belize/231771/PDFs/Remarks%20in%20Recognition%20of%20International%20Human%20Rights%20Day.pdf (accessed 20 January 2016).

Table 2.1 Descriptive statistics of the European LGBT organizations (N = 150)

Category	Score	
Average number of paid employees	4.7	
Average number of volunteers	29.4	
Annual budget (in euros)	20%	Under 5000
	12%	5000–15,000
	10%	15,001–30,000
	10%	30,001–50,000
	10%	50,001–100,000
	14%	100,001–200,000
	19%	200,001+
	5%	Don't know
Budget includes external funding sources	58%	

THE POLISH CASE AND TRANSNATIONAL CONTENTION

The difficulties that LGBT activism in Poland encountered made headlines in Europe, as activists and media highlighted Poland's struggle to recognize LGBT people. Despite some institutional changes associated with EU accession, like passing the anti-discrimination in employment directive, Poland showed itself resistant to many protective policy measures, societal attitudes toward sexual minorities remained largely negative, and cases of state-sponsored discrimination abounded (Bączkowski, 2008), especially in the three years following European accession (2004–07). Several city governments violated the freedom of assembly for LGBT marches, despite the fact that the march has a long history within the tactical repertoire for expressing political grievances in Poland. While other EU countries (old and new) also experienced backlashes, a socially conservative and vocally homophobic government coalition of the Law and Justice Party (PiS), the League of Polish Families (LPR) and the Self-Defense of the Polish Republic (SRP) from 2005 to 2007, coupled with an emerging civil society and several engaged LGBT organizations, made Poland a focal case for improving the situation of sexual minorities in Central and Eastern Europe (Chetaille, 2011; European Parliament Resolution on Homophobia in Europe, 2006; O'Dwyer, 2012). Polish LGBT activists made progress in the three years leading up to accession by implementing innovative campaigns and founding a new national LGBT organization, Kampania Przeciw

Homofobii (KPH).[7] The euphoria associated with EU membership – and the potential its human rights mandate might have for Poland and the work of local LGBT activists – was not long-lived, however, as hostile political and social opposition began forming in response. In large part, allies from abroad aided local Polish activism by helping organize demonstrations and placing demands on the Polish state from foreign contexts during this time.

When the Polish President and former Mayor of Warsaw, Lech Kaczyński, banned marches for LGBT equality in 2005, LGBT organizations planned to hold the event illegally on 11 June 2005.[8] What was unique about illegal Equality March, compared to similar gay pride events in other major cities where LGBT visibility has become commonplace, was that a transnational group of activists, described below, helped organize the event from both Poland and neighboring Germany. Many of these activists were expatriate Poles who used resources made available to them in Berlin. By 2006, an estimated 2000 of the 5000 illegal marchers in Warsaw came from foreign contexts and included prominent European politicians (interview nos. 124, 125; Bączkowski, 2008, p. 37). According to Tomasz Bączkowski, the central figure behind the organization of the march and one of the activists who later brought a case against Poland to Strasbourg:[9]

> I thought, in these times . . . it shouldn't be a problem organizing from the outside. Naturally, through the personal contacts with [German Green Party Chairwomen] Claudia Roth and others, it was much easier for me to organize it from [Germany] than for Polish activists in Poland, where the environment in general is very hostile. In retrospect, these international political pressures were much more important than if I would have just done this in Poland. (Interview no. 124)[10]

Polish LGBT activism illustrates the increasing influence that internationalization – which in the EU includes open borders – has on the political mobilization of actors and their tactics. This chapter reflects on

---

[7] According to the former president of KPH, the debate on homosexuality most visibly entered the public realm leading up to EU accession (interview no. 8). In 2003, the *Niech Nas Zobaczą* (Let Them See Us) campaign – where 27 billboards funded substantially by the Dutch Embassy showed same-sex couples holding hands – fueled national debate on the issue. The Kultura dla Tolerancji festival in 2004 and 2005 also generated international attention.

[8] The march was also banned in 2004, to which activists responded by organizing an illegal rally.

[9] In 2007, Bączkowski and four Polish activists brought a successful case against Poland (for prohibiting the protest) before the Council of Europe's Court of Human Rights (see also Sandholtz, this volume).

[10] Translated from German by the author.

transnational LGBT activism in Europe, emphasizing the implications it has on the structures of political opportunities that social movement scholars have traditionally theorized within national borders. The more recent literature on transnational social movements departs from earlier scholarship by suggesting that social movement actors in one state increasingly have ties to those in another and that actors in one state can target another state's government (Brysk, 2000; Keck and Sikkink, 1998; Tarrow, 2005). In what follows, I argue that available political opportunities and mobilizing structures in Germany partially substituted absent ones in Poland. I show that in the case of LGBT activism, internationalization has an effect on contentious politics by altering the actors, targets and opportunities traditionally theorized within the nation state – all of which contribute to the expansion of human rights.

DIFFERING OPPORTUNITIES FOR LGBT MOBILIZATION ACROSS STATES

This section makes the case that the abundance of social spaces and organizational resources in neighboring Germany were important variables for bringing together actors, defining their common identity, and empowering them with the necessary resources for transnational activism in Poland. By LGBT social spaces, I refer to the centers for gay life that make the community visible and serve as safe spaces where LGBT people can meet and express their identity. Social spaces ferment ties "by demonstrating the co-presence of others, thus showing people that issues they thought taboo can be discussed, and strengthening collective identity by providing tangible evidence of the existence of a group" (Polletta, 1999, p. 25). Social spaces can foster collective consciousness by making the issue visible to potential movement actors (Stockdill, 2003). For LGBT people, these spaces often take the form of cafes, bars and clubs (Kane, 2003). Organizational capacity refers to the presence of LGBT organizations that endow LGBT communities with resources and capabilities, including "money, expertise, legitimacy, and (pre-)existing networks" (Princen and Kerremans, 2008, pp. 1131–2). Organizational capacity also exists at the European level (for example, ILGA-Europe), but it serves a different function, as these umbrella gatekeeper organizations are more likely to pursue formal lobbying than domestic organizations, which are often devoted to public sphere work (Lang, 2013). Social spaces and organizational capacity in other EU member states provided the mobilizing structures that engendered a process less available in Poland.

The topography of LGBT recognition – both socially and legally – is complex, with stark variation from one state to another and within states from rural to urban areas.[11] In Europe, Europeanization processes facilitate the access to centers of gay life through the free movement of people, goods and services, making established gay communities, such as those in Berlin, more accessible to non-nationals. This creates especially dense nodes of gay social spaces and activist kinships in specific national contexts and urban areas that outpace their surroundings – for example, Amsterdam, London and Berlin became known as "gay capitals" at various points in the 1970s, 1980s and 1990s. European integration accelerates access to such spaces, where openly gay populations and social spaces are more visible. This is especially true for post-socialist countries, where social spaces and organizational resources are comparatively less developed.

In Germany, openly LGBT people have a long history as part of the state's fabric – including both persecution and tolerance – which has resulted in long-term LGBT organizations and visibility in some parts of the public space in cities such as Berlin, Cologne and Hamburg. Berlin, in particular, became a hotbed for activism focused on Poland, providing a host of opportunities for mobilization absent in Poland that were also different from those available at the EU level.[12] Berlin's large Polish expatriate community, its geographic proximity to the Polish border and its status as an LGBT friendly European city provided fertile ground for transnational activism to take root there beginning in the late 1990s. First, a long history of immigration by Polish workers to Germany has left a visible mark on German demography.[13] Berlin's second largest immigrant group is Polish, numbering nearly 41,000 registered Polish citizens (Amt fuer Statistik Berlin-Brandenburg, 2011). The population of Berliners of Polish descent is estimated to be 130,000, counting both undocumented Polish immigrants and those who were born and raised in Poland but have since taken German citizenship. In particular, Berlin is

---

[11] LGBT movements also consider legal recognition to be deeply intertwined with socio-cultural recognition, which is more about the acceptance of specific identities and LGBT visibility in everyday contexts.

[12] While I focus on Berlin and Warsaw here, similar connections exist between other cities in Germany and Poland. For example, the mayor of Nuremberg addressed the importance of LGBT rights as part of cooperation on a visit to Cracow – one of Nuremberg's sister cities (interview no. 103). Activists from Cologne – another center of gay life with a large Polish community – were also engaged in Poland. Alongside Warsaw, targets included Cracow, Poznan and other cities with banned marches.

[13] Similarly, the work of Binnie and Klesse (2013) shows that Polish migration flows in other European countries have developed activist networks.

appealing to Polish sexual minorities who seek it out as a destination to reside and travel because of the comparatively high level of LGBT visibility within the city (interview no. 5). A Polish presence – for example, flags, pamphlets, information booths – is renowned and visible at all of Berlin's major LGBT events, including the annual Christopher Street Day Parade and the Gay-Lesbian Street Fair. Second, geographic proximity is a critical factor, since Berlin is just over 60 kilometers from the Polish border, and train and plane connections such as the Berlin-Warszawa Express make travel between the two capitals quick and affordable.

Alongside Berlin's Polish population and geographic convenience, a third factor for LGBT mobilization is the city's long history as a center of gay life, as a discussion of Hirschfeld illustrated earlier in the chapter. Especially after German reunification, Berlin's status as a gay capital has flourished. In 2001, the then newly elected mayor, Klaus Wowereit, ended speculation by saying, "Ich bin schwul und das ist auch gut so" ("I am gay, and it's alright that way"). In sum, the LGBT issue is highly visible, both socially and politically. The city's gay history has led to an abundance of LGBT social spaces and organizations, which I will argue are mobilizing structures for local, national and transnational activism.

Compared to Warsaw, the center of gay life and activism in Poland, the differences in social spaces and organizational capacity are sharp (Figure 2.1). I use 15 years of issues of *Spartacus*, an international gay travel guide, to measure the number of gay social spaces and organizations leading up to the 2005 Equality March (Frank, Camp and Boutcher, 2010). The *Spartacus* guides have appeared yearly since 1970 and provide a systematic way to measure the presence of gay life across cities in over 160 countries because they use the same categories to list the presence of LGBT organizations and businesses. I code "LGBT social spaces" by counting the presence of LGBT restaurants, cafes, bars and clubs in each city. I code "LGBT organizations" broadly by counting all political, religious and health/counseling LGBT organizations and groups in each city. The fact that the march took place in June 2005 explains the time period, which ranges from (the post-fall of the Berlin Wall) 1990/91 *Spartacus* issue to the 2004/05 issue, depicted in the figure.

The figure shows the discrepancies between Warsaw and Berlin in terms of potential mobilizing structures.[14] In the last 20 years, Europeanization

---

14 Spaces for LGBT activism and LGBT organizations certainly also existed in Poland (Chetaille, 2011) but they existed in far smaller quantities than in Germany (and many other EU member states). Other EU member states had more resources, experience and openly LGBT publics that could be used to work with local activists in a politically closed context like Poland.

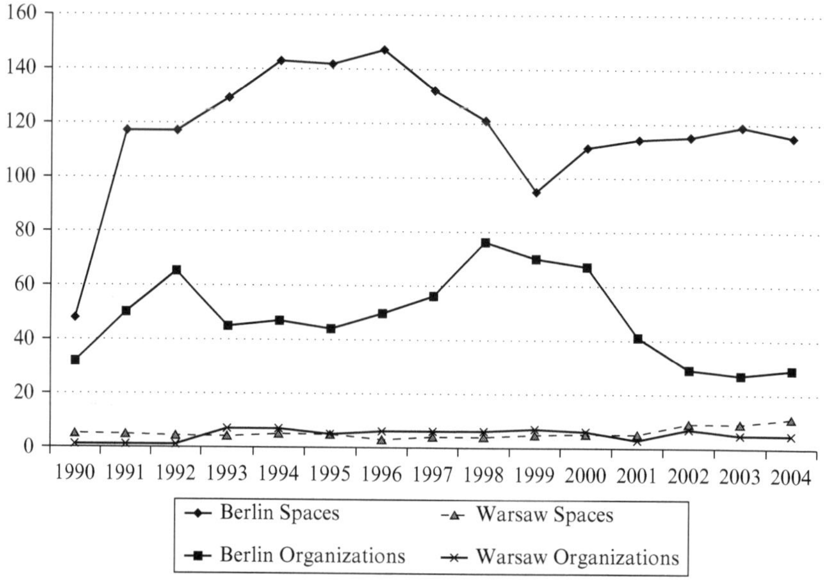

Figure 2.1 Number of LGBT social spaces and organizations in Berlin and Warsaw

has made this cleft less relevant by increasing the mobility of European citizens and providing new channels to access foreign contexts within the EU's institutional framework. As a result, the above variables – available social spaces and organizational capacity in some member states – have established the necessary personal networks that brought together a new group of transnational actors involved in Polish LGBT activism. In many ways, this European story is also representative of the shift in human rights more generally, and the increasing presence of LGBT actors in human rights activism and rhetoric.

EXPANDING ACTORS: NEW NETWORKS OF TRANSNATIONAL ACTORS

This section discusses the expanding types of transnational activists that have aided this process. I define transnational activists as "individuals and groups who mobilize domestic and international resources and opportunities to advance claims on behalf of external actors, against external opponents, or in favor of goals they hold in common with transnational allies" (Tarrow, 2005, pp. 8–9). It discusses both those mobilized between

Germany and Poland, which include expatriate Poles and German activists, celebrities, and ordinary citizens, and those who were mobilized at the European level, which include European and German parliamentarians. Cross-border spaces and resources are important for giving LGBT people, who remain invisible in many domestic contexts, a space for interaction.

Mobilization of Polish and German Actors Based in Germany

Expatriate Polish activists discussed the strength they felt to become politically active after leaving Poland. According to one activist from the Fundacja Równosci/Stiftung für Gleichberechtigung (Equality Foundation[15]), she now holds hands with her girlfriend when she visits Warsaw, which she attributes to socialization in Berlin and the comfort she takes in knowing that she can "escape" back to Berlin (interview no. 5). "When you leave a country, you suddenly feel more brave – to show yourself." Like her, many of the actors involved were expatriate Poles who used mobilizing structures available to them in Berlin. The role of expatriate Poles and their interactions with German allies is crucial because they provide a competent understanding of the Polish domestic context – through their personal experiences, language competence and associational ties to Polish activists – and draw attention to the Polish situation by putting it on the agenda of German LGBT organizations.

One such activist, Bączkowski, came to Berlin in the 1990s to continue his studies in economics, international relations and European law. He became actively engaged in LGBT politics, with "the background thought that these skills [could] be . . . transported to Poland later" (interview no. 124). His partner, a volunteer at Maneo (a local Berlin gay organization), introduced Bączkowski to the organization's president. At this point in the late 1990s, Maneo's president – who had previously worked as part of a transnational campaign to combat violence in Northern Ireland – was looking to deepen the organization's political cooperation abroad, and Bączkowski's volunteer work brought Poland to the forefront of the discussion (interview no. 125). In 1998, Maneo organized its first roundtable meeting in Warsaw with Polish activists, establishing a largely symbolic transnational network of LGBT organizations in five European capitals called *Tolerantia*.

As Maneo expanded its realm of activities to address Poland-related issues, it acted as a magnet for the involvement of Berlin's expatriate Poles.

---

[15] It should be noted that the Fundacja Równosci was funded by three domestic Polish organizations, whose presidents at times were at odds with Bączkowski's leadership of it (interview no. 129).

"[A]s Maneo started having more contacts to Poland, expatriate Poles approached us wanting to be involved" (interview no. 124). What emerged in 2005 was Tolerancja po Polsku/Toleranz auf Polnisch, a subsidiary of Maneo, which provided both a social space for expatriate Poles to gather and a mobilizing structure for using resources in Berlin to address LGBT politics in Poland. It encouraged "[g]ays and lesbians from both countries to meet regularly to cooperate against violence and discrimination towards homosexuals in Germany and Poland, and to exchange information and develop projects" (Maneo-Tolerancja, 2005). Similar projects fostering transnational dialogue and cooperation between Germany and Poland have been organized since 1998. Alongside the personal and symbolic support provided by expatriate networks, they generate material support for new transnational activism. Through Maneo's organizational connections to Berlin's Gay-Lesbian Street Fair, for example, Fundacja Równosci was given rent-free spaces to sell beverages and raise funds for the marches.

In 2005, most of the foreign participants in the Warsaw march were German (Bączkowski, 2008, p. 37). In Berlin, personal networks garnered the involvement of various German celebrities who aided Polish activism, among others through the *Warschauerpakt* (Warsaw Pact) organization. This group was founded in 2005 by German media personalities – Thomas Herrmanns, Georg Uecker, Wolfgang Macht and Holger Wicht – who knew the organizers through their personal networks and wanted to support their cause by increasing awareness and collecting material funds for Polish demonstrations. Their mission statement reads:

> The *Warschauerpakt* is a consortium of convinced Europeans, who volunteer to support the Equality March in Warsaw. We stand for the emancipation of LGBT Poles, whose chartered rights are continually ignored by the Administration. Since 2005 we successfully support the Polish movement by building solid networks, which remain strong today. Through this network we foster the partnership and cooperative engagement of institutions between Germany and Poland (Warschauerpakt, 2007).[16]

From 2006 to 2009, the group grew to include the support of over 300 German celebrities who sponsored activism in Poland through (1) press work in the German media; (2) fundraising for the Warsaw marches; (3) organizing the participation of Germans at those marches; and (4) collecting signatures for various petitions of solidarity with LGBT Poles (Warschauerpakt, 2007). These efforts included printing T-shirts

---

[16] Translated from German by the author.

and hosting concerts to generate funds, as well as organizing buses to take Berliners to attend Polish marches. They promoted their campaign to Berlin's LGBT community. Posters calling for involvement in Poland were visible at many of the social spaces described above, including gay bars and clubs, LGBT health and social service centers, and at the yearly Gay-Lesbian Street Fair and the Christopher Street Day (CSD) Parade – where floats and information booths were adorned with flyers calling for action in Poland (interview no. 6). Berlin's LGBT community is also connected and accessible through free magazines, such as *Die Siegessäule* and *Blu*, which published interviews and press releases on the Polish situation. Such press releases, framed in a language of European solidarity, are explicit in their call for action. For example, a press release by the organization Maneo states:

> On the occasion of President Kaczyński's visit, we invite all brave and engaged persons who care about German-Polish relations and European solidarity in the struggle for equality for all, to come to Cracow and Warsaw with us. Polish NGOs are organizing CSDs and need international support. Marches will be held in Cracow on April 28th, 2006 and in Warsaw on June 10th, 2006. (Maneo-Tolerancja, 2006)[17]

While I do not explore framing processes in detail here (see Brysk, Chapter 5, this volume), it is important to note that such European framing was particularly important for the movement at the time of the 2005 mobilization. Not only did it motivate German participation, it also quelled the Polish opposition's argument that Germany – which has militarily occupied Poland in the past – was imposing its German values (see Ayoub, 2016). Adapting frames in response to various forms of movement/counter-movement interaction, including frames of shared European values at that time, have facilitated effective responses to backlash (Ayoub and Chetaille, 2017).

Mobilization of Outside Actors from Leading States

Similar to the process described above, the organizers of the equality marches explained their connections to the prominent European politicians who supported them through networks of European LGBT organizations and friendships that were formed at social events in Germany (interview nos. 124 and 125). According to Volker Beck, a German Green Party parliamentarian who attended Warsaw marches in 2005, 2006

---

[17] Translated from German by the author.

and 2010, he first became involved in the Polish equality marches after a friend at the German Lesbian and Gay Union (LSVD) contacted him (interview no. 1). Activists said shared ideas on LGBT rights brought them into contact with Beck and Roth: "We have similar political ideas. They knew what [we were] working on . . . We became friends over beers and dinner" (interview no. 124).

In turn, these politicians had connections to sympathetic colleagues at the European level and in other EU member states. Alongside the German parliamentarians, state representatives from Ireland, Norway, Sweden and the United Kingdom attended the marches in 2005 and 2006. This support was organized through the contacts of German parliamentarians and activists within the network of European LGBT organizations, such as ILGA-Europe's umbrella network (interview no. 124). ILGA-Europe serves as a gatekeeper as it regularly writes letters to authorities in states where marches will take place, to "point out safety problems and to let them know they will be watched from the outside" (interview no. 143). The EU Parliament's Intergroup of LGBTI Rights can also financially support the attendance of some MEPs at LGBT marches (interview no. 126). While the efforts of groups connected to EU institutions primarily involve lobbying, they can be active in mobilizing a political elite – especially after the 2005 Equality March generated so much attention among domestic LGBT organizations. By 2006, 32 representatives from 15 different European parliaments attended the Warsaw Equality March (interview no. 124). Transnational German-Polish contention is not a singular event in activism by LGBT people. As LGBT groups have taken a seat alongside members of broader networks of human rights advocacy, they bring with them a transnational dimension that they have developed and maintained since the time of Hirschfeld.

CONCLUSION

This chapter has described the transnational nature of LGBT activism, using the European case to show how ties to Berlin were used to make claims for LGBT recognition in Poland. It discusses the new venues and pathways for mobilizing actors at multiple levels, in a process that expands human rights discourses. Since the geography of LGBT acceptance is so varied among states, the chapter has emphasized the importance of transnational resources – social spaces and organizational capacity – that were scarce in Poland and readily available in Berlin. These resources served as mobilizing structures for activism, bringing together networks of distinct actors who were connected by common identities. Transnational activism did support domestic Polish activism in its struggle to put LGBT issues on the map of contemporary Polish politics. The fluidity of sexuality – like gender – across national borders has given it a natural place alongside other universal human rights issues.

While the analysis here did not explore the effect of cooperative transnationalism on tactical outcomes in the state, it is worth noting the importance of the role these cross-border interactions have played in the lives of LGBT people. Tactical outcomes in Poland included gaining the support of some political elites, police protection for protestors, media visibility and international attention – and similar dynamics have been charted across a series of new adopter states (Ayoub, 2015).[18] For example, in 2011 Poland elected Robert Biedroń and Anna Grodzka, its first openly LGBT parliamentarians – both activists and former presidents of Polish LGBT organizations (KPH and Trans-Fuzja). However small these steps may be in repainting the broader picture, they are fundamentally important steps toward recognition nonetheless, in that they provide support for the domestic activism that has started to change the human rights debate in various domestic contexts. It is no coincidence, for example, that issues like same-sex unions have become a reality in dozens of states and across multiple world regions in the last 20 years (Kollman, 2007). While successes for LGBT human rights are apparent, it is important to note that such successes rarely happen in a linear and steady fashion. Indeed, the expansion of human rights to include LGBT people has happened in a contested terrain, and backlash and resistance to such claims and mobilization is common, if not expected.

The chapter has had less room to describe such complexities of transnational LGBT mobilization, though I want to end by highlighting some challenges that come with expanding human rights. For one, cooperative transnationalism may come with cultural misunderstandings that trigger hostile reactions from some domestic groups who see such activism in light of outside imposition. In the Polish case, a religious-nationalist opposition, centered on the protection of Polish sovereignty and values, fomented an activist resistance against what it saw as meddling by historically unwelcome neighbor states (Ayoub, 2014). As a result, there is neither rapid change nor smooth diffusion associated with sexual minority rights in Poland. Homophobic views on LGBT issues are still expressed in the state

---

[18] I should note that it is particularly difficult to tease out and assess the effect of transnational action separately from that of the local/domestic activism to which it is so closely tied. Furthermore, this study is based largely on interviews with actors who, given their own position, might over-estimate the role of transnational action, a caveat I wish to emphasize.

and social spheres (as they are elsewhere), and political action to oppose the recognition of LGBT people reoccurs (Ayoub and Chetaille, 2017; O'Dwyer, 2012). The 2015 Polish election, which returned a nationalist and socially conservative government, is a case in point. Whether their outspoken opposition to gender and sexual rights is counterproductive to the movement in the long run remains unclear, but activists of various liberal social justice groups have taken to the street in the thousands to denounce the politics of the new government. In sum, the fluidity of LGBT identities – ones that can benefit them in human rights discourses – has also made them particularly threatening to national identities, which are usually more fixed, provoking opposition.

Furthermore, the process of expanding human rights to include LGBT people comes with a series of challenges associated with that discursive construction. First, dominant ("one size fits all") understandings of LGBT identities within human rights frameworks do not always fit neatly with local identities and understandings of same-sex love and desire (Waites, 2009). They may trivialize or make invisible indigenous understandings of sexuality. Second, LGBT rights have been used by states to overshadow human rights abuses in other realms. Classic examples of this process have been the use of gender and LGBT rights to justify anti-immigrant policies (Mepschen, Duyvendak and Tonkens, 2010) and Palestinian occupation (Puar, 2007). For example, at Berlin's gay street parade in 2010 Judith Butler criticized the exclusionary politics and lack of cooperation among dominant LGBT organizations with LGBT organizations representing migrants and people of color. Especially in light of the recent refugee crisis, the problematic portrayal of migrant communities as disproportionately homophobic deserves more scholarly attention. Third, existing scholarship often conceptualizes transnational actors as "good" moral entrepreneurs, while remaining silent about transnational counter-movements as an element of domestic and international opportunity structures and competing advocacy networks (Bob, 2012; Weiss and Bosia, 2013). Such phenomena are central to LGBT politics, however. While internationalization has engendered progress in the political and social realms by facilitating support for the work started by Polish activists, the financial support from foreign Evangelical groups to Polish organizations that demonize LGBT people has not (interview no. 8). Finally, recent scholarship is also noting the polarization of norms on gender and sexuality at the global level, demonstrating how some states (for example, Russia) are purporting a new paradigm of "traditional and moral" values that explicitly excludes LGBT rights from human rights (Altman and Symons, 2016; Ayoub and Paternotte, 2014b). Scholars need to also be aware of precisely these ambivalences of transnational mobilization as we chart the exciting new frontier of LGBT rights as human rights. In sum, this chapter illustrates a dynamic process for expanding rights, one that involves ever-changing actors, repertories, venues and pathways.

ACKNOWLEDGEMENT

Some of the text in this chapter (*c*. 50 percent) has appeared in my earlier work (Ayoub, 2013). Those portions are reprinted with the permission of Cambridge University Press.

REFERENCES

Websites were last accessed 20 January 2016.

Acharya, A. (2004). "How Ideas Spread: Whose Norms Matter? Norm Localization and Institutional Change in Asian Regionalism." *International Organization*, **58**(2), 239–75.

Adam, B., J.W. Duyvendak and A. Krouwel (1998). *Global Emergence of Gay & Lesbian Politics*. Philadelphia, PA: Temple University Press.

Allen, J. (1996). *Growing Up Gay: New Zealand Men Tell Their Stories*. Auckland: Godwit Publishing.

Altman, D. and J. Symons (2016). *Queer Wars* (1st edn). Cambridge, UK and Malden, MA: Polity.

Amt fuer Statistik Berlin-Brandenburg (2011, February). "Über 457 000 Ausländer aus 190 Staaten in Berlin gemeldet. Amt für Statistik Berlin-Brandenburg." Retrieved from http://www.statistik-berlin-brandenburg.de/pms/2011/11-02-04 pdf.

Ayoub, P.M. (2013). "Cooperative Transnationalism in Contemporary Europe: Europeanization and Political Opportunities for LGBT Mobilization in the European Union." *European Political Science Review*, **5**(2), 279–310.

Ayoub, P.M. (2014). "With Arms Wide Shut: Threat Perception, Norm Reception, and Mobilized Resistance to LGBT Rights." *Journal of Human Rights*, **13**(3), 337–62.

Ayoub, P.M. (2015). "Contested Norms in New-adopter States: International Determinants of LGBT Rights Legislation." *European Journal of International Relations*, **21**(2), 293–322.

Ayoub, P.M. (2016). *When States Come Out: Europe's Sexual Minorities and the Politics of Visibility*. New York: Cambridge University Press.

Ayoub, P.M. and A. Chetaille (2017). "European Poles and Polish Patriots." *Social Movement Studies*, **16**(4).

Ayoub, P.M. and D. Paternotte (2014a). "Challenging Borders, Imagining Europe: Transnational LGBT Activism in a New Europe." In J. Bickham-Mendez and N. Naples (eds), *Border Politics, Social Movements and Globalization*. New York: NYU Press, pp. 230–60.

Ayoub, P.M. and D. Paternotte (eds) (2014b). *LGBT Activism and the Making of Europe: A Rainbow Europe?* Houndmills, Basingstoke: Palgrave Macmillan.

Bączkowski, T. (2008). "Diese widerwärtigen Päderasten." *Berliner Debatte Initial*, **19**(6), 33–41.

Balzer, C. and J.S. Hutta (2014). "Trans Networking in the European Vortex: Between Advocacy and Grassroots Politics." In P.M. Ayoub and D. Paternotte (eds), *LGBT Activism and the Making of Europe: A Rainbow Europe?* Houndmills, Basingstoke: Palgrave Macmillan, pp. 171–92.

Beachy, R. (2014). *Gay Berlin: Birthplace of a Modern Identity*. New York: Knopf Doubleday.

Binnie, J. (2004). *The Globalization of Sexuality*. London: Sage.

Binnie, J. and C. Klesse (2013). "'Like a Bomb in the Gasoline Station': East-West Migration and Transnational Activism around Lesbian, Gay, Bisexual, Transgender and Queer Politics in Poland." *Journal of Ethnic and Migration Studies*, **39**(7), 1107–24.

Bob, C. (2012). *The Global Right Wing and the Clash of World Politics*. Cambridge: Cambridge University Press.

Brysk, A. (2000). *From Tribal Village to Global Village*. Palo Alto, CA: Stanford University Press.

Chetaille, A. (2011). "Poland: Sovereignty and Sexuality in Post-socialist Times." In M. Tremblay, D. Paternotte and C. Johnson (eds), *The Lesbian and Gay Movement and the State*. Surrey: Ashgate, pp. 119–34.

Dececco, J. and V.L. Bullough (2002). *Before Stonewall: Activists for Gay and Lesbian Rights in Historical Context*. Binghamton, NY: Routledge.

European Parliament Resolution on Homophobia in Europe, 2005/2666(RSP) 2005/2666(RSP) (2006). Retrieved from http://www.europarl.europa.eu/sides/getDoc.do?type=TA&reference=P6-TA-2006-0018&language=EN&ring=B6-2006-0040.

Frank, D.J., B.J. Camp and S.A. Boutcher (2010). "Worldwide Trends in the Criminal Regulation of Sex, 1945 to 2005." *American Sociological Review*, **75**(6), 86793. doi: 10.1177/0003122410388493.

Imig, D. and S. Tarrow (2001). *Contentious Europeans*. Lanham, MD: Rowman and Littlefield.

Kane, M. (2003). "Social Movement Policy Success: Decriminalizing State Sodomy Laws, 1969–1998." *Mobilization: An International Journal*, **8**(3), 313–34.

Keck, M.E. and K. Sikkink (1998). *Activists Beyond Borders: Advocacy Networks in International Politics*. Ithaca, NY: Cornell University Press.

Kneefel, B. (2016, 9 February). "What Do LGBTQ Rights Have to Do With Black Lives Matter?" *The Huffington Post*. Retrieved from http://www.huffingtonpost.com/brandon-kneefel/what-do-lgbtq-rights-have_b_9142164.html.

Kollman, K. (2007). "Same-sex Unions: The Globalization of an Idea." *International Studies Quarterly*, **51**(2), 329–57. doi: 10.1111/j.1468-2478.2007.00454.x.

Kollman, K. and M. Waites (2009). "The Global Politics of Lesbian, Gay, Bisexual and Transgender Human Rights: An Introduction." *Contemporary Politics*, **15**(1), 1–37.

Lang, S. (2013). *NGOs, Civil Society, and the Public Sphere*. New York: Cambridge University Press.

Maneo-Tolerancja (2005, 23 November). "Grundrechte gelten auch für Lesben und Schwule!" Press release. Retrieved from http://www.maneo.de/infopool/flyer-und-infopakete.html?eID=dam_frontend_push&docID=288.

Maneo-Tolerancja (2006, 8 March). Europäische Solidarität gegen Homophobie in Polen. Berlin, Germany. Press release. Retrieved from http://www.maneo.de/infopool/flyer-und-infopakete.html?eID=dam_frontend_push&docID=288.

Mepschen, P., J.W. Duyvendak and E.H. Tonkens (2010). "Sexual Politics,

Orientalism and Multicultural Citizenship in the Netherlands." *Sociology*, **44**(5), 962–79.
Nadelmann, E.A. (1990). "Global Prohibition Regimes: The Evolution of Norms in International Society." *International Organization*, **44**(4), 479–526.
O'Dwyer, C. (2012). "Does the EU Help or Hinder Gay-rights Movements in Post-communist Europe? The Case of Poland." *East European Politics*, **28**(4), 332–52. doi: 10.1080/21599165.2012.721094.
Polletta, F. (1999). "'Free spaces' in collective action." *Theory and Society*, **28**(1), 1–38. doi: 10.1023/A:1006941408302.
Princen, S. and B. Kerremans (2008). "Opportunity Structures in the EU Multi-level System." *West European Politics*, **31**(6), 1129–46. doi: 10.1080/01402380802370484.
Puar, J.K. (2007). *Terrorist Assemblages: Homonationalism in Queer Times*. Durham, NC: Duke University Press.
Rupp, L.J. (2011). "The Persistence of Transnational Organizing: The Case of the Homophile Movement." *American Historical Review*, **116**(4), 1014–39. doi: 10.1086/ahr.116.4.1014.
Stockdill, B.C. (2003). *Activism Against AIDS: At the Intersection of Sexuality, Race, Gender, and Class*. Boulder, CO: Lynne Rienner.
Tarrow, S. (2005). *The New Transnational Activism*. Cambridge: Cambridge University Press.
Thoreson, R.R. (2014). *Transnational LGBT Activism: Working for Sexual Rights Worldwide*. Minneapolis, MN: University of Minnesota Press.
Tremblay, M., D. Paternotte and C. Johnson (2011). *The Lesbian and Gay Movement and the State: Comparative Insights into a Transformed Relationship*. Surrey: Ashgate.
Waites, M. (2009). "Critique of 'Sexual Orientation' and 'Gender Identity' in Human Rights Discourse: Global Queer Politics Beyond the Yogyakarta Principles." *Contemporary Politics*, **15**(1), 137–56.
Warschauerpakt (2007, 1 January). "Warschauerpakt: Europa = Tolerancja." Retrieved 3 January 2011 from http://warschauerpakt2007.de/.
Weiss, M.L. and M.J. Bosia (2013). *Global Homophobia: States, Movements, and the Politics of Oppression*. Urbana-Champaign, IL: University of Illinois Press.

SOURCES OF INTERVIEW REFERENCES

1. Lesben und Schwulen Verband Deutschland (LSVD) (in German), Lobbyist, 20 June 2009.
5. Fundacja Równosci (translated from German), Activist, 2 July 2009.
6. Bündnis 90/Die Grünen (translated from German), Representative for LGBT Issues, 22 June 2009.
8. Kampania Przeciw Homofobii (KPH), President, 17 July 2009.
103. Ogólnopolskie Porozumienie Związków Zawodowych, Activist, 29 October 2010.
124. Fundacja Równosci (translated from German), President, 21 February 2011.
125. Maneo/LSVD: Berlin Bradenburg (translated from German), President, 24 March 2011.

126. European Parliament's Intergroup on LGBT Rights, Secretary, 26 April 2011.
129. Kampania Przeciw Homofobii (KPH), Project Coordinator, 12 October 2011.
143. ILGA-Europe, Senior Policy Coordinator, 3 March 2012.

3. How do global human rights expand?: A case of Japan's Burakumin going global

Kiyoteru Tsutsui

INTRODUCTION

This chapter examines how local actors become part of the international human rights system and contribute to the reinforcement and expansion of the system. As Ayoub, Gómez, and Hertel in this volume also demonstrate, unpacking these processes is critical in understanding how the international human rights system has reached its current status. My analysis demonstrates how global human rights can expand to accommodate many new claims. It also points to a concern about the current system, namely, that it has too many different bodies dealing with too many different kinds of rights, or "hypertrophy of human rights" (Posner, 2014).

Here, I examine one instance of the establishment of a new type of rights issue, discrimination based on descent and work. Drawing on my work on minority rights activism in Japan (Tsutsui, 2017), I focus on a discriminated minority group in Japan called Burakumin, which led the process of establishing a new norm about descent-based discrimination. Burakumin have a long history of activism dating back to the 1920s and started using universalistic language long before the Universal Declaration of Human Rights (UDHR). Their activism achieved some level of success in the domestic arena but they needed further progress in tackling the social discrimination that continued to plague them. In the 1970s, as the international human rights system expanded and engulfed Japan, Burakumin activists went global, seeking to leverage global human rights for change in the domestic arena. Since then, their steady participation in international human rights forums has navigated their activism increasingly toward international promotion of human rights. Collaborating with other international actors, they made concerted efforts to establish discrimination based on descent and work as a new human rights issue in the international system, and eventually succeeded in passing resolutions in United Nations (UN) forums regarding this type of discrimination.

In the following, I trace the history of Burakumin activism, focusing on their foray into international forums since the 1970s and their efforts to establish a new rights issue since the 1990s. I note that this is one of many cases in which local actors added to the international human rights agenda and that for a more complete picture of the evolution of global human rights many more cases need to be examined. Nonetheless, this analysis sheds light on the iterative, cumulative efforts of these local actors who work with dedicated international actors to sustain and expand the edifice of global human rights institutions.

BACKGROUND

Burakumin are a group of people who face discrimination based primarily on their ancestors' occupations and outcaste status in the stratification system of premodern Japan. The Meiji government abolished the caste system in 1871 as a part of its effort to modernize Japan, but discrimination persisted, as Burakumin were confined to their hamlet (*buraku*), in which living conditions were visibly inferior. Burakumin are not a distinct people racially, nationally, religiously, or linguistically.[1] When non-Burakumin contend that Burakumin are racially or ethnically different from mainstream Japanese, they typically do so with an intent to disparage and discriminate.

Burakumin have vigorously challenged such discourse and mobilized collectively to fight discrimination and achieve greater equality since the 1920s. In 1922, they formed the first large-scale Burakumin organization, Suiheisha, and advocated universalistic anti-discrimination principles. After a halt in their activism during World War II, Suiheisha-related activists returned onto the political scene in the postwar period and established a national organization that eventually became the Buraku Liberation League (BLL) in 1955. The BLL has led the Buraku liberation movement[2]

---

[1] Ethnic distinction of Burakumin is a more complicated issue and depends on the definition of ethnicity. As John Lie argues, "(t)he designation of the Burakumin as an ethnic group is controversial because most contemporary Japanese equate ethnicity with race . . . if shared descent and common culture, as well as discrimination, characterize an ethnic group, then the Burakumin are as ethnic as the Ainu or Okinawans" (Lie, 2001, p. 85).

[2] Since the 1960s, internal disputes about the BLL's direction intensified and prompted those affiliated with the Japan Communist Party to splinter and form

since then, deploying two main tactics: (1) denunciation campaigns that publicly admonish organizations and individuals for displaying discriminatory attitudes toward Burakumin and (2) protest campaigns for grants to improve their substandard community infrastructure that initially targeted local governments and then the national government. In 1969, these campaigns resulted in the Special Measures on Dowa Communities, intended for Burakumin community improvement. It was the largest government project for minorities in Japan and would be renewed repeatedly until its amicable demise in 2002. Despite these successes in formal policies, Burakumin continued to face social discrimination in private spheres, especially in employment and marriage. As I detail below, this issue emerged as one of the main foci of Burakumin activism in subsequent decades, and global human rights seemed appealing in addressing this issue.

Against this background of Burakumin activism, global human rights entered Japanese politics in the 1970s. In 1976, the International Covenant on Civil and Political Rights (ICCPR) and the International Covenant on Economic, Social, and Cultural Rights (ICESCR) entered into force after collecting the required number of ratifications. Three years later, in 1979, the Japanese government ratified the two Covenants. Since then, both the government and civil society have deepened their engagement with international human rights institutions, and that has changed the dynamics of minority politics in Japan. Below, I examine how Burakumin activism has changed since the 1970s.

MOVEMENT REORIENTATION BY BURAKUMIN

After the 1969 Special Measures started addressing their living conditions, more insidious forms of social discrimination, especially in employment

---

the National United Buraku Liberation Movement Association (henceforth the Association) in 1976. The Association's main claim was that Burakumin discrimination would disappear over time and that disruptive activism was counterproductive. Based on this argument, the Association did not engage in much visible activism except to counter and criticize BLL's activities. There is a third line of Burakumin advocacy that promotes quiet integration into mainstream society. This integrationist (*Yuwa*) line was promoted by groups representing the interests of ruling elites, who engaged in few public protests. Thus, as a social movement organization, the BLL was by far the most active carrier of the Buraku liberation movement that started in 1922 with Suiheisha. The BLL has also been the most dominant Burakumin organization, drawing support from a vast majority of Burakumin and spearheading most large-scale mobilizations. For these reasons, my analysis will focus on BLL's activities.

and marriage, became the focal point of BLL activities. As Japanese citizens, their citizenship rights were fully secured in principle. And it has become increasingly difficult to identify Burakumin, as the key markers – their occupation, residential area, and registration record – were no longer automatically linked to Burakumin background. Yet, some employers and parents would still investigate descent background, using professional detectives, and reject those deemed to have Burakumin heritage. The denunciation campaigns reduced the number of flagrant cases (Upham, 1987), but social discrimination persisted underground. To break this impasse, the BLL sought a new law that would ban discriminatory acts against Burakumin, including background checks, and promoted educational campaigns that would spread universal human rights ideas and change public perception about Burakumin (McLauchlan, 2003).

International human rights treaties emerged as an attractive instrument for that goal in this period, and the BLL launched a campaign for Japan's ratification of the ICCPR and the ICESCR. A BLL leader recounts the motivation for this campaign as follows:

> The campaign started after the two Covenants (the ICCPR and ICESCR) entered into force in 1976. The Covenants were not that well known prior to that, but their entry into force, coupled with the fact that Japan had not ratified them, led to much attention to UN human rights activities . . . After the 1969 Measures, infrastructure in Burakumin communities was improving, but many incidents of social discrimination continued, and the BLL was exploring how to address these issues. It was along these lines that global human rights emerged as possibly useful tools for the movement . . . We hoped that ratification of the two Covenants by the Japanese government would prompt legislation of a Buraku Liberation Basic Law, which would promote human rights and reduce social discrimination. (Interview 2005/8/16)

BLL activists expected that ratification of the two Covenants would provide the legal basis for a new anti-discrimination law (Tomonaga, 1978). They also anticipated socializing effects of the treaties, hoping to leverage the UN's authority into greater respect for human rights principles in general and reduction in prejudice against Burakumin in particular (Interview 2004/12/1).

With these motivations, the BLL launched a campaign for ratification of the human rights treaties in 1976. It organized various seminars and symposia, inviting experts on international human rights law and human rights practitioners from the UN and other international organizations, and lobbied many ministries and politicians domestically (Wajima, 1977, pp. 221–32). In one of the first events of the campaign in 1977, the BLL invited the former head of the UN Center for Human Rights, Marc Schreiber, as a keynote speaker. This visit was brokered by

Kazunari Inoue, a Japan Socialist Party Diet member from a Burakumin community in Osaka, who had visited the UN and met Schreiber (Interview 2005/8/16). Through this personal connection, the first encounter of the BLL with the UN human rights system materialized. Soon after Schreiber's visit, the Japanese government ratified the two Covenants in 1979. Following this success, the BLL continued to organize events almost yearly featuring international human rights activists to pressure the Japanese government to ratify other human rights treaties and improve domestic practices.

Encouraged by Schreiber, BLL activists began to attend UN human rights forums in the late 1970s. Their first official participation in UN forums was in 1983, when they issued a statement about Burakumin discrimination in a meeting of a Working Group of the UN Sub-Commission on Prevention of Discrimination and Protection of Minorities (henceforth the Sub-Commission).[3] In order to make a statement, they had to borrow the credential of a UN consultative status non-governmental organization (NGO), the Minority Rights Group (MRG) (Sekai Jinken Sengen 35 Shunen Chuo Jikko Iinkai, 1983, pp. 68–72). In 1984, when they came back to make another statement in the Sub-Commission, they had to rely on the credential of a different consultative status NGO, the Religions for Peace (Uesugi, 1984). As they repeatedly borrowed other NGOs' consultative status to make an intervention at UN forums, they began to realize the importance of having their own seat at the table. As one activist put it, it was "like taking a train ride with somebody else's pass" (Interview 2005/8/16).

Through these international activities, BLL leaders' networks with international human rights activists expanded. They observed the tireless work of UN officials and NGO representatives and understood the importance of international alliances. They were also encouraged repeatedly by other activists to contribute to international human rights activities. For example, during their early visits to the UN, BLL representatives met Yo Kubota, a UN human rights official who was originally from Japan. Observing the way the BLL representatives presented their problems, Kubota argued that they should:

---

[3] The Sub-Commission on Prevention of Discrimination and Protection of Minorities was established in 1947, under the UN Commission on Human Rights. Its name changed to the Sub-Commission on the Promotion and Protection of Human Rights in 1999, and then to Human Rights Council Advisory Committee in 2008, but in this text, I will refer to all of them as the Sub-Commission.

> be recognized internationally as a true human rights organization by making appeals about other issues of discrimination and human rights violations, not just (their) own problems . . . and by forming an alliance with other anti-discrimination organizations in the world to establish an international organization with a consultative status at the UN. (Tomonaga, 2003, p. 11)

As a resourceful minority group in a rising economic superpower, the BLL faced expectations to not just address their plight but also contribute to global human rights advocacy.

Before their international engagements, the BLL was focused almost exclusively on Burakumin discrimination, and their entry into international arenas was primarily to address their domestic problems. Through their international experiences, they embraced a more global view:

> The world today is deeply interconnected and one discrimination does not stand isolated from other kinds of discrimination . . . looking at Buraku discrimination from this perspective, we need to further deepen international alliances. (Tomonaga, 1984, p. 88)

By the late 1980s, international human rights activities had become one of the three core mandates of the BLL, along with elimination of social discrimination against Burakumin and forging alliances with other disadvantaged groups in Japan (Buraku Kaiho Kenkyusho, 1989, pp. 306–10). Their activist orientation had shifted from a domestic minority movement focused on their own issues to a broader human rights and anti-discrimination movement that sought alliances with other disadvanged groups. Correspondingly, becoming an international human rights organization with UN consultative status emerged as a central goal of the BLL.

BECOMING A UN CONSULTATIVE STATUS NGO

The BLL quickly took concrete steps to accomplish this goal. In 1987, five BLL representatives went on a fact-finding mission to Europe to investigate how to become a consultative status NGO. They first visited the UN Committee on NGOs in Geneva to learn about application processes and necessary qualifications for consultative status, which entailed purposes that align with UN's goals, independence from any governments, and representation from at least several countries[4] (Tomonaga, 1990, p. 85).

---

4 This requirement is no longer in place; NGOs operating in only one country can obtain consultative status today.

They then visited international human rights NGOs in Europe and learned about their operations. They were especially impressed with the Minority Rights Group and Anti-Slavery Society for their substantial contributions to global human rights work with much smaller resources than the BLL. BLL leaders were inspired and heartened to realize the BLL's potential as an international human rights organization and noted that "we became painfully aware of our obligation to work tirelessly toward elimination of discriminations across the globe" (Tomonaga, 1990, pp. 98–9).

After this preparatory period, on 25 January 1988, the BLL established an affiliated but independent international organization, the International Movement Against All Forms of Discrimination and Racism (IMADR). IMADR professed its commitment to work with UN human rights instruments in advancing human rights principles and tackling intractable discriminations across the world. To fulfill the requirements for UN consultative status, it included board and secretariat members from Austria, Belgium, Ecuador, England, France, Korea, South Africa, Sierra Leone, Sweden, the USA, and West Germany, most of whom were international activists who BLL leaders had encountered in their earlier activities. Its goals are aligned with UN goals, and its independence from the government was not in question. Thus, IMADR seemed to have all the qualifications for UN consultative status.

The UN Committee on NGOs examined IMADR's first application for consultative status in 1989. IMADR leaders engaged in extensive lobbying activities, meeting all 19 members of the Committee. However, because of its short history and anchoring in one country, its application was tabled for continuing examination (Tomonaga, 1989, pp. 87–91). To counter the image of a heavily Japan-focused organization, IMADR increased its international activities in the next several years, establishing an office in Geneva, attending all major UN human rights forums, organizing many events not just in Japan but in other countries, and inviting members from many more countries (Buraku Kaiho Kenkyusho, 1994, pp. 76–80; Tomonaga, 1994, p. 57). Since consultative status is typically accorded to an NGO that has been in existence for more than four or five years, their application was tabled again in 1991 (Tomonaga, 1991, pp. 123–4). In its third trial in 1993, however, IMADR's persistent efforts to promote global human rights and anti-discrimination were recognized, and it received the coveted consultative status.

This marked a successful transformation of a national minority organization into an international human rights organization. This movement reorientation began as an attempt to change the Japanese public's understanding of Burakumin issues and to reduce anti-Burakumin discrimination. As BLL activists deepened their engagement with global human rights, taking advantage of international political opportunities at the UN and international networks of human rights activists and organizations, they internalized the altruistic norms shared by international activists and received encouragement to contribute to the global human rights effort. Through these experiences, they transformed themselves from a minority organization working only for its constituents to an international human rights organization for disadvantaged populations throughout the world.

This movement reorientation has served Burakumin activists well. When government measures to improve Burakumin communities' infrastructure ended in 2002 by mutual agreement that they had served their purposes, the movement could have fizzled out if its focus had been exclusively on Burakumin issues. Because it had already transformed itself and spun off an international wing, the movement continues to thrive in promoting human rights domestically and internationally.[5] This was, however, not what BLL activists anticipated in the 1970s, but rather an unintended consequence of their international engagements.

GLOBAL NORM EXPANSION BY BURAKUMIN

With the newly established IMADR, Burakumin activists sought to contribute to global human rights. IMADR has advocated for various minority groups in the world and made many statements condemning violating governments in international forums. In recent years, it has issued statements and reports on ethnic conflict in Sri Lanka, human rights violations against the Roma in Europe, and violence against indigenous peoples in Guatemala and Argentina. It has also promoted ratification of international human rights treaties, publicized international conferences such as the Durban World Conference against Racism, and launched international campaigns against human trafficking and racial discrimination in the criminal justice system.[6] Their focus on minority rights issues, especially those in the relatively under-examined Asia-Pacific

---

[5] While movement reorientation was most dramatic for the BLL, the other two lines of advocacy among Burakumin, the Association and the integrationist groups, also shifted to promotion of human rights. They do not have an international wing like the BLL, but their ideology is aligned with global human rights principles, and therefore movement reorientation affected the Buraku liberation movement as a whole, not just the BLL.

[6] Some examples of its vast ambit of activities can be found in the website: http://www.imadr.org/ (accessed 11 July 2009).

region, is particularly valuable to UN human rights activities.[7] Once it gained UN consultative status, IMADR lent its status to other groups that lack sufficient resources and experience to become a consultative status NGO, much like the NGOs that helped Burakumin activists in the 1980s.[8] These efforts directly contributed to reinforcement of global human rights norms.

More importantly, IMADR has contributed to the expansion of global human rights norms by adding discrimination based on descent to the international human rights agenda. BLL activists had their eyes on norm expansion from early on. In 1983, in their first statement in UN forums, BLL activists made a request that the UN establish an official unit that focuses on issues such as Burakumin discrimination and caste discrimination in India. This was an important goal for Burakumin activists, because if the UN recognizes discrimination based on former outcaste status as similar to racial and ethnic discrimination, they would be able to resolve the issue of their sameness/difference dilemma. Ever since the Meiji period, Burakumin activists have emphasized their ethno-racial sameness in claiming equality with non-Burakumin Japanese but also had to highlight differences in their treatment in calling for a government budget for community improvements. The dilemma was that if they talk about their disadvantages too much, their social discrimination might be exacerbated, but that stressing their sameness could undermine their claim for special remedies. Establishing descent-based discrimination as an internationally legitimated issue would enable them to claim at once their ethno-racial sameness, which fortifies demands for equality, and their socio-economic disadvantages, which justify special measures by the government.

They found their legal footing in the Convention on the Elimination of all Racial Discrimination (CERD), which had specific stipulations about discrimination based on descent. The Sub-Commission on the Prevention of Discrimination and Protection of Minorities, where the impetus for CERD originates and the issue of descent-based discrimination was raised first, was also an important forum for this. BLL activists' promotion of descent-based discrimination took place mostly in these two forums, the CERD Committee and the Sub-Commission. The developments in these

---

7 For example, in the 1994 session of the UN Sub-Commission, IMADR reported on a previously little known issue of discrimination against minority Nepalese in Bhutan based on their own research (Suzuki, 1994, p. 40).

8 For example, in their second UN Commission on Human Rights session as a consultative status NGO in 1995, they made statements on eight occasions, in four of which they lent their credential to Asian NGOs without consultative status (Tanaka, 1995, pp. 55–6).

two forums are intertwined but for ease of understanding, I will describe them separately below.

The Sub-Commission was where the issue of discrimination based on occupation and descent first emerged. As mentioned earlier, in their very first statement at the UN in 1983, at the Sub-Commission, BLL activists had already argued for a unit at the UN on issues such as Burakumin discrimination and caste discrimination in India. BLL activists have participated in Sub-Commission sessions almost every year since then and made various claims including the need for focused attention on discrimination based on occupation and descent. Groups from India were also active on this issue. In 1998, they formed the National Campaign on Dalit Human Rights (NCDHR) and campaigned for elimination of discrimination against Dalit. In March 2000, with the support from international NGOs such as the Minority Rights Group and Human Rights Watch, activists from Japan, India, and other countries that have similar discrimination gathered in London to form the International Dalit Solidarity Network (IDSN) to promote the issue at the UN. In August of the same year, these activists, including a Burakumin activist, participated in a session on caste discrimination to explain this type of discrimination to members of the Sub-Commission and the CERD Committee (Tomonaga, 2003, pp. 12–13). Two days later, the Sub-Commission adopted a resolution on discrimination based on occupation and descent, which explicitly included Burakumin discrimination (E/CN.4/Sub.2/Res/2000/4, 11 August 2004). The resolution declared that international human rights law prohibits this type of discrimination and called on UN member states to take measures to prevent and punish such discrimination. It also appointed a member of the Sub-Commission, Rajendra Kalidas Wimala Goonesekere from Sri Lanka, to submit a working paper on this issue at the next session. IMADR and the BLL were active in lobbying for this resolution. They engaged in NGO briefing with members of the Sub-Commission (and the CERD Committee) and informed them of the history of Burakumin discrimination and its similarity to Dalit discrimination in India (Nakajo, 2000, pp. 59–60).

It was very important for the supporters of this resolution to establish that it is not just about India. When the first Goonesekere report was presented to the Sub-Commission, the Indian government reacted strongly against it, criticizing the report for targeting India. There was a rule in the Sub-Commission against targeting a specific country in a resolution, and some members of the Sub-Commission also expressed unease about excessive references to India in the report. Thus, it was critical that Japan, Nepal, and Sri Lanka were mentioned in the report. This issue was also a main motivation for further research to establish global prevalence of this type of discrimination (Bando, 2001, pp. 46–9).

This reveals the potential of global human rights to expose many cases of discrimination that were largely unknown to the world. In the case of descent-based discrimination, groups from Nigeria, Senegal, and other countries have discovered their descent-based discrimination as a human rights issue in the process of the global campaign by other groups. Because global forums encourage actors to present human rights issues as having a broader relevance rather than an issue for one specific group, the initiator groups, Burakumin in Japan and Dalit in India in this case, are often likely to expand their ambit to identify similar issues in other parts of the world. This often leads to "discovery" of hitherto uncovered human rights violations, thus empowering previously disadvantaged and suppressed groups.

In August 2001, Goonesekere submitted the result of his research as a working paper on discrimination based on occupation and descent to the Sub-Commission (E/CN.4/Sub.2/2001/16). The resolution listed India, Sri Lanka, Nepal, Pakistan, and Japan as countries afflicted by this type of discrimination, and estimated the number of victims to be as many as 250 million people. It also called for more research on similar situations in Africa, South America, and other places. He received much information from the IDSN – and the BLL for Burakumin issues – in preparing for this report, and the report's focus on Asian cases clearly reflected the lead taken by the BLL, IMADR, and the NCDHR (Tomonaga, 2003, pp. 12–14).

Meanwhile, at the World Conference Against Racism in Durban in 2001, the issue of discrimination based on occupation and descent attracted much attention. Due to strong opposition by the Indian government, the issue was not included in the Declaration and Programme of Action adopted by governments. However, the Action Plan for NGOs included it. The World Conference Against Racism was the first international forum in which Burakumin activists officially participated in its earlier iteration in 1983. Unfamiliar with the surroundings, they were unable to make official statements and were only able to circulate documents (Tomonaga, 1987, pp. 394–9). They played active roles 18 years later in the preparation of the World Conference and in the Conference proceedings, and their issue has become a legitimate topic of discussion in the Conference (Tomonaga, 2003, pp. 17–18).[9]

---

[9] Human Rights Watch also studied this issue and released a report at the World Conference with cases in India, Nepal, Japan, and others, along with policy prescriptions for resolving this problem. This report influenced subsequent UN documents such as the CERD Committee General Recommendation 29 and the draft Guideline published by the Human Rights Council in 2009, both of which I describe below.

Back at the Sub-Commission, two other members, Asbjørn Eide from Norway and Yokota Yozo from Japan, were appointed to write a follow-up report in August 2002 (Goonesekere was not re-elected to the Sub-Commission). Eide and Yokota submitted their working paper in the next session of the Sub-Commission in 2003. The working paper reported on groups facing discrimination based on work and descent in Africa, the Middle East, and Europe, called for more research on this issue, and requested that the Sub-Commission and the CERD Committee put more pressure on relevant governments to address the issue. Days later, the Sub-Commission adopted a resolution based on the Eide/Yokota working paper. This resolution reaffirmed the commitment made by CERD Article 1, the 2000 Sub-Commission resolution, the 2001 Goonesekere working paper, and the 2002 CERD Committee General Statement 29, and called on governments to design and implement policies to eliminate this type of discrimination. It also authorized further research by Eide and Yokota, to be reported in 2004, for continued discussion of this issue (Murakami, 2002, p. 24; Tomonaga, 2003, pp. 14–17).

By 2006, when the Sub-Commission was reorganized with the transition from the Commission on Human Rights to the Human Rights Council, the Sub-Commission had received two working papers and three reports on the issue of descent-based discrimination, first by Goonesekere, and then by Eide and Yokota (International Dalit Solidarity Network, 2015, p. 7). As one of its final tasks, in 2005, the Commission on Human Rights appointed Yokota and Chin-Sung Chung from South Korea "as Special Rapporteurs with the task of preparing a comprehensive study on discrimination based on work and descent, on the basis of the three working papers submitted to the SubCommission on this topic (E/CN.4/Sub.2/2001/16, E/CN.4/Sub.2/2003/24 and E/CN.4/Sub.2/2004/31)" (Commission on Human Rights decision 2005/109 of 19 April 2005; E/CN.4/2005/2 E/CN.4/Sub.2/2004/48:13). Then, the Sub-Commission gave Yokota and Chung the mandate to write "the Draft UN Principles and Guidelines for the Effective Elimination of Discrimination Based on Work and Descent" (A/HRC/Sub.1/58/L.11, 24 August 2006: 58–60).[10]

[10] The Draft Principles and Guidelines defined discrimination based on work and descent as "any distinction, exclusion, restriction, or preference based on inherited status such as caste, including present or ancestral occupation, family, community or social origin, name, birth place, place of residence, dialect and accent that has the purpose or effect of nullifying or impairing the recognition, enjoyment, or exercise, on an equal footing, of human rights and fundamental freedoms in the political, economic, social, cultural, or any other field of public life. This type of discrimination is typically associated with the notion of purity

The draft was received in 2007 and published in 2009 by the UN Human Rights Council, a newly reorganized core human rights forum at the UN (A/HRC/11/CRP.3, 18 May 2009). In developing the draft UN Principles and Guidelines for the Effective Elimination of Discrimination based on Work and Descent, IMADR made many contributions as Yokota and Chung prepared the document (Tomonaga, 2013, pp. 72–3). IMADR and the IDSN organized a special side event and over 100 participants attended on that occasion. They then visited the office of Navi Pillay, the High Commissioner for Human Rights, to make an appeal for elimination of descent-based discrimination. Pillay responded with a statement calling for the Human Rights Council to formally adopt and promote the Guideline (Komori, 2009, pp. 11–12). Although the Guideline has not been officially adopted yet (as of February 2015), it serves as a useful blueprint for governments and civil society actors to follow in addressing discrimination based on descent.

Turning to the other major international forum, how did BLL activists leverage CERD to establish descent-based discrimination as a distinct category that includes Burakumin discrimination? CERD ratification had been a key focus of BLL activists ever since the ICCPR and the ICESCR were ratified in 1979 (until the Japanese government ratified the CERD in 1995). The BLL, and also IMADR from 1988, organized annual events to promote CERD ratification, inviting experts at the CERD Committee as speakers. The CERD was a particularly important treaty for Burakumin because its Article 1 prohibits discrimination based on "any distinction, exclusion, restriction or preference based on race, colour, descent, or national or ethnic origin."[11] No other core UN human rights treaties included the term "descent." The UDHR and the CCPR include the term "social origin" and "birth" in prohibiting various types of discrimination, but not "descent." The term "descent" had ambiguous meanings, as admitted by a secretary general of the CERD Committee (Buraku Kaiho Kenkyusho, 1985, p. 117). Nonetheless, the inclusion of the term "descent" indicated to Burakumin activists that Burakumin discrimination is part

and pollution and practices of untouchability, and is deeply rooted in societies and cultures where this discrimination is practiced" (A/HRC/11/CRP.3, Scope and Application para. 2).

[11] Notably, the term "descent" is listed in Article 1: "race, colour, descent, or national or ethnic origin" but not in Article 5: "States Parties undertake to prohibit and to eliminate racial discrimination in all its forms and to guarantee the right of everyone, without distinction as to race, colour, or national or ethnic origin." This is said to be due to an input from an Austrian representative in the process of negotiating the treaty provision (Buraku Kaiho Kenkyusho, 1985, p. 116).

of "racial discrimination" that the treaty addresses. While this seemed evident to Burakumin activists, the Japanese government did not agree. The government's first report to the CERD Committee submitted in 2000 did not mention Burakumin, and it has consistently held the position that Burakumin does not fall under the jurisdiction of CERD in its second and third report to the CERD Committee in 2010 and 2014, respectively.

Burakumin activists briefed the members of the CERD Committee in the hope that the committee examination and resulting recommendations would reflect their views (IMADR-JC, 2001, pp. 86–8; Tomonaga, 2003, pp. 8–10). Correspondingly, CERD Committee's Concluding Observations for Japan's first report clearly stated that Burakumin discrimination is within the scope of the treaty: "With regard to the interpretation of the definition of racial discrimination contained in article 1 of the Convention, the Committee, unlike the State party, considers that the term 'descent' has its own meaning and is not to be confused with race or ethnic or national origin. The Committee therefore recommends that the State party ensure that all groups including the Burakumin community are protected against discrimination and afforded full enjoyment of the civil, political, economic, social and cultural rights contained in article 5 of the Convention" (CERD/C/304/Add.114, para. 8:2).

Similar debates had emerged in 1996, when the CERD Committee examined the Indian government's periodic report. Regarding the caste system in India, the CERD Committee acknowledged that caste discrimination falls under the jurisdiction of CERD, stating "that the role of the Committee included the examination of social as well as racial discrimination" (CERD/CR/S1531, para. 5:2). But the Indian government did not accept this claim (Murakami, 2002, p. 4). In addition to India and Japan, the issue of discrimination based on descent emerged when reports from Nepal and Bangladesh were examined in 2000 and 2001, respectively. In these cases also, the government claimed that these types of discrimination fall outside the purview of the CERD, but the Committee rejected these claims (Tomonaga, 2013, pp. 71–2).[12]

---

[12] In the following few years, descent-based discrimination was discussed in examination of periodic reports of Senegal, Mali, Ghana, UK, South Korea, Madagascar, Mauritania, and Nigeria (Murakami, 2005, pp. 89–91). The IDSN reports that "caste discrimination is found in varying degrees in India, Nepal, Pakistan, Bangladesh, Sri Lanka, Japan, Micronesia, Yemen, Senegal, Burkina Faso, Mali, Chad, Cameroon, Ghana, Mauritius, Mauritania, Madagascar, Nigeria, Kenya, Ethiopia and Somalia, and possibly more countries. It also occurs in Diaspora communities in Europe, North America, and Asia" (International Dalit Solidarity Network, 2015, p. 7).

In response to these repeated claims by governments and in light of the development in the Sub-Commission described above, the CERD Committee had a "Thematic Discussion on Discrimination Based on Descent" and issued a resolution in 2002 (CERD/C/SR.1531).[13] The BLL and IMADR both played a key role in the adoption of this resolution, as they invited committee members, Lagaban Basdeban Pillai and Patrick Thornberry to Japan for symposiums on this issue and also had them visit Burakumin communities. In addition, members of both the BLL and IMADR participated in the thematic discussion at the CERD Committee. One of the members, Masanao Murakami, left a mark in the resulting document: "Mr. Murakami, who had spoken the previous day, contending that the broadest interpretation of the term 'descent' was the most appropriate, and would not lead to an unjustifiable expansion of the role of the Convention" (CERD/C/SR.1531, para. 5:3; Tomonaga, 2003, pp. 9–10). The same document also specifically mentioned Japan and India and urged them to recognize descent-based discrimination as a part of the CERD: "Japan and India must reconsider their views with respect to the competence of the Committee to consider the issue of descent-based discrimination" (CERD/C/SR.1531, para. 7:3).

After these debates, the CERD Committee adopted a resolution, known as general recommendation 29 (CERD/C/61/Misc. 29), that explicitly recognized descent-based discrimination as an important type of discrimination under the jurisdiction of the CERD that is distinct from discrimination based on race, color, national or ethnic origin. This was not a new interpretation of the treaty at all, as the Committee had made the same claim before, but repeated disagreements about this from member states prompted the Committee to reconfirm that descent-based discrimination is a distinct type of discrimination that the CERD prohibits (Murakami, 2002, p. 20). The general recommendation also specified measures to address this type of discrimination in various areas such as marriage, employment, housing, education, gender, media, political participation, and law enforcement, and served as a basis for future discussions and resolutions on this issue at the UN. In measures such as the restriction of background checks and affirmative action, Japanese NGOs such as IMADR publicized Burakumin's experiences as successful examples,

---

[13] The CERD Committee did not offer a precise definition of "descent" but presented seven factors commonly found in descent-based groups: restrictions on changing their status; restrictions on intermarriage; segregation in public and private life; restrictions on changing inherited occupation; indentured servitude; theories about impurity and untouchability; and lack of respect for human dignity and equality (Murakami, 2005, pp. 88–9).

and the outcome document reflected these examples. This general recommendation was the first international document that specifically focused on descent-based discrimination, and in it, Japanese NGOs have, perhaps for the first time, exported a Japanese model of anti-discrimination efforts to the world (Murakami, 2002, pp. 20–1).[14] This recognition of descent-based discrimination has ramifications beyond the CERD Committee, because it establishes obligations to promote and address descent-based discrimination throughout the UN system.

The Japanese government, on the other hand, continues to deny Burakumin issues as part of the CERD. It argues that in the process of drafting CERD Article 1, the term "descent" was proposed along with "place of origin" simply to avoid the confusion that "national origin" can bring, and therefore it is about racial and national origin, not about social origin, and does not apply to Burakumin, who are neither racially nor nationally distinct (Ministry of Foreign Affairs, 2001). In the CERD Committee examination of its periodic reports in 2010 and 2014, Committee members repeatedly urged Japan to change its stance, and the Committee expressed "regret" in the Concluding Observations both times.[15]

---

[14] In addition to the CERD Committee, three other UN treaty bodies have referred to "caste" as a prohibited form of discrimination in their general comments: CESCR No. 20 on non-discrimination (2009), CEDAW No. 25 on temporary measures (2004), and CEDAW No. 28 on core obligations (2010) (International Dalit Solidarity Network, 2015, p. 7).

[15] In its most recent examination in 2014, the CERD Committee stated the following in its Concluding Observations. "The Committee regrets the position of the State party which excludes the Burakumin from the application of the Convention on the grounds of descent. It is concerned that the State party has not yet adopted a uniform definition of Burakumin, as raised by the Committee in its previous concluding observations. The Committee is concerned about the lack of information and indicators to assess the impact of concrete measures implemented by the State party upon the termination of the Dowa Special Measures in 2002, including measures to counter discrimination against the Burakumin. The Committee is also concerned about the persistent socio-economic gaps between the Burakumin and the rest of the population. The Committee is further concerned at reported abuses of the illegal access to the family registration system, which may be used for discriminatory purposes against Burakumin (art. 5). Bearing in mind its general recommendation No. 29 (2002) on descent, the Committee recalls that discrimination on the ground of descent is fully covered by the Convention. The Committee recommends that the State revise its position and adopt a clear definition of Burakumin in consultation with Buraku people. The Committee also recommends that the State party provide information and indicators on concrete measures taken upon the termination of the Dowa Special Measures in 2002, in particular on living conditions of Burakumin. The Committee further recommends that the

The Japanese government might continue to resist accepting Burakumin as a group that should be protected under the CERD. However, descent-based discrimination has been firmly established as a global human rights issue, and all UN members are expected to combat this type of discrimination. Armed with the UN resolutions and principles, IMADR continues to report on descent-based discrimination and promote solutions to this problem, in alliance with the UN and other international organizations.

CONCLUSION

This case demonstrates how global human rights can draw local actors into the system, transform their orientations in the international direction, and turn them into valuable contributors to the consolidation and expansion of global human rights. Local groups come to global arenas seeking to achieve their own goals. But once they start engaging in international forums and become a fixture in them, their orientation tends to shift in the direction of more international, altruistic work. Pursuit of their own domestic success never completely disappears from their international activities, but over time international contributions become increasingly important for the local groups.

Burakumin initially came to the UN human rights system seeking to advance their domestic goals of eliminating social discrimination against them. As they started participating in UN forums regularly, their orientations got transformed, and they established a UN consultative status international NGO that promotes human rights across the globe. Motivated to gain the UN's legitimacy for their activism, they sought to establish discrimination based on work and descent as a new category of human rights issue and succeeded in doing so.

These international activities have helped Burakumin activists achieve their domestic goals to a certain extent. There are some signs that social discrimination has declined, especially in urban areas. Opinion polls show that fewer Japanese see Burakumin status as a hurdle for marriage, although there are some regional variations. A 2002 survey conducted in Tokyo, an urban area where population mobility is high and Burakumin

---

State party effectively apply its legislation to protect Burakumin against illegal access to their family data which may expose them to discriminatory acts, investigate all incidents relating to illegal abuses of the family registration and punish those responsible" (CERD/C/JPN/CO/7-9, para. 22).

presence is low, shows that 4.2 percent of respondents would oppose their children's marriage to a Burakumin person; a different survery conducted in 2004 in Mie prefecture, a much less urbanized area with much greater Burakumin presence, shows that 30.7 percent of respondents would encourage their children to reconsider their marriage if it was with a Burakumin person (Kurokawa, 2011, p. 249). Considering that the rate of intermarriage among Burakumin (marriage with a non-Burakumin person) was 1–3 percent in the early 20th country, this constitutes significant improvement. Migration from and to traditionally Burakumin areas has increased significantly. One survey in Osaka City shows that over 40 percent of households in Burakumin communities in Osaka City immigrated from outside (Noguchi, 2000, p. 31). To be sure, the precise impact of international activities on these improvements is hard to gauge, and social discrimination against Burakumin has not completely disappeared. In recent years, online space has emerged as a forum for disparaging language against Burakumin that is particularly difficult to regulate. What is more certain is that Burakumin activism in international forums has made great contributions in raising the standards of global human rights and in empowering the populations facing descent-based discrimination in the world.

This is one example of the expansion of global human rights in recent decades, but similar processes have added many new human rights items on the agenda of international institutions. Does this "hypertrophy of human rights" harm human rights efforts and prevent improvement of human rights practices in the world? It is entirely possible that the growing number of rights issues that international institutions have to attend to have paralysed and incapacitated them. In terms of measurable rights that typically feature personal integrity rights, cross-national evidence on improvement in the past few decades ranges from mixed to negative (Hafner-Burton, 2013). However, the kind of improvement that Burakumin experienced would not be picked up by those quantitative measures. As this case demonstrates, the legitimacy that international institutions confer can have a subtle but far-reaching impact on local practices. The UN's authority may have reduced discrimination against Burakumin, and the new UN norm they helped establish might empower those in other countries who suffer discrimination based on descent. These subtle improvements cannot be easily quantified, but they do matter for people on the ground facing this type of discrimination.

REFERENCES

Websites last accessed 30 October 2016.

Bando, Nozomi. 2001. "2001 Nen Natsu, Kokuren ni Okeru 'Monchi' Sabetsu no Atsukaware Kata." *Buraku Kaiho Kenkyu* **146**, 46–55.

Buraku Kaiho Kenkyusho. 1985. "Jinshusabetsu Teppai Joyaku no Soki Hijiun wo Mezashite." *Buraku Kaiho Kenkyu* **44**, 114–31.

Buraku Kaiho Kenkyusho. 1989. *Buraku Kaihoshi Ge Kan: Netsu to Hikari wo.* Osaka: Kaiho Shuppansha.

Buraku Kaiho Kenkyusho (ed.). 1994. *Kokuren to Jinken NGO: Han Sabetsu Kokusai Undo to ha?* Osaka: Kaiho Shuppansha.

Hafner-Burton, Emilie M. 2013. *Making Human Rights a Reality*. Princeton, NJ: Princeton University Press.

IMADR-JC. 2001. *Kokuren kara Mita Nihon no Jinshu Sabetsu*. Osaka: Kaiho Shuppansha.

International Dalit Solidarity Network. 2015. "Caste Discrimination and Human Rights." http://idsn.org/wp-content/uploads/2015/02/UNcompilation1.pdf.

Komori, Megumi. 2009. "'Shokugyo to Sekei ni Motozuku Sabetsu' no Kokateki Teppai ni Mukete." *IMADR-JC Tsuushin* **160**, 11–12.

Kurokawa, Midori. 2011. *Kindai Burakushi: Meiji kara Gendai Made*. Tokyo: Heibonsha.

Lie, John. 2001. *Multi-ethnic Japan*. Cambridge, MA: Harvard University Press.

McLauchlan, Alastair. 2003. *Prejudice and Discrimination in Japan: The Buraku Issue*. Lewiston, NY: Edwin Mellen Press.

Ministry of Foreign Affairs. 2001. "Jinshu Sabetsu Teppai Iinkai no Nihon Seihu Houkoku Shinsa ni Kansuru Saishu Kenkai ni Taisutu Nihon Seihu no Iken no Teishutsu." http://www.mofa.go.jp/mofaj/gaiko/jinshu/iken.html.

Murakami, Masanao. 2002. "Jinshu Sabetsu Teppai Iinkai ni okeru 'Sekei Sabetsu' ni Kansuru Kyogi to Kankoku." *Buraku Kaiho Kenkyu* **149**, 2–24.

Murakami, Masanao. 2005. "Jinshu Sabetsu Teppai Iinkai no Doko". In Buraku Kaiho Jinken Kenkyusho (ed.), *Nihon kara Sekai he no Hasshin: Shokugyo to Sekei ni Motozuku Sabetsu*. Osaka: Kaiho Shuppansha, pp. 86–117.

Nakajo, Orga. 2000. "Kokuren Jinken Sho iinkai Dai 52 Kaiki Hokoku." *Buraku Kaiho Kenkyu* **137**, 51–63.

Noguchi, Michihiko. 2000. *Buraku Mondai no Paradaimu Tenkan*. Tokyo: Akashi Shoten.

Posner, Eric A. 2014. *The Twilight of Human Rights Law*. New York: Oxford University Press.

Sekai Jinken Sengen 35 Shunen Chuo Jikko Iinkai. 1983. *Sekai Jinken Sengen 35 Shunen to Buraku Kaiho*. Tokyo: Kaiho Shuppansha.

Suzuki, Mieko. 1994. "Kokuren no Jinken Katsudo to NGO." In Buraku Kaiho Kenkyusho (ed.), *Kokuren to Jinken NGO: Han Sabetsu Kokusai Undo to ha?* Osaka: Kaihou Shuppansha, pp. 22–46.

Tanaka, Atsuko. 1995. "Dai 51 Kaiki Kokuren Jinken Iinkai." *Buraku Kaiho Kenkyu* **107**, 47–57.

Tomonaga, Kenzo. 1978. "Kokusai Jinken Kiyaku Hijun Undou No Igi Ni Tsuite." *Buraku Kaiho Kenkyu* **14**, 1–23.

Tomonaga, Kenzo. 1984. "Kokusai Rentai wo Tsuyome Buraku Kaiho wo." *Buraku Kaiho* **220**, 80–8.

Tomonaga, Kenzo. 1987. *Buraku Kaiho to Han Sabetsu Kokusai Rentai.* Osaka: Kaiho Shuppansha.
Tomonaga, Kenzo. 1989. "Kokuren Toroku NGO ni Mukete Ookiku Zenshin Sita 'Hansabetsu Kokusai Undou'." *Buraku Kaiho* **291**, 82–94.
Tomonaga, Kenzo. 1990. *Suiheisen ni Ima.* Osaka: Kaihou Shuppan Sha.
Tomonaga, Kenzo. 1991. "Saranaru Hatten wo Mezasu 'Hansabetsu Kokusai Undo'." *Buraku Kaiho* **324**, 121–7.
Tomonaga, Kenzo. 1994. "Hansabetsu Kokusai Undo no Kessei, Ayumi, Kadai." In Buraku Kaiho Kenkyusho (ed.), *Kokuren to Jinken NGO: Han Sabetsu Kokusai Undo to ha?* Osaka: Kaihou Shuppansha, pp. 47–65.
Tomonaga, Kenzo. 2003. "Kokuren to Buraku Mondai: Rekishi, Genjo, Kadai." *Buraku Kaiho Kenkyu* **155**, 2–25.
Tomonga, Kenzo. 2013. "Sabetsu Naki Sekai no Kochiku wo Mezashita Buraku Kaiho Undo no Yakuwari." *Buraku Kaiho* **681**, 66–81.
Tsutsui, Kiyoteru. n.d. "Rights Make Might: Global Human Rights and Minority Social Movements in Japan." Manuscript.
Tsutsui, Kiyoteru. 2017. "Human Rights and Minority Activism in Japan: Transformation of Movement Actorhood and Local-global Feedback Loop." *American Journal of Sociology.*
Uesugi, Saichiro. 1984. "Buraku Sabetsu wo Hajime Issaino Sabetsu no Teppai wo." *Buraku Kaiho Kenkyu* **42**, 51–60.
Upham, Frank K. 1987. *Law and Social Change in Postwar Japan.* Cambridge, MA: Harvard University Press.
Wajima, Iwakichi. 1977. *Kokusaijinken Kiyaku to Ningen Kaiho.* Osaka: Kaiho Shuppansha.

4. Indigenous peoples: from objects of protection to subjects of rights

Felipe Gómez Isa

To the memory of Bertha Cáceres[1]

INTRODUCTION

Indigenous peoples have lived through a process of invisibility and systematic exclusion since the era of conquest. The arrival of republican states in Latin America following the decolonization process did not involve a substantial change in the traditional relationship of subjection and submission endured by native peoples in the Americas. In the mid twentieth century, the international community began to pay attention to the marginalized situation of indigenous peoples. The main objective was to integrate some peoples that were considered to be backward and in need of protection. It was within this paradigm that most of the interactions with indigenous peoples have occurred, such as the first international treaty adopted in this field, Convention No. 107 of the International Labour Organization (ILO, 1957). This situation began to change with the adoption of Convention No. 169 by the ILO in 1989, and especially with the recently adopted United Nations Declaration on the Rights of Indigenous Peoples (UNDRIP, 2007). From this point onwards, indigenous peoples have moved from being considered as populations to be protected, to being regarded as distinct peoples, with rights that deserve to be recognized and secured both domestically and internationally. This

---

[1] At the time of writing this chapter, March 2016, Bertha Cáceres was assassinated due to her role as indigenous leader of the Lenca people in Honduras and as an environmental activist opposing the construction of the Agua Zarca Dam. We are witnessing a backlash against indigenous human rights defenders in the context of the expansion of extractive industries and mega-development projects. The increasing indigenous resistance to the extractive paradigm is facing violent repression and the criminalization of social protest (Rojas-Páez, 2014).

chapter aims to analyse this interesting albeit contradictory process of expansion of both norms and mechanisms to promote and protect indigenous peoples' rights.

INDIGENOUS PEOPLES UNDER INTERNATIONAL LAW: FROM EXCLUSION TO INCLUSION

Traditional international law has played a major role in the dramatic history of conquest, usurpation of indigenous peoples' sovereignty, and dispossesion of their lands, territories and resources (Keal, 2003). The emerging international legal order in Europe became a powerful instrument in the hands of conquerors to dominate and subjugate indigenous peoples in the Americas (Anaya, 2004; Anghie, 2004). Since its inception, given the role played by the main European powers in its creation, and the subordinate position of indigenous peoples and other non-Western countries and societies, international law could be characterized as a hegemonic discourse and as a source of domination (Rajagopal, 2003). Accordingly, Elvira Pulitano (2012, p.4) has referred to international law as "quintessentially Eurocentric." At the same time, in a highly contradictory move, the so-called Spanish School of International Law (Scott, 1934), based on the Aristotelian and Thomist idea of the natural sociability and rationality of human beings, defended the essential humanity and freedom of the Indians in the context of the Spanish conquest of the Americas (Gómez Isa, 2015a). The ideas of scholars such as Francisco de Vitoria or Bartolomé de las Casas opened the door to the consideration of the Indians as full human beings in need of protection (Carozza, 2003, p.291). But, unfortunately, the conquest of the Americas did not follow in practice the teachings of these precursors of contemporary human rights law.

This situation continued unaltered until very recently, when contemporary international law progressively changed its approach to indigenous peoples. But it is highly shocking that even in the first half of the twentieth century the West still believed that it was entrusted with a "civilizing mission" to save non-European peoples from ignorance and backwardness.[2] In line with this approach, the first international

---

[2] This is the essence of some provisions found in the Covenant of the League of Nations (1919), the constitutive treaty of the first international organization. According to Article 22, a provision that has to be read in a colonial context, "to those colonies and territories which as a consequence of the late war have ceased to be under the sovereignty of the States which formerly governed them and which are inhabited by *peoples not yet able to stand by themselves* under the strenuous

treaty adopted by the ILO in 1957 to deal specifically with indigenous issues was still dominated by an assimilationist paradigm (Thornberry, 2002, pp. 329–33). As stated in Article 2 of the Indigenous and Tribal Populations Convention (No. 107, 1957), "Governments shall have the primary responsibility for developing co-ordinated and systematic action for the protection of the populations concerned and their *progressive integration* into the life of their respective countries" [3] (emphasis added).

The 1970s and 1980s witnessed the so-called "indigenous emergence" (Bengoa, 2000; Brysk, 2000), and international law, particularly international human rights law, became a very powerful discursive resource for indigenous peoples to advance their demands both at domestic and international fora. In Rhiannon Morgan's view, "the global indigenous movement is just one example of a movement that has grasped the transformative, dynamic potential lodged in the discourse of human rights, drawing on its manipulability and malleability to foster the reform of human rights" (Morgan, 2011, p. 43). But the human rights discourse also has some inherent contradictions when approached from an indigenous perspective. We have to admit that the very idea of human rights has certain features reminiscent of colonialism. Like colonialism, "human rights discourse contains implicit assumptions about the nature of civilized and backward societies . . . Concepts of civilization and savagery, rationality and passion, that were fundamental binaries of thinking during the imperialist era creep back into debates over human rights and social justice. The practice of human rights is burdened by a colonialist understanding of culture" (Engle Merry, 2006, p. 226). Along the same lines, Makau Mutua (2009, p. 901) sees the way the most dominant proponents have constructed human rights as "part of the colonial project that forms the unbroken chain of the Christian missionary, the early merchant of capital, and the colonial administrator."

At the same time, and as part of the process of empowerment of indigenous peoples, since the 1970s the United Nations (UN) has been increasingly receptive to claims by indigenous peoples (Willemsen-Diaz, 2009, pp. 16–31), opening institutional spaces and avenues for their participation and for the advance of their demands.[4] Indigenous peoples

---

conditions of the modern world, there should be applied the principle that the well-being and development of such peoples form a *sacred trust of civilization*" (emphasis added).

3 Also, ILO Convention No. 107 refers to indigenous "populations" instead of peoples. The recognition as true peoples and nations is one of the main claims of the global indigenous movement.

4 A number of bodies were created to deal specifically with indigenous issues (Working Group on Indigenous Peoples; Working Group on a Draft Declaration

used the UN as a mobilizing structure to increase visibility of their marginalized position and to pursue some strategic goals in terms of recognition and protection (Bellier and Préaud, 2012). In a sense, we witnessed a very promising process of decolonization of both international law and the UN.[5] This process has allowed indigenous peoples to transform from solely victims to actors, and from objects of protection to subjects of rights, thus opening the door to their acquisition of some forms of international legal personality (Meijknecht, 2001; Sambo Dorough, 2009, p. 265). The culmination of this legal and institutional development is the creation of the UN Permanent Forum on Indigenous Issues in 2000, a unique body in which states and indigenous representatives participate on an equal footing (García-Alix, 2003), and, above all, the adoption of the UNDRIP in 2007. As the Committee on the Rights of Indigenous Peoples of the International Law Association has affirmed, all these developments demonstrate that "indigenous persons and peoples are back not only as fully entitled holders of individual human rights, but as collective actors with distinct rights and status under international law" (ILA, 2010a, p. 2).

---

on Indigenous Peoples' Rights; Permanent Forum on Indigenous Issues; Special Rapporteur on the Rights of Indigenous peoples; and Expert Mechanism on the Rights of Indigenous Peoples). The General Assembly of the UN also proclaimed two consecutive UN Decades on Indigenous Peoples (1994–2003 and 2005–14). The UN Permanent Forum on Indigenous Issues has recently called for a Third International Decade of the World's Indigenous Peoples. In its view, "over the course of the two Decades, we have seen some progress . . . However, we need to ensure and reinvigorate momentum to genuinely implement the UN Declaration . . . A Third Decade can provide a framework and consolidate clear milestones for the achievement of the UN Declaration" (A Third International Decade of the World's Indigenous Peoples, United Nations Permanent Forum on Indigenous Issues, Dalee Sambo Dorough, Chairperson, 7 November 2014, http://www.un.org/esa/socdev/unpfii/documents/Communication-UNPFII%20Chair-3decade.pdf, accessed 15 March 2016).

[5] Post-1945 international law and institutions have been used by the West (an imagined community itself) to construct and impose a new set of rational truths based on particular values, norms and socio-political organizations that were defined as universal. Post-colonial studies have demonstrated that international law and institutions, among many other structures of power, were used by the West to maintain its hierarchies and modes of domination. Indigenous peoples' struggles have aimed to decolonize both the theory and practice of the "ideological-institutional complex" known as international law. On this challenging process see the illuminating essay by Sundhya Pahuja (2011).

PROGRESSIVE RECOGNITION OF INDIGENOUS PEOPLES' RIGHTS

One of the most significant developments in the field of human rights in recent decades has been the gradual recognition of the rights of indigenous peoples, both in the domestic and international legal arenas. The ILO was the first international organization to pay attention to the situation of marginalization and exclusion suffered by indigenous peoples. The adoption of ILO Convention 169 in 1989 substituting ILO Convention No. 107 (1957)[6] was a relevant step forward for the recognition of indigenous rights (Rodríguez-Piñero, 2005), but states have been very reluctant to ratify it.[7] Against the background of the negative experience with the two existing ILO Conventions, the global indigenous movement established as a priority the adoption of a declaration of universal reach to recognize its rights. After a lengthy process of negotiation in which indigenous peoples themselves were the main drivers (Bellier, 2012), the UNDRIP was finally adopted on 13 September 2007 by the UN General Assembly by an overwhelming majority.

Main Innovations of the UNDRIP

The UNDRIP has incorporated a whole range of new rights, thus expanding significantly the scope of existing human rights. The main conceptual innovation refers to the recognition of collective rights as complementary to the classical individual rights. Collective rights have been alien to the process of emergence and recognition of human rights in Western legal culture. The multiculturalism that indigenous peoples advocate in addressing human rights clearly challenges, and eventually enriches, a concept of human rights that has been essentially mono-cultural so far. As recognized and reaffirmed in the preamble of the UNDRIP,

---

[6] Twenty-seven states ratified this convention. Since the adoption of ILO Convention 169, Convention 107 is no longer open for ratification. However, it is still in force in 18 countries that have not yet ratified Convention 169.

[7] As of January 2016, only 22 states have ratified ILO Convention No. 169 (Argentina, Plurinational State of Bolivia, Brazil, Central African Republic, Chile, Colombia, Costa Rica, Denmark, Dominica, Ecuador, Fiji, Guatemala, Honduras, Mexico, Nepal, the Netherlands, Nicaragua, Norway, Paraguay, Peru, Spain and Bolivarian Republic of Venezuela), http://www.ilo.org/dyn/normlex/en/f?p=1000:11300:0::NO:11300:P11300_INSTRUMENT_ID:312314, accessed 15 March 2016.

> indigenous individuals are entitled without discrimination to all human rights recognized in international law, and that indigenous peoples possess *collective rights which are indispensable for their existence, well-being and integral development as peoples.* (emphasis added)

The second expansion of rights put forward by the UNDRIP is the recognition of some so-called third generation human rights, also known as solidarity rights. These rights emerged in the 1980s but faced strong opposition from Western countries. The most relevant solidarity right enshrined in the UNDRIP is the right to development (Gómez Isa, 2015b). In light of Article 23 of the UNDRIP, "indigenous peoples have the right to determine and develop priorities and strategies for exercising their right to development." Along the same lines, Article 29.1 of the UNDRIP establishes that "indigenous peoples have the right to the conservation and protection of the environment and the productive capacity of their lands or territories and resources."

A final step forward by the UNDRIP is the recognition of the need for free, prior and informed consent of indigenous peoples when states take legislative or administrative measures that may affect them (Rombouts, 2014). While ILO Convention 169 is based on consultation with indigenous peoples, the UNDRIP takes a new step and requires that consultation must lead to obtaining their free, prior and informed consent. As stated in Article 19 of the UNDRIP,

> States shall consult and cooperate in good faith with the indigenous peoples concerned through their own representative institutions in order to obtain their free, prior and informed consent before adopting and implementing legislative or administrative measures that may affect them.

The UNDRIP and Historical Injustices

Another major innovation of the UNDRIP is the recognition of historical injustices as an impediment to the enjoyment of human rights by indigenous peoples. Actually, it is one of the first references to this issue that can be found in an international legal instrument.

The adoption of the UNDRIP in 2007 reflects the deepest aspirations of the world's indigenous peoples and their confidence in international law and human rights law as powerful tools to modify entrenched patterns of domination and exclusion that have affected indigenous peoples since colonial times (Glenn, 2011, p. 174). The very adoption of the UNDRIP can be interpreted as an attempt to repair historical wrongs suffered by indigenous peoples (Gómez Isa, 2011). Significantly, the wording of the Declaration includes an explicit reference to historical injustices. In the preamble of this Declaration, the General Assembly of the UN emphasized that

> indigenous peoples have suffered from *historic injustices* as a result of, inter alia, their colonisation and dispossession of their lands, territories and resources, thus preventing them from exercising, in particular, their right to development in accordance with their own needs and interests.[8] (emphasis added)

In addition to the concern about historic injustices[9] expressed by the General Assembly, we can also see a cause-effect link between colonization and the dispossession of land, territories and resources suffered by indigenous peoples in the past, and the inability to effectively exercise their right to development, the consequences of which are still being felt (Concha Malo, 2007, p.321).

The substantive text of the Declaration contains a significant number of provisions on the right of redress for indigenous peoples, some of which have clear links to the past and to historical injustices. In this regard, Article 11 recognizes the right of indigenous peoples to "practise and revitalise their cultural traditions and customs," which includes the right to "maintain, protect and develop the *past*, present and future manifestations of their cultures, such as archaeological and historical sites, artefacts, designs, ceremonies" (emphasis added). Sometimes the enforcement of this right involves a process of restitution of property and objects that indigenous peoples were deprived of in the past. As stated in paragraph 2 of Article 11, "States shall provide redress through effective mechanisms, which may include restitution . . . with respect to their cultural, intellectual, religious and spiritual property taken without their free, prior and informed consent or in violation of their laws, traditions and customs." Article 12, meanwhile, refers to the "repatriation of ceremonial objects and human remains" by the states that possess them.

Article 20 of the Declaration recognizes that "indigenous peoples deprived of their means of subsistence and development are entitled to just and fair redress." Although this provision does not specify whether or not it refers to the hardship suffered by indigenous peoples in the past, it could be argued that past injustices largely explain the exclusions of the present

---

8 Paragraph 6 of the preamble.

9 The issue of historical injustices is also present in Kiyoteru Tsutui's chapter in this volume, where he develops the patterns of exclusion and discrimination suffered by the Burakumin in Japan's history.

and, therefore, indigenous peoples should be entitled to redress to that effect. In the same vein, Article 28.1 states that

> indigenous peoples have the right to redress, by means that can include restitution, or, when this is not possible, just, fair and equitable compensation, for the lands, territories and resources which they have traditionally owned or otherwise occupied or sued, and which have been confiscated, taken, occupied, used or damaged without their free, prior and informed consent.

Paragraph 2 of this provision details more types of redress that are relevant to the deprivation of land, territories and resources owned by indigenous peoples. Thus, "unless freely agreed upon by the peoples concerned, compensation shall take the form of lands, territories and resources in equal quality, size and legal status of monetary compensation or other appropriate redress." As regards development projects related to lands, territories and other indigenous resources, Article 32.2 of the Declaration demands the "free and informed consent" of indigenous peoples before approval is given by the state, especially when a project involves "the use or exploitation of mineral, water or other resources." In this context, paragraph 3 of Article 32 provides that "States shall provide effective mechanisms for just and fair redress for any such activities, and appropriate measures shall be taken to mitigate adverse environmental, economic, social, cultural or spiritual impact."

Another important provision from the point of view of the redress to which indigenous peoples are entitled is Article 15 of the Declaration, which deals with education and the media. As we have seen, in order to ensure that past abuses do not take place again, some aspects of indigenous cultures and worldviews have to be incorporated into the educational system and the media. In this regard, Article 15.1 states that "indigenous peoples have the right to the dignity and diversity of their cultures, traditions, histories and aspirations which shall be appropriately reflected in education and public information." To reinforce this right, "States shall take effective measures, in consultation and cooperation with the indigenous peoples concerned, to combat prejudice and eliminate discrimination and to promote tolerance, understanding and good relations among indigenous peoples and all other segments of society."

As has been seen, the right of indigenous peoples to compensation, including some key provisions to seek to ensure redress for historical injustices, is at the forefront of the UNDRIP, unlike other international instruments to protect indigenous peoples' rights mentioned previously.

The UNDRIP and Existing International Law

To a great extent, many of the provisions embodied in the UNDRIP do not create new rights, but can be considered as a reaffirmation of existing customary international law (Anaya and Wiessner, 2007). As James Anaya (2008, p. 43), former Special Rapporteur on the situation of human rights and fundamental freedoms of indigenous people, has argued, the Declaration "reflects the existing international consensus regarding the individual and collective rights of indigenous peoples in a way that is coherent with, and expands upon, international developments, including the interpretations of other human rights instruments by international bodies and mechanisms." The same conclusion can be found in a recent resolution adopted by the International Law Association (ILA, 2012, para. 2). According to this very authoritative opinion, "the 2007 UNDRIP as a whole cannot yet be considered as a statement of existing customary international law. However it includes several key provisions which correspond to existing state obligations under customary international law." Among the norms of the UNDRIP that can be regarded as evidence of customary international law, the ILA included the following: the right of indigenous peoples to self-determination, autonomy and self-government; the right to participate in national decision-making with respect to decisions that may affect them; the right to free, prior and informed consent (FPIC) on projects significantly impacting their rights and ways of life; the right to cultural identity; the right to lands, territories and resources, including restitution of ancestral lands of which they have been deprived in the past; the right to establish their own educational institutions and media; and the right to reparation and redress for wrongs indigenous peoples have suffered.

This position was explicitly rejected by those states that voted against the UNDRIP (United States, Canada, Australia and New Zealand). The clearest opposition came from the United States, denying

> any possibility that this document is or can become customary international law . . . As this declaration does not describe current state practice or actions that states feel obliged to take as a matter of legal obligation, it cannot be cited as evidence of the evolution of customary international law. (United States, 2007)

The Canadian representative also shared this approach, when it stated that the Declaration "has no legal effect in Canada, and its provisions do not represent customary international law."[10] In the same vein, the Australian

---

[10] UN Doc. A/61/PV.107, p. 13.

government emphasized that the UNDRIP "is an aspirational declaration with political and moral force but no legal force . . . it is not intended itself to be legally binding or reflective of international law."[11] While recognizing the relevance of the position of these states, we must underline that they "represent only a minority of states specially affected by the Declaration" (Barelli, 2009, p. 967). It seems quite clear that the position of these states would not be able to prevent the emergence of international customary law (Meza-Lopehandía, 2013, p. 466), but they probably could have been considered as persistent objectors, given that they opposed the text of the UNDRIP from the very early stages of its drafting. Although, fortunately for the cause of indigenous peoples, these four states have changed their official positions vis-à-vis the UNDRIP and have endorsed it, they have repeatedly reiterated that the Declaration is neither legally binding nor a statement of current international law. According to the United States, "while not legally binding or a statement of current international law," the Declaration "has both moral and political force," and "expresses both the aspirations of indigenous peoples around the world and those of States in seeking to improve their relations with indigenous peoples."[12] Along the same lines, Australia declared that "while it is non-binding and does not affect existing Australian law, it sets important international principles for nations to aspire to." And, more importantly from an international legal perspective, "Australia's existing obligations under international human rights treaties are mirrored in the Declaration's fundamental principles."[13]

---

[11] Ibid., p. 12.

[12] Announcement of U.S. Support for the United Nations Declaration on the Rights of Indigenous Peoples, 16 December 2010, http://www.state.gov/documents/organization/184099.pdf, accessed 15 March 2016. A very similar position was expressed by the Canadian government. In its view, "the Declaration is a non-legally binding document that does not reflect customary international law nor change Canadian laws . . . In 2007, at the time of the vote during the United Nations General Assembly, and since, Canada placed on record its concerns with various provisions of the Declaration . . . These concerns are well known and remain. However, we have since listened to Aboriginal leaders who have urged Canada to endorse the Declaration and we have also learned from the experience of other countries. We are now confident that Canada can interpret the principles expressed in the Declaration in a manner that is consistent with our Constitution and legal framework"; Canada's Statement of Support on the United Nations Declaration on the Rights of Indigenous Peoples, 12 November 2010, http://www.aadnc-aandc.gc.ca/eng/1309374239861/1309374546142, accessed 15 March 2016.

[13] Statement on the United Nations Declaration on the Rights of Indigenous Peoples, Parliament House, Canberra, 3 April 2009, http://www.un.org/esa/socdev/unpfii/documents/Australia_official_statement_endorsement_UNDRIP.pdf, accessed 15 March 2016.

Irrespective of the legal nuances expressed by these countries, we must recognize that these endorsements, an unprecedented move as regards an instrument of this nature, represents a clear signal of the growing acceptance of indigenous peoples' rights as an integral part of the contemporary human rights regime.[14] In this sense, the words by the Minister of Maori Affairs of New Zealand when she announced its support to the UNDRIP are very illustrative: "New Zealand now adds its support to the Declaration both as an affirmation of fundamental rights and in its expression of new and widely supported aspirations."[15]

Legal Scope of the UNDRIP

When trying to ascertain the legal value of the UNDRIP, three elements are of utmost importance: the circumstances of adoption of the instrument; the precision and normative nature of its content; and the existence of implementation mechanisms.

The adoption of the UNDRIP in 2007 is the result of more than 25 years of intense and controversial negotiations in which indigenous peoples and their close allies achieved very significant levels of participation. We can affirm that the way in which this process was conducted, and the very positive outcomes, will eventually influence international norm-creation exercises in other areas of international law, in general, and international human rights law, in particular. H. Patrick Glenn (2011, p. 174) situates the Declaration as part of a broader movement of international law. In his view, the Declaration "would represent not simply a use or application of international law, in novel circumstances, but a major shift in the nature and direction of international law itself." The inclusiveness of the process and the support from a number of bodies and instances within the UN, and from states themselves, provide the Declaration with high degrees of legitimacy that will definitely increase compliance.

---

[14] A less optimistic view has been expressed by some scholars. In relation to Australia's endorsement, "it remains to be seen whether the international legislation underpinning the UNDRIP can be brought to bear on Australia, or whether the current government's endorsement of UNDRIP is indeed little more than an empty gesture designed to enhance the country's reputation in the eyes of the world" (Collingwood-Whittick, 2012, p. 136).

[15] Statement by Hon Dr Pita Sharples, Minister of Maori Affairs, Announcement of New Zealand's support for the Declaration on the Rights of Indigenous Peoples, 19 April 2010, http://www.mfat.govt.nz/Media-and-publications/Media/MFAT-speeches/2010/0-19-April-2010.php, accessed 15 March 2016.

The final vote on the UNDRIP at the UN General Assembly is also an indication of the international consensus around the document. As we know, 144 states voted in favor of the Declaration, 11 abstained[16] and four voted against. An interesting evolution has taken place since 2007, and the four states that voted against have all endorsed the Declaration. Along the same lines, two of the abstaining states, Colombia and Samoa, have also made up their mind. This overwhelming support to the UNDRIP shows a clear commitment on the part of the international community to support the protection of the rights enshrined in the Declaration and promote compliance, and can be considered as clear evidence of *opinio iuris* that, if accompanied by consistent state practice, may give rise to new rules of customary international law.

The final determining factor to calibrate the legal value of the UNDRIP is the existence of mechanisms for its implementation. The UNDRIP does not create specific follow-up mechanisms, but relies on existing bodies both at international and state levels. The only body explicitly mentioned is the Permanent Forum on Indigenous Issues (PFII), thus placing it "at the forefront in ensuring the effective implementation of the Declaration" (Barelli, 2009, p. 978). In light of Article 42 of the Declaration,

> The United Nations, its bodies, including the Permanent Forum on Indigenous Issues, and specialized agencies, including at the country level, and States shall promote respect for and full application of the provisions of this Declaration and follow up the effectiveness of this Declaration.

According to the interpretation developed by Luis Rodríguez-Piñero (2009a, pp. 74–5), the main goal of this provision is "mainstreaming and operationalizing" the promotion of the rights enshrined in the Declaration within the activities of UN bodies, specialized agencies, regional organizations and states. Therefore, implementation measures of the UNDRIP will need to be taken at three parallel and inter-related levels: international, regional and national.

At the international level, it must be acknowledged that a high number of UN bodies and specialized agencies are increasingly using the UNDRIP as a parameter of reference when interpreting international legal standards and their mandates. First of all, the mechanisms created to specifically address indigenous issues refer explicitly to the UNDRIP as an interpretive guide. Given the relevant coordinating role of the PFII aimed at

---

[16] Azerbaijan, Bangladesh, Bhutan, Burundi, Colombia, Georgia, Kenya, Nigeria, Russian Federation, Samoa and Ukraine.

mainstreaming indigenous issues throughout the whole UN system,[17] its position is key for the implementation of the UNDRIP. In its 2008 session, the PFII welcomed the adoption of the Declaration and stated that it will be "its legal framework" (UN Permanent Forum on Indigenous Issues, 2008).[18] Similarly, the Special Rapporteur on the situation of human rights and fundamental freedoms of indigenous people (SR) was also entrusted with the mandate of promoting the UNDRIP (Human Rights Council, 2007), and it has worked very hard to make it possible. As James Anaya (2008, para. 85), former SR, stated, the UNDRIP

> represents an authoritative common understanding, at the global level, of the minimum content of the rights of indigenous peoples, upon a foundation of various sources of international human rights law . . . The principles and rights affirmed in the Declaration constitute or add to the normative frameworks for the activities of United Nations human rights institutions, mechanisms and specialized agencies as they relate to indigenous peoples.

Finally, the recently created Expert Mechanism on the Rights of Indigenous Peoples (EMRIP) is also a body that can significantly contribute to the implementation of the UNDRIP. Given its technical and advisory function as a body composed of five independent experts, the EMRIP is in a "privileged position to contribute to promoting authoritative interpretations of the standards of the Declaration" (Rodríguez-Piñero, 2009b, p. 334).

The UN human rights treaty bodies have also gradually interpreted the human rights conventions incorporating indigenous peoples' rights (Thornberry, 2002, p. 116), and more recently they have referred explicitly to the UNDRIP as a parameter of reference when interpreting the international human rights legal standards. Along these lines, the recent World Conference on Indigenous Peoples invited the human rights treaty bodies "to consider the Declaration in accordance with their respective

---

[17] In 2002, the Inter-Agency Support Group on Indigenous Issues (IASG) was created to support the PFII in the goal of promoting dialogue and cooperation between UN bodies and agencies dealing with indigenous issues. The IASG is composed of 31 bodies, departments, funds and agencies of the UN (Burger, 2009, pp. 309–10).

[18] Some members of the PFII have claimed that given the special legitimacy and radical novelty of the UNDRIP, it should have some legally binding effects. This view has been expressed, among others, by Bartolomé Clavero (2008, p. 9), for whom "although the Declaration is not a treaty between states, it constitutes a convention or covenant between states and peoples, between the member states of the United Nations and indigenous peoples."

mandates," and encouraged states "to include . . . information on the situation of the rights of indigenous peoples, including measures taken to pursue the objectives of the Declaration, in reports to those bodies" (World Conference on Indigenous Peoples, 2014, para. 29).

At the regional level, both the Inter-American Court of Human Rights and the African Commission on Human and Peoples' Rights[19] are using the UNDRIP as one of the legal bases for their findings and decisions. The UNDRIP, and the positive vote by Suriname at the UN General Assembly, were used by the Inter-American Court of Human Rights in its judgment on *Saramaka People vs. Suriname*,[20] a case in which the Court affirmed the indigenous peoples' rights over land, territories and natural resources. The Court affirmed that states have the obligation "to obtain the consent of indigenous and tribal peoples to carry out large-scale development or investment projects that have a significant impact on the right of use and enjoyment of their ancestral territories."[21] This is a very far-reaching decision, since the Court is implicitly recognizing that these standards are operative principles of international law irrespective of the normative scope of the Declaration and despite the fact that the state involved in this specific case is not a party to ILO Convention 169.

The African Commission on Human and Peoples' Rights (ACHPR) has also been open to incorporate the UNDRIP in the legal framework it has to apply. Just some two months after the approval of the UNDRIP, the ACHPR welcomed its adoption and stated that "the Declaration will become a very valuable tool and a point of reference for its efforts to ensure the promotion and protection of indigenous peoples' rights on the African continent."[22] In a memorable decision dated May 2009,[23]

---

[19] On the conflicting emergence of indigenous peoples' rights in the African context see Viljoen (2012) and Mukwiza Ndahinda (2011). On the position of African states vis-à-vis the process of adoption of the UNDRIP and the UNDRIP itself see Barume (2009).

[20] Inter-American Court of Human Rights, *Saramaka People v. Suriname (Preliminary Objections, Merits, Reparations, and Costs)*, Judgment of 28 November 2007, Series C No. 172, paras. 131 and 138.

[21] Ibid., para. 129.

[22] ACHPR, Resolution 121 (XXXXII) on the UN Declaration on the Rights of Indigenous Peoples, 28 November 2007.

[23] *Centre for Minority Rights Development (Kenya) and Minority Rights Group International on behalf of Endorois Welfare Council v. Kenya*, Communication 276/2003, para. 232. The African Commission relied to a great extent on the indigenous jurisprudence of the Inter-American Court of Human Rights, in a clear example of cross-fertilization between regional human rights systems.

the African Commission stated that the forcible eviction of the Endorois people from their traditional lands near Lake Bogoria by the government of Kenya without prior consultation and with no provision for compensation was a violation of a number of rights under the African Charter on Human and Peoples' Rights (ACHPR) and under the UNDRIP (Borraz, 2013).

At the national level, indigenous peoples' rights have also been gradually recognized both at the legislative and judicial levels,[24] opening avenues for their effective implementation. First of all, many states, especially in Latin America, have gone through constitutional changes to incorporate indigenous peoples' rights. The most significant development took place in Bolivia,[25] where a law[26] was adopted to explicitly incorporate the UNDRIP in its domestic legal system. At the judicial level, both the Colombian Constitutional Court (Gómez Isa, 2014), the Constitutional Court of Peru[27] and the Supreme Court of Belize have used the UNDRIP in some of their decisions. It is worth noting that the Supreme Court of Belize issued "the first court judgment ever to apply the UNDRIP . . . barely a month after its adoption" (Campbell and Anaya, 2008, p. 377). The Supreme Court referred specifically to Belize's vote in favor of the UNDRIP as a clear commitment on future compliance in the *Case of the Maya Villages of Belize*. As stated by the Supreme Court, "General Assembly resolutions are not ordinarily binding on member states. But where these resolutions or Declarations contain principles of general international law, states are not expected to disregard them."[28] And the Court continues emphasizing that "it is of some signal importance . . . that

---

[24] Countries that have affirmed the right of indigenous peoples to their cultural identity, their cultural rights, land rights, right to autonomy and participatory rights include Argentina, Australia, Bangladesh, Botswana, Brazil, Cambodia, Canada, Chile, Colombia, Costa Rica, India, Laos, Malaysia, Mexico, New Zealand, Nicaragua, Norway, Paraguay, Peru, South Africa and Taiwan, among many others (ILA, 2010b, pp. 49–50).

[25] The new Constitutions of Bolivia (2009) and Ecuador (2008) are leading examples of a new wave of constitutionalism known as plurinational constitutionalism. See Almut Schilling-Vacaflor and René Kuppe (2012).

[26] Ley 3760 de los derechos de los pueblos indígenas, 7 November 2007.

[27] The Constitutional Court of Peru has also referred to ILO Convention 169, the jurisprudence of the Inter-American Court of Human Rights and the UNDRIP to reaffirm the rights of indigenous peoples to their lands and territories in the *Tres Islas indigenous community Case*, Sentencia del Tribunal Constitucional, Exp. No. 01126-2011-HC/TC, 11 September 2012, para. 23.

[28] *Manuel Coy, Maya Village of Conejo, Manuel Caal, Perfecto Makin, Melina Makin Claimants v. Attorney General of Belize, Minister of Natural Resources, and Environmental Defendants*, Supreme Court of Belize, 18 October 2007, para. 131.

Belize voted in favor of the Declaration."[29] Finally, the Court is of the view that Article 26 of the UNDRIP reflects "the growing consensus and the general principles of international law on indigenous peoples and their lands and resources."[30]

In sum, there is a significant emerging practice at international, regional and domestic levels that constitutes a solid basis to defend that the UNDRIP has become a parameter of reference when interpreting and applying indigenous rights, and that at least some of the key provisions of the UNDRIP have already become customary international law, or are in the process of emerging as new rules of customary law.

CONCLUSIONS AND THE WAY FORWARD

Indigenous peoples have used contemporary international law and international institutions as very close allies in their struggle for recognition and in their efforts to put an end to historically rooted patterns of subjugation, dispossession and cultural assimilation. As part of this evolution, indigenous peoples have become subjects of rights under international law rather than objects of protection, thus becoming protagonists of a far-reaching process of expansion of human rights. The UNDRIP, adopted in 2007 by the UN General Assembly, has to be seen as the culmination of a long and difficult journey in which indigenous peoples themselves and their representatives have been the driving force and key participants. Irrespective of the uncertain legal nature of the UNDRIP per se, one can conclude that it has become an unavoidable parameter of reference when dealing with indigenous peoples' rights. The recent experience of UN bodies, specialized agencies, human rights treaty bodies, regional human rights courts and commissions, and some domestic courts, clearly shows the strong persuasive authority and the interpretive function of the UNDRIP. But in spite of all these promising legal and institutional developments, indigenous peoples' rights still face what Rodolfo Stavenhagen (2006) has termed "the implementation gap." Indigenous peoples continue to suffer from situations of vulnerability and poverty in most countries where they live, as well as growing threats to their lands, territories and natural resources. There is a huge gap between the formal proclamations at the UN and other international organizations, and the harsh realities encountered by indigenous peoples in their daily life.

29 Ibid.
30 Ibid.

REFERENCES

Websites last accessed 15 March 2016.

Anaya, James (2004), *Indigenous Peoples in International Law*, Oxford: Oxford University Press.

Anaya, James (2008), *Report of the Special Rapporteur on the Situation of Human Rights and Fundamental Freedoms of Indigenous People, S. James Anaya*, UN Doc. A/HRC/9/9, 11 August.

Anaya, James and Siegfried Wiessner (2007), "The UN Declaration on the Rights of Indigenous Peoples: Towards Re-empowement," *Jurist*, 3 October, http://jurist.org/forum/2007/10/un-declaration-on-rights-of-indigenous.php.

Anghie, Antony (2004), *Imperialism, Sovereignty and the Making of International Law*, Cambridge: Cambridge University Press.

Barelli, Mauro (2009), "The Role of Soft Law in the International Legal System: The Case of the United Nations Declaration on the Rights of Indigenous Peoples," *International and Comparative Law Quarterly*, **58** (4), 957–83.

Barume, Albert (2009), "Responding to the Concerns of the African States," in Claire Charters and Rodolfo Stavenhagen (eds), *Making the Declaration Work. The United Nations Declaration on the Rights of Indigenous Peoples*, Copenhagen: IWGIA, pp. 170–83.

Bellier, Irène (2012), "Les peuples autochtones aux Nations Unies: un nouvel acteur dans la fabrique des normes internationales," *Critique Internationale*, **54** (1), 61–80.

Bellier, Irène and Martin Préaud (2012), "Emerging Issues in Indigenous Rights: Transformative Effects of the Recognition of Indigenous Peoples," *International Journal of Human Rights*, **16** (3), 474–88.

Bengoa, José (2000), *La emergencia indígena en América Latina*, México: Fondo de Cultura Económica.

Borraz, Patricia (2013), "The Endorois case: Indigenous Peoples' Rights in the African Regional Human Rights System," in Loreto Ferrer and Patricia Borraz (eds), *Indigenous Peoples' Human Rights in Domestic Courts*, Madrid: Almaciga, pp. 211–16.

Brysk, Alison (2000), *From Tribal Village to Global Village. Indian Rights and International Relations in Latin America*, Stanford, CA: Stanford University Press.

Burger, Julian (2009), "Making the Declaration Work for Human Rights in the UN System," in Claire Charters and Rodolfo Stavenhagen (eds), *Making the Declaration Work. The United Nations Declaration on the Rights of Indigenous Peoples*, Copenhagen: IWGIA, pp. 304–13.

Campbell, Maia and James Anaya (2008), "The Case of the Maya Villages of Belize: Reversing the Trend of Government Neglect to Secure Indigenous Land Rights," *Human Rights Law Review*, **8** (2), 377–99.

Carozza, Paolo G. (2003), "From Conquest to Constitutions: Retrieving a Latin American Tradition of the Idea of Human Rights," *Human Rights Quarterly*, **25**, 281–313.

Clavero, Bartolomé (2008), *Nota sobre el Alcance del Mandato contenido en el Artículo 42 de la Declaración sobre los Derechos de los Pueblos Indígenas y el Mejor Modo de Satisfacerlo por parte del Foro Permanente para las Cuestiones Indígenas*, UN Doc. E/C.19/2008/CRP.6, 26 March.

Collingwood-Whittick, Sheila (2012), "Australia's Northern Territory Intervention and Indigenous Rights on Language, Education and Culture: An Ethnocidal Solution to Aboriginal 'Dysfunction'?," in Elvira Pulitano (ed.), *Indigenous Rights in the Age of the UN Declaration*, Cambridge: Cambridge University Press, pp. 110–42.

Concha Malo, Miguel (2007), "Lucha por la dignidad y los derechos humanos individuales y colectivos de los pueblos de América Latina," in Reyes Mate (ed.), *Responsabilidad Histórica. Preguntas del nuevo al viejo mundo*, Barcelona: Anthropos, pp. 313–32.

Engle Merry, Salle (2006), *Human Rights and Gender Violence. Translating International Law into Local Justice*, Chicago, IL: University of Chicago Press.

García-Alix, Lola (2003), *The Permanent Forum on Indigenous Issues*, Copenhagen: IWGIA.

Glenn, Patrick (2011), "The Three Ironies of the UN Declaration on the Rights of Indigenous Peoples," in Stephen Allen and Alexandra Xanthaki (eds), *Reflections on the UN Declaration on the Rights of Indigenous Peoples*, Oxford: Hart Publishing, pp. 171–82.

Gómez Isa, Felipe (2011), "Repairing Historical Injustices: Indigenous Peoples in Post-conflict Scenarios," in Gaby Oré Aguilar and Felipe Gómez Isa (eds), *Rethinking Transitions. Equality and Social Justice in Societies Emerging from Conflict*, Cambridge and Antwerp: Intersentia, pp. 265–300.

Gómez Isa, Felipe (2014), "Cultural Diversity, Legal Pluralism, and Human Rights from an Indigenous Perspective: The Approach by the Colombian Constitutional Court and the Inter-American Court of Human Rights," *Human Rights Quarterly*, **36** (2), 722–55.

Gómez Isa, Felipe (2015a), "The First Cry for Justice in the Americas – From Antonio de Montesinos to the Laws of Burgos (1512)," in Markku Suksi, Kalliope Agapiou-Josephides, Jean-Paul Lehners and Manfred Nowak (eds), *First Fundamental Rights Documents in Europe. Commemorating 800 Years of Magna Carta*, Cambridge: Intersentia, pp. 93–105.

Gómez Isa, Felipe (2015b), "The Right to Development, Translating Indigenous Voice(s) into Development Theory and Practice," in Jan Wouters, Alberto Ninio, Teresa Doherty and Hassane Cissé (eds), *The World Bank Legal Review Volume 6. Improving Delivery in Development: The Role of Voice, Social Contract, and Accountability*, Washington, DC: World Bank Publications, pp. 91–102.

Human Rights Council (2007), Resolution 6/12, 28 September.

ILA (International Law Association) (2010a), *Rights of Indigenous Peoples*, Report of The Hague Conference.

ILA (International Law Association) (2010b), *Rights of Indigenous Peoples*, Interim Report, The Hague Conference.

ILA (International Law Association) (2012), Resolution No. 5/2012, 75th Conference of the ILA, Sofia, 26–30 August.

Keal, Paul (2003), *European Conquest and the Rights of Indigenous Peoples: The Moral Backwardness of International Society*, New York: Cambridge University Press.

Meijknecht, Anna (2001), *Towards International Personality: The Position of Minorities and Indigenous Peoples in International Law*, Oxford: Intersentia.

Meza-Lopehandía, Matías (2013), "El Derecho Internacional de los Derechos Humanos y los Pueblos Indígenas," in José Aylwin (ed.), *Los Pueblos Indígenas y el Derecho*, Santiago de Chile: LOM Ediciones, pp. 441–521.

Morgan, Rhiannon (2011), *Transforming Law and Institution. Indigenous Peoples, the United Nations and Human Rights*, Farnham: Ashgate.

Mukwiza Ndahinda, Felix (2011), *Indigenousness in Africa: A Contested Legal Framework for Empowerment of Marginalised Communities*, The Hague: Asser Press.

Mutua, Makau (2009), "The Transformation of Africa. A Critique of the Rights Discourse," in Felipe Gómez Isa and Koen De Feyter (eds), *International Human Rights Law in a Global Context*, Bilbao: Deusto Univesity Press, pp. 899–924.

Pahuja, Sundhya (2011), *Decolonising International Law. Development, Economic Growth and the Politics of Universality*, Cambridge: Cambridge University Press.

Pulitano, Elvira (2012), "Indigenous Rights and International Law: An Introduction," in Elvira Pulitano (ed.), *Indigenous Rights in the Age of the UN Declaration*, Cambridge: Cambridge University Press, pp. 1–25.

Rajagopal, Balakrishnan (2003), *International Law from Below. Development, Social Movements and Third World Resistance*, Cambridge: Cambridge University Press.

Rodríguez-Piñero, Luis (2005), *Indigenous Peoples, Post-colonialism and International Law. The ILO Regime (1919–1989)*, Oxford: Oxford University Press.

Rodríguez-Piñero, Luis (2009a), "La 'implementación' de la Declaración: las implicaciones del Artículo 42," in Natalia Álvarez, Daniel Oliva and Nieves Zúñiga (eds), *La Declaración sobre los derechos de los pueblos indígenas. Hacia un mundo intercultural y sostenible*, Madrid: Los Libros de la Catarata, pp. 65–106.

Rodríguez-Piñero, Luis (2009b), "Where Appropriate: Monitoring/Implementing of Indigenous Peoples' Rights under the Declaration," in Claire Charters and Rodolfo Stavenhagen (eds), *Making the Declaration Work. The United Nations Declaration on the Rights of Indigenous Peoples*, Copenhagen: IWGIA, pp. 314–43.

Rojas-Páez, Gerardo (2014), "Whose Nature? Whose Rights? Criminalization of Social Protest in a Globalizing World," *Oñati Socio-Legal Series*, **4** (1), 1–12.

Rombouts, Sebastiaan Johannes (2014), *Having a Say. Indigenous Peoples, International Law and Free, Prior and Informed Consent*, Oisterwijk: Wolf Legal Publishers.

Sambo Dorough, Dalee (2009), "The Significance of the Declaration on the Rights of Indigenous Peoples and its Future Implementation," in Claire Charters and Rodolfo Stavenhagen (eds), *Making the Declaration Work. The United Nations Declaration on the Rights of Indigenous Peoples*, Copenhagen: IWGIA, pp. 264–79.

Schilling-Vacaflor, Almut and René Kuppe (2012), "Plurinational Constitutionalism: A New Era of Indigenous-State Relations?," in Detlef Nolte and Almut Schilling-Vacaflor (eds), *New Constitutionalism in Latin America: Promises and Practices*, Farnham: Ashgate, pp. 347–70.

Scott, James Brown (1934), *The Spanish Origin of International Law: Francisco de Vitoria and his Law of Nations*, London: Clarendon Press.

Stavenhagen, Rodolfo (2006), *Report of the Special Rapporteur on the Situation of Human Rights and Fundamental Freedoms of Indigenous People*, Mr Rodolfo Stavenhagen, UN Doc. E/CN.4/2006/78, 16 February.

Thornberry, Patrick (2002), *Indigenous Peoples and Human Rights*, Manchester: Manchester University Press.

UN Permanent Forum on Indigenous Issues (2008), *Report of the Seventh Session*, UN Doc. E/C.19/2008/23.

United States (2007), "Observations of the United States with respect to the Declaration on the Rights of Indigenous Peoples: Explanation of Vote by Robert Hagen, U.S. Advisor, on the Declaration on the Rights of Indigenous Peoples, to the UN General Assembly," 13 September.

Viljoen, Frans (2012), *International Human Rights Law in Africa*, Oxford: Oxford University Press.

Willemsen-Diaz, Augusto (2009), "How Indigenous Peoples' Rights Reached the UN," in Claire Charters and Rodolfo Stavenhagen (eds), *Making the Declaration Work. The United Nations Declaration on the Rights of Indigenous Peoples*, Copenhagen: IWGIA, pp. 16–31.

World Conference on Indigenous Peoples (2014), *Outcome Document of the High-level Plenary Meeting of the General Assembly Known as the World Conference on Indigenous Peoples*, UN Doc. A/RES/69/2, 22 September.

PART III

Expanding claims

5. Expanding rights: new frames for violence against women

Alison Brysk

A generation of research on the politics of human rights shows that critical factors for challenging all forms of human rights violations include bringing transnational pressure "from above and below," naming and framing abuse, using information politics, empowering vulnerable groups, and institutionalizing change through law. Communication power operates through introducing new and effective voices, frames, and performances of human rights claims that resonate with an audience due to bridging narratives (Brysk, 2013). All human rights campaigns for "private wrongs" must work additionally to reframe customary and hidden forms of coercion, reclaim recognition of objectified or dependent others, and extend state acknowledgement that "the personal is political" (Brysk, 2005).

Using, bridging, and creating frames can expand the power of human rights, even for hidden abuse of powerless people. These new frames then expand the global repertoire of rights struggles. The dynamics of fitting, bridging, and crafting frames is distinct at the local, national, and global levels. Moreover, the response to human rights frames is filtered by the availability of democratic citizenship claims. For violence against women, bridging frames has a special power to cross the public-private divide, but conversely lagging rights norms in the private sphere may undermine mobilization.

The international human rights regime establishes a toolbox of frames that are constructed and reconstructed by dialectic among transnational networks and campaigns, international institutions, state promoters, and global grassroots initiatives. The lowest barriers to entry and strongest regime response for a human rights claim will be when a clearly visible social problem fits a well-established frame. When an existing frame does not fit completely or garners counter-mobilization, activists may strategically bridge to a different or overlapping frame that elicits greater consensus and coalitions. It is more demanding, but often necessary for a privatized, naturalized, emerging or invisible problem to create a new frame – and construct corresponding institutional response. Finally, it is important to consider unsuccessful or missing frames, and the cost for advocacy efforts (Brysk, 2013). This chapter reviews the pattern of expanding claims for violence against women, and then considers a range of framing strategies by global campaigns against sexual violence: fitting the war crimes frame, bridging official rape as torture and ethnic rape as discrimination, crafting a new frame for sexual harassment, and lagging frames for reproductive rights.

In the area of women's rights, "NGOs attempt to influence states' interests by framing problems, solutions, and justifications for political action" (Joachim, 2003, p. 247). From the 1993 Vienna World Human Rights Conference onwards, the global community has reframed "women's rights as human rights." In the analysis that inspired the movement, activist Charlotte Bunch pointed out the extent of violence and its threat to life and fundamental freedoms, questioned the distinction between public and private violence, and showed that gender violence is a structural result of male dominance (Bunch, 1990) – and the theme was powerfully articulated by Hilary Clinton at the Beijing World Conference on Women. Attention to violence against women benefits from its universal humanitarian appeal and apparent political neutrality, the widespread vulnerability to gendered violence of diverse constituencies of women across countries, cultures, and classes, and a clear fit with the international human rights regime's core commitment to end bodily harm to innocent victims (Keck and Sikkink, 1998).

Acting globally to end violence against women leads to an expansion of human rights frames, claims, and mechanisms. Within the overarching frame of violence against women as a human rights issue, activists and international law initially extended the CEDAW (Convention on the Elimination of Discrimination Against Women) framework of discrimination and framed violence – especially traditional practices – as a barrier to the exercise of established civil and political rights and freedoms. As patterns of wartime assault and fatal domestic violence are taken up by mainstream human rights organizations such as Human Rights Watch and regional institutions such as the Inter-American Convention, gender violence from all sources is bridged to human rights norms of physical integrity established for state actors. At the same time, transnational networks, global institutions like the World Health Organization (WHO), and modernizing states mobilize against violence as a threat to public health, security, and development. While at the beginning of the regime, rape was variously denied, seen as a crime, a personal tragedy, or a humanitarian problem, a generation of rights-based feminism crafts a frame of sexual violence – visible in the establishment of United Nations (UN) Special Campaigns and Rapporteurs.

	Fit	*Bridge*	*Shift*	*Craft*	*Missing*
Violence against women (VAW)	discrimination	physical integrity	health, development, security	sexual violence	reproductive rights
Child marriage	freedom				
Trafficking		slavery	security		sex workers
FGM			health		
Domestic violence			development	femicide	marital rape
Son preference	infanticide			gendercide	
Rape	war crime	torture	discrimination	harassment	marital rape, conflict abortion

Figure 5.1 Rights frames for gender violence

But issues connected to the lagging area of reproductive rights are the least salient and consistent.

Within the larger rubric of gender violence, differentiating genres of abuse also expands frames that influence the fate of advocacy efforts. The successful campaign to frame rape as a war crime installs a formerly privatized wrong in the international human rights regime. The globalized commodification of sex in human trafficking gains attention when it is described as a form of pre-modern slavery. Reframing FGM/C (female genital mutilation/cutting) as a health rights claim facilitates coalition-building on global public health, with similar patterns on domestic violence. Campaigns craft new frames: gender-based killing worldwide is framed as "femicide" by activists and a series of UN conferences, revealing new patterns of abuse and responsibility and inspiring waves of legislation and mobilization. But the systematic silences of reproductive rights pose critical challenges to policies on trafficking, domestic violence, and conflict rape – among others.

Even within campaigns against a single genre of abuse, differences in the location and framing influence the repertoire of global, legal, and campaign response. In general, response to rape diminishes as it moves from interstate to public to private. As we examine below, the campaign against rape as a war crime is a good fit with the oldest body of humanitarian law and global institutions established for an interstate abuse. State-sponsored or tolerated assault by public officials bridges to human rights standards for torture and police abuse; it is readily contested in democracies, and incorporated by mainstream human rights organizations in condemnation of dictatorships. Framing and mobilization are more difficult when sexual assault is perpetrated by private actors and tolerated in the community – but when rape is a targeted strategy of ethnic, religious, or descent-based dominance, campaigns can borrow from anti-discrimination rubrics and movements. While individual cases of public assault are framed as an exceptional crime, worldwide campaigns are just beginning to gain recognition and response to more systematic patterns of sexual violence as an assault on women's right to freedom of movement and public space, through the construction of a frame of sexual harassment. But lagging rights for reproductive self-determination impedes framing of the most widespread form of sexual violence: marital rape.

The relative power of framing to secure human rights claims for sexual violence is demonstrated in microcosm through the evolution of rape legislation in India, with very different timing and penalties for the same crime depending on the frame, location, and identity of victims and perpetrators. The very limited treatment of public sexual assault by strangers inherited from the 1860 colonial code stood for more than a century, with rare reporting, prosecution, and conviction highly dependent on the race and class of victim and perpetrator – rape was fundamentally framed as an offense against honor or social boundaries. In 1983, after public protest by a burgeoning women's movement and highly publicized cases of police assault of detained women, a major reform was enacted that introduced the frame of custodial rape and specifically penalized sexual abuse by responsible authorities, bridging to broader rights frames of police abuse. After further protest and publicity by a rising lower-caste movement introduced the frame of caste-based rape as part of anti-discrimination struggles, in 1989 the Scheduled Castes (Prevention of Atrocities) Act recognized the chronic, widespread crime – but offered only economic compensation without criminal penalties. Further recognition of ethnic conflict rape did not come until 2013, when a decade of investigations and trials for the 2002 Gujarat riots secured one conviction for the widely reported rape of Muslim women by Hindu nationalists. But Hindu nationalist governments continue to resist parallel claims of conflict rape by Indian troops in Kashmir documented by international human rights groups. After the widely protested 2012 Delhi gang rape shifted the agenda to urban insecurity and systematic threats to the mobility of middle-class women, the government's Verma Commission drafted a modernized 2013 rape law that raised penalties and facilitated prosecution of stranger rape – but explicitly excluded marital rape (unless the wife was under 15). The same year, pressure by increasing numbers of working women and advocacy by labor unions for women's rights led to India's first Sexual Harassment in the Workplace Act. Around the same time, as long-standing child protection efforts produced non-governmental organization (NGO) reports and media coverage of sexual abuse of children by criminals, orphanages, and families, India passed the unprecedented 2012 Protection of Children from Sexual Offenses Act. Finally, a 2014 Supreme Court case forbidding a village vendetta rape ordered by an officially authorized tribal council asserted universal rights over the legalization of cultural relativist violence.

BRINGING OLD WRONGS INTO EXISTING FRAMES: RAPE AS A WAR CRIME

Sexual assault can be framed as a crime, a security problem, an offense against honor, a humanitarian tragedy, a marker of cultural difference by an "uncivilized" enemy, a war crime, or a human rights violation. Even in wartime, rape may serve the social function of a systematic foreign policy, a tool of identity politics, a human "scorched-earth" policy to promote forced displacement, a form of torture, a side-payment to maintain military cohesion, or an opportunistic side effect of a generalized breakdown in social order. Perpetrators may include official militaries, police, civil authorities, paramilitaries, and private parties. The turn to law, and the preference for international humanitarian law and the war crimes frame, must be explained. The conflict frame of "rape as a weapon of war" has the potential to overcome patriarchal notions of consent and legitimate victims as representatives of the aggrieved national or ethnic community, turning shame to martyrdom. For example, recently in Libya, women survivors of rape during the uprising were reclassified as wounded war veterans (Schlanger, 2014).

One important factor facilitating the framing of rape as a war crime is the symbolic politics of wartime sexual violence. Once it is acknowledged, conflict rape is perhaps the most individually visible, gratuitously brutal violation of a widespread norm against "physical harm to innocent victims." Victims are personified, causal responsibility is clear, tribunals provide a stage for testimonials, media are present to cover the conflict, and the receptive audience for claims expands from humanitarian forces to feminists to international peace-keeping and refugee institutions. Wartime violence is the most visible, recognizable, and reparable disruption of normal social order.

Another factor is agency, as the appearance of new conflicts provided a shock to global governance and international law that created space for global civil society mobilization. Even the earliest recognition of wartime sexual violence in the Geneva Conventions (Article 27) was sparked by women's groups changing the International Red Cross' initial Draft (Inal, 2013, p. 97). During the 1990s, the exogenous shock was the resurgence of war in Europe after 50 years, which allowed activists to graft a new norm to an existing frame by linking rape as violence against women to genocide in Bosnia (Inal, 2013, p. 159). A transnational movement by Asian survivors of World War II sexual slavery revealed the hidden history of that conflict and Japanese state sponsorship, hosting numerous testimonials and eventually receiving limited reparations from a state-managed private "Comfort Women's Fund." From the early 1990s, the Women's International War Crimes Tribunal provided agenda-setting and evidence for historical accountability and laid the groundwork for the next wave of international law. The push for the inclusion of sexual violence in the Charter of the International Criminal Court followed a decade of women's movement mobilization (Spees, 2003).

Wartime sexual assault is only mentioned obliquely in the Geneva Conventions as an offense against honor and dignity, and is not included among the "grave breaches" that merit universal prosecution. Similarly, the extensive use of numerous forms of sexual violence by the Nazis was not mentioned at the Nuremberg trials. Perhaps the first international prosecution for wartime rape was at the Tokyo War Crimes trials, centering on the massive and bloody assault on tens of thousands of Chinese women by Japanese forces known as the Rape of Nanking. However, the judgment distinguished between "understandable" battlefield rapes and persisting rapes in pacified areas, and established a hierarchy of victims by class and race. For example, these trials castigated the assault and sometimes enslavement of Dutch women in Indonesia but ignored the massive systematic enslavement of hundreds of thousands of Southeast Asian so-called Comfort Women, mainly from Korea – an issue which later generated a transnational social movement, private reparations fund, and ongoing bilateral controversy (Henry, 2011, p. 51).

The international legal status of conflict rape is silent throughout the Cold War, but returns to prominence with the emergence of systematic sexual violence as a strategy of ethnic cleansing in the Balkan wars of the 1990s, extremely visible in the heart of Europe. The International Criminal Tribunal for the Former Yugoslavia (ICTY) followed the finding of a UN Commission of Experts that found patterns of rape with looting and intimidation of target groups, rape with fighting and deportation, rape in detention camps, detention for rape and forced impregnation, sexual enslavement and "entertainment" of soldiers, most prominently by Bosnian Serb forces but carried out by several parties to the conflict. Accordingly, the Tribunal successfully prosecuted sexual violence in a series of landmark cases. The ICTY's Tadic case convicts the perpetrators of ordering rape as an "instrument of terror," while the Celebic case highlights command responsibility and the status of rape as torture. Finally, the 2001 Foca verdict establishes rape and sexual enslavement as crimes against humanity (De Vito, 2011).

During the contemporaneous conflict in Rwanda, it is estimated that over 250,000 women survived extremely violent rape – and many of the women murdered among the 800,000 victims of the genocide were sexually assaulted before being killed. As in Bosnia, forced pregnancy was often an explicit goal of repeated gang rape by enemy ethnic perpetrators. The pattern of long-term sexual enslavement was more present in Bosnia, but brutal rape of children and elderly women was more common in Rwanda. The original indictment of the International Criminal Tribunal for Rwanda (ICTR) that did not include rape was amended after a push by women's and human rights groups, and catalysed when a prosecution witness spontaneously recounted the rape of her six-year old daughter by three Hutu Interahamwe (Henry, 2011). The resulting Akayesu case of the ICTR established rape as a form of genocide and a violation of group as well as individual rights. While the Rwanda tribunal established an extremely valuable record of the prevalence and patterns of genocidal rape, poor investigations and prosecutions diminished the number of convictions for massive sexual violence to a handful, and also excluded crimes that did not fit the genocide frame (Buss, 2010).

More recently, another notable development of transitional justice jurisprudence has come through the hybrid international-domestic Sierra Leone Special Court on war crimes. In that protracted civil war, extensive sexual violence against civilians by rebel groups was mixed with other egregious war crimes such as forced amputations, kidnapping, and brutalization of child soldiers. Accordingly, that tribunal included sexual violence in four of five indictments, and added forced marriage as a "crime against humanity" punishable by the International Criminal Court (ICC). But in a checkered pattern of human rights accountability, sexual violence was separated from other forms of physical harm, war rape separated from other kinds, and wartime forced marriage separated from harmful traditional arranged child marriage – by the consent of family (Grewal, 2012).

The pinnacle of the international legal regime is the incorporation of rape as a war crime in the statute of the ICC. The ICC recognizes rape and forced pregnancy as crimes against humanity with universal jurisdiction and potential autonomous prosecution (not requiring Security Council referral). This milestone in global governance was attributed to the influence of a coalition of dozens of NGOs, the Women's Caucus for Gender Justice, which revised the 1994 civil society coalition draft of the Rome Statute. Then, from 1997 on, the Women's Caucus coordinated with the USA and other key states for gender-friendly provisions – Australia, Bosnia, Canada and the Netherlands (which consecutively chaired the conference), Costa Rica, Mexico, Sweden, and South Africa (which chaired working groups). This experience drew on and in some cases mobilized policy within the active states – such that despite the US subsequent equivocation on the ICC, it retains an active engagement on war crimes against women. Moreover, the mobilization went beyond norms to procedures, securing guidelines for gender representation and expertise in judges, the Prosecutor, and procedures regarding collection of evidence and protection of witnesses. During the ICC's difficult Democratic Republic of Congo case (*vs. Katanga 2008*), the Court did not drop charges of sexual violence – due to pressure from victim groups (Cakmak, 2011).

The frame of rape as a war crime has continued to diffuse at the national and regional levels. Colombia's post-conflict truth commission includes an accounting for sexual violence. In 2016, Guatemala saw landmark convictions of former military officers for rape, murder, and sexual enslavement of indigenous women during the 1982 civil war (BBC, 2016).

BRIDGING FRAMES: RAPE AS TORTURE

In some stable authoritarian regimes, rape is used regularly as a weapon of intimidation and torture by military, paramilitary, and police forces – and once the women's rights as human rights frame was established in the 1990s, transnational human rights networks added condemnation of sexual violence to their chronicle of torture and police abuse. In Zimbabwe, a 2002 Amnesty International report on rape and abductions by government-sponsored paramilitary forces shows how a National Youth Service ("Green Bombers") force was recruited and trained to punish political opponents and terrorize contested social sectors and regions (AI Index AFR 46/032/2002). Similarly, opposition activists in Iran's 2009 Green Uprising decried and mobilized transnational support around an increase in the rape of dissidents – including men – by the Islamic regime's police, Revolutionary Guards, and paramilitary Basij (Iran Human Rights Documentation Center, 2011).

In corrupt democracies, as chronicled above in India, police rape is often one of the first leverage points for accountability for sexual violence – and sexual abuse is one of the most powerful indictments of widespread malfeasance by security forces. In Bangladesh, until 2003, police would put women who had been trafficked, raped, complained of domestic violence, suspected of prostitution, or detained under the 1974 Special Powers Act into "safe custody" – initially one month without review. In 1996 a female garment worker, arrested with her boyfriend for walking unaccompanied in public, questioned her arrest and was gang raped by the police. After she complained upon release, she was detained from the hospital where she was receiving treatment. Despite a local women's organization and family protests as well as legal actions, she was not released and was sent to the same prison where the accused were being detained for investigation – and within a few months was murdered in detention. This finally mobilized a government investigation committee, but the four accused police were acquitted. After media and MPs pressed further, the government filed an appeal in the High Court. Meanwhile, in 1995 a 16-year old domestic worker returning home was abducted, gang raped, murdered, and dumped by police in their patrol car. After mass public protest (repressed by police with seven demonstrators killed) and later riots, the local movement went national, a human rights organization filed a new legal case, and three of the nine accused police in that case were convicted. Following these widely publicized and protested cases, numerous other police rape charges were brought – one women's group reports 21. In 2002, the government transferred "safe custody" from police to shelters. After 2003, in response to a human rights organization lawsuit, the government limited the Special Powers Act and ordered the release of rape victims and 400 children jailed with adults (Anwary, 2012).

CROSSOVER FRAMES: ETHNIC RAPE AS DISCRIMINATION

Another form of linkage, which yields the first and strongest response to systematic non-state sexual violence, is the crossover anti-discrimination frame and associated minority rights advocacy. Pervasive private sexual terror against oppressed sectors is often mobilized at the national level alongside citizenship struggles in democracies.

In India, by the mid 1990s, government studies began to report on the high rate of sexual abuse of "scheduled caste" women – and the inefficacy of the justice system in relieving their vulnerability. Beyond conventional criminal liability for rape, a 1989 Scheduled Castes and Scheduled Tribes (Prevention of Atrocities) Act mandates monetary compensation to victims of violence, apparently to repair their damaged marriage prospects and perhaps facilitate relocation – indicating the additional social cost of sexual abuse for this population, above the universal burdens of medical care and psychological trauma (Tekchandani et al., 1995). Women in Dalit communities are assaulted as punishment for challenges to caste boundaries or rights claims by family members. In a typical recent case in July 2004, when a teenaged village girl eloped with her Dalit boyfriend, in revenge 30 men of the Yadav group raped his mother and two aunts (Bhattacharjee, 2008). Within a significant lower-caste rights movement that includes protection from rape in its protest demands, a specific Dalit Women's Self-Respect Movement has formed to contest sexual violence.

State-sponsored, state-delegated, and state-tolerated rape is also a routine tool of inter-ethnic conflict in India and has met with increasing condemnation but checkered accountability. Sexual violence has been tolerated during ethnic riots, and there are credible linkages between state authorization and massive rape in the anti-Muslim riots in Gujarat in 2002. The genocidal intent of the assaults can be seen in witness testimonies that while raping Indian Muslim women, gangs shouted, "Go to Pakistan, why are you in Hindustan?" Local police hit the stomachs of pregnant Muslim women saying, "Kill them before they are born!" Some rapists stated their attempt to impregnate their victims, while others were killed after rape. In terms of facilitating political forces, the influential Hindu nationalist movement RSS published pamphlets that encouraged Hindu men to rape Muslims. The Hindu nationalist BJP government in Gujarat, which had strong ties to the movement, had earlier dismantled the violence against women unit of the police when it came to power. Instead, the local BJP government had started a police cell on inter-religious marriages, claiming abuse and coercion of Hindu women who married Muslims (International Initiative for Justice, 2008). While Gujarat's female former MP and Minister of Women Maya Kodnani was convicted of murder in 2013 for presiding over one site of mob violence, after a special investigation the region's Chief Minister Nahendra Modi (now Prime Minister) was acquitted of command responsibility. The continuing nature of sexual assault during sectarian riots – and its link to resource conflicts – is highlighted by 2013 land riots in Muzaffarnagar in which a dominant Hindu caste attacked, killed, and displaced 42,000 Muslims. Six unprecedented gang rape complaints were filed in India's changing legal climate – but the police have failed to investigate them, in a district 75≈miles from Delhi (Raina, 2013).

In March 2014, three men were convicted of the gang rape of a Catholic nun during ethnic riots in Orissa in 2008. After a Hindu religious leader was shot by avowed Maoist rebels who have been especially active in marginalized tribal and religious minority communities, hard-line Hindu groups attacked the minority Christian community, killing dozens, assaulting hundreds, and destroying churches. Nine people were arrested for the gang rape of the nun, who was dragged from hiding, raped by a mob, and paraded naked through the streets. Six of the accused were acquitted, one was sentenced to 11 years, and two to 26 months (BBC News India, 2014).

CRAFTING A NEW FRAME: SEXUAL HARASSMENT

When public sexual assault is widespread and the state fails to protect half its citizens, sexual terror becomes a threat to women's right to freedom of movement. Recent human rights framing by local activists combines naming and shaming of private perpetrators with a call for state accountability – in authoritarian regimes and democracies alike. Victims begin to reveal hidden or personalized aggression, document common patterns of assault, and relabel abuse from a shame to a crime. Monitoring, mobilization, and demands for legal reform increasingly use the term "sexual harassment" (in Spanish, *acoso sexual*) and refer to transnational trends and social media.

In Egypt, all three recent regimes since 2011 – Mubarak, Morsi, and the military – have seen an explosion of public sexual assaults of female protesters, journalists, and ordinary women in increasingly conflictual and impoverished urban spaces. As Egyptian women have emerged in the public sphere since the Arab Spring, a study by UN Women shows that over 90 percent have suffered harassment, and in many cases sexual assault, in the streets (BBC, 2013). During the 2011 Egyptian Revolution, numbers of women were assaulted by mobs of unclear provenance, in public view and despite male accompaniment – including foreigners and journalists like Lara Logan. By 20 December 2011, thousands marched to protest army violence against female protesters, while the army used a 2002 law on associations to attack women's NGOs. Egyptian and international human rights groups reported ongoing assaults in Tahrir Square during the public occupation before and following the regime change (Amnesty International, 2013; www.nazra.org). A March 2011 Women's Day march celebrating women in the revolution was attacked by groups of angry men, shouting, "This is not the time!" and "A woman's voice is a shame!" Amnesty International reported that the next day 18≈women were held in military detention and beaten, as well as subjected to official medical rape via "virginity tests." Women's activist Samira Ibrahim filed a lawsuit against the transitional government, and in December 2011 Egypt's Court of Administrative Justice ruled the detentions and abuse violated the Egyptian Constitution. Murky street assaults on women continued during the 2012–13 Islamist Morsi regime with little government response, and some women appear to have joined the call for the mid-year military coup seeking basic public security. During 2012, the Ministry of Interior recorded over 20,000 cases of rape, and NGOs reported over 100 incidents of sexual assault of women activists in June and July (US State Department, 2013).

We are now witnessing the re-emergence of women's anti-harassment movements as one of the few spaces of human rights resistance in Egypt. In 2012, Egyptian women established movements such as Basma, Anti-Harassment Movement, and Operation Anti-Sexual Harassment/Assault (OpAntiSH), successfully lobbied for 2014 legal reform, and created security apps such as HarassMap. Activists have also fostered a tremendous increase in media discussion and reframing of harassment – including a shift in talk shows contesting victim blaming and justification by dress (Langohr, 2016).

Similarly, chronic street crime and sexual violence in Mexico has surged in an era of economic and political crisis, and is often targeted at women perceived as empowered: workers, activists, journalists, and foreigners. In a context where hundreds of women have disappeared or been found raped and murdered along the US-Mexico border, transnational activists have been campaigning since the 1990s for recognition and response to "femicide" – the mass murder of women. The femicide campaign led to an Inter-American Human Rights Court judgment against Mexico and passage of 2007 landmark legislation by that country.

Now, throughout the country but especially in Mexico City, women report thousands of street rapes, sexual torture of activists and journalists, along with constant groping, sexual battery, and threats in the street, public transport, workplaces, and schools. Two-thirds of women on public transport in Mexico City report sexual aggression. State measures such as dedicated metro cars for women are inconsistent and overwhelmed by invading gangs of men, while several notorious cases of rape and kidnapping by privileged youth have not yet been prosecuted – at least one victim has gone into exile after death threats when she reported the assault and pressed charges (Machado, 2016).

From above, a World Bank-funded campaign with government agencies in Mexico's transport system publicizes the unacceptability of abuse, defines harassment (*acoso*), and encourages bystanders to report it (Paullier, 2016). Meanwhile, survivors of sexual aggression have formed a human rights framed campaign on social media with almost three million views: Grupo de Accion por los Derechos Humanos y Justicia Social. Their video shows a kidnapped activist, a foreign journalist, and a university student each reporting their experience, defining harassment, and denouncing the failure of authorities to prosecute – despite each woman providing footage and forensic evidence of their assaults. They call for women to come forward and report harassment with the slogan *Notecalles* ("don't be silent"), solidarity by women to respond as a group, and the demand "*Calle sin acoso*" ("harassment-free streets") (Grupo de Accion por los Derechos Humanos y la Justicia Social, 2016). A grassroots youth initiative confronts street rape culture with direct intervention, under the name "Hijas de la Violencia" (Daughters of violence) – also framing the victims in family roles echoing the Latin American human rights repertoire. The guerrilla theater group counters street harassers with confetti guns and a punk feminist anthem against abuse, somewhat reminiscent of the Russian punk feminist group Pussy Riot, and often involves turning the camera on aggressors. Their *Sexista Punk* video has over ten million views, and begins with the line: "What you have done to me is called *harassment* – and every time I will respond . . . you have no right to do this: sexist, machista, disgusting pig . . . don't talk to me as if you want to rape me!" (Roiz, 2016).

MISSING FRAMES, LAGGING RIGHTS: REPRODUCTIVE RIGHTS AND SEXUAL SELF-DETERMINATION

Reproductive rights are the most recent, contingent, and contested rights in both international and domestic law. Reproductive rights are defined as the right to choose sex and partner, pregnancy, the number and spacing of children, sexual health including safe pregnancy, and freedom from sexual violence. Rights to marital and reproductive self-determination garner the most reservations in the widely subscribed CEDAW treaty. Women's reproductive roles increase vulnerability to violence, while sexual self-determination lags behind women's rights as workers, citizens, and civilian victims of war and disaster. Many states do not recognize marital rape or a woman's right to terminate a pregnancy, and displaced or migrant women often lack access to reproductive health services and legal protection from sexual abuse. Sex workers almost everywhere are more vulnerable to violence, systematically denied protection, and often abused by police. In many countries, prosecution of sexual assault or trafficking for sexual exploitation demands proof of failure to consent – in contrast to response to parallel forms of non-sexual violence like robbery or debt bondage.

Weak reproductive rights repertoires undermine response to violence against women even within the well-established frame of wartime rape. There is uneven and contested availability of abortion for victims of sexual violence, within countries, post-war, and especially for refugees. International agencies and humanitarian aid providers who govern refugees' access to health care have monitoring, interventions, and preventive measures for sexual violence – but inconsistent policies and access to abortion. The Global Justice Center advocacy group mounted a campaign in 2010 calling for humanitarian access to abortion under the Geneva Convention health protocols, which was adopted in principle by only the

UK, the Netherlands, and France – and implemented only by the UK. The European Union defers to national legislation of the conflict or refugee host country in this matter (though not other rights of refugees), and the USA explicitly forbids overseas funding of abortion services in any humanitarian operation. The UK went on to co-sponsor a series of UN Security Council resolutions in 2013, which called for: "nondiscriminatory and comprehensive health services, including sexual and reproductive health" and "access to the full range of sexual and reproductive health services, including regarding pregnancies resulting from rape, without discrimination" (Global Justice Center, 2015; McGinn and Casey, 2016).

Similarly, lagging standards on consent and sexual self-determination undermine emerging frames such as sexual harassment even in relatively progressive states. In Germany, for example, a lingering requirement that victims of sexual assault demonstrate "resistance" complicated the prosecution of the mass street assaults in Cologne during New Year – inspiring review of the rape law in 2016. Although the law had been under discussion due to women's movement pressure, lawmakers' hesitation was overcome only when the attacks by apparent migrants and ethnic minority men triggered a protectionist nationalist frame.

The lack of sexual self-determination limits framing for marital rape – the most common, least acknowledged, and most legitimized form of sexual violence. For example, India's National Family Health Survey 2005–06 found that 35 percent of Indian women faced physical or sexual abuse at the hands of their husbands; 14.7 percent specifically reported sexual violence (Rajesh, 2010). In dozens of countries, the marriage contract negates women's basic self-determination by requiring irrevocable sexual consent; like a certain form of dictatorship, it is "one woman, one vote, one time." According to a 2011 UN report, only 52 countries had criminalized marital rape, usually in response to either powerful women's movements or modernization projects (including the USA, UK, Canada, Australia, Denmark, Sweden, Spain, Turkey, Brazil, South Africa). Spousal rape remains legal in at least three dozen states, including most of the Middle East, about half of Africa, and several Southeast Asian nations. Underlining this lack of rights to bodily integrity for married women, in many Arab and African codes and traditions, a wife's refusal to have sex is also justifiable grounds for other forms of violence such as assault and battery (De Silva and Klugman, 2015).

Campaigns to include marital rape in domestic violence legislation have struggled to counter norms of patriarchal ownership with self-determination. An instructive illustration of norm contestation comes from the "Three To Be Free" campaign, a transnational legal effort by

African feminists modeled on Canada's Equality Effect that seeks to criminalize marital rape in Kenya, Malawi, and Ghana. Thus far, it has resulted in legal reform in Ghana in 2007, and Malawi in 2015.

But in Kenya, the contestation of the frame is still visible in response to public debate of the measure. In a town 90 minutes from Nairobi, the 40-year old head of a town council told a journalist: "I own her. The dowry I paid for her means she's my property. If my wife refuses to have sex with me, I will rape her. And then I'll beat her because she didn't obey me." Yet a reforming younger woman in the same village, whose educated husband works in the capital says, "We need a delegation to come from Nairobi and tell the people here to change the way we behave. They need to say that women have feelings, that a bully in the house is not good and women are the same as men. The men in the village will listen to people who come from outside" (Armstrong, 2014, pp. 205–14).

CONCLUSION

After a generation of campaigns for women's rights as human rights, the one out of three women in the world who suffer gender violence now have a vocabulary to claim their freedom, dignity, and survival. Since framing is only the beginning phase of human rights campaigns, institutionalization and fulfillment of the new claims are critical themes for further analysis.

This case suggests a general pattern that fitting border-crossing problems to global frames like war crimes is a strong strategy for institutionalization, while bridging to national norms such as torture or discrimination will rely on the general dynamics of state compliance and capacity. Further afield, constructing new frames can help with monitoring, mobilization, and social change, but is less likely to result in new mechanisms or leverage. Moreover, as seen in other chapters, we must understand that gaps in rights reform may result from conflicting or missing rights frames – not just insufficient mobilization or lack of political will.

In the 21st century, women's movements around the world have begun to raise their voice to champion the fundamental freedom of sexual self-determination – from the battlefield to the prison, from the home to the street. Understanding and expanding the toolbox of communication power can make an important contribution to that struggle.

REFERENCES

Websites last accessed 17 January 2016.

Amnesty International. *Zimbabwe: Assault and Sexual Violence by Militia*. London: Amnesty International, 2002.

Amnesty International. *Egypt: Gender-based Violence Against Women Around Tahrir Square*. London: Amnesty International, 2013.

Anwary, Afroza. "State Sponsored Gang Rape and Murder of Women in Bangladesh: The Gendered Nature of Legal Institutions." *Pakistan Journal of Women's Studies* **19** (1), 2012, 23.

Armstrong, Sally. *Uprising: A New Age is Dawning for Every Mother's Daughter*. New York: St. Martin's Press, 2014.

BBC. "Egypt 'Worse for Women' Out of 22 Countries in Arab World." 12 November 2013.

BBC. "Guatemala: Rape Sentences in Landmark Military Trial." 27 February 2016.

BBC News India. "Three Convicted Over India Nun Rape." 14 March 2014.

Bhattacharjee, Swati. *A Unique Crime: Understanding Rape in India*. Kolkata: Gangchil, Distributor, Doyel, 2008.

Brysk, Alison. *Human Rights and Private Wrongs: Constructing Global Civil Society*. New York: Routledge, 2005.

Brysk, Alison. *Speaking Rights to Power: Constructing Political Will*. Oxford: Oxford University Press, 2013.

Bunch, Charlotte. "Women's Rights as Human Rights: Toward a Re-vision of Human Rights." *Human Rights Quarterly* **12** (4), 1990, 486–98.

Buss, Doris. "Learning Our Lessons? The Rwanda Tribunal Record on Prosecuting Rape." In Clare McGlynn and Vanessa Munro (eds), *Rethinking Rape Law: International and Comparative Perspectives*. London: Routledge-Cavendish, 2010, pp. 61–75.

Cakmak, Cenap. "The Rome Statue of the International Criminal Court (2002): The Impact of the Coalition of Women's Groups." In David Wingeate Pike (ed.), *Crimes Against Women*. New York: Nova Science Publishers, 2011.

De Silva de Alwis, Rangita and Jeni Klugman. "Freedom from Violence and the Law: A Global Persoective." FXB Center for Health and Human Rights, 2015.

De Vito, Daniela. *Rape, Torture and Genocide: Some Theoretical Implications*. New York: Nova Science Publishers, 2011.

Global Justice Center. "The Right to Non-discriminatory Medical Care, Including Safe Abortion, for Rape Victims in Armed Conflict under International Humanitarian Law (Ihl)." http://www.globaljusticecenter.net/index.phpoption=com_mtree&task=att_download&link_id=617&cf_id=34, 2015.

Grewel, Kiran. "International Criminal Justine: Advancing the Cause of Women's Rights?" In Tonia St. Germain and Susan Dewey (eds), *Conflict-related Sexual Violence: International Law, Local Responses*. Sterling, VA: Kumarian Press, 2012.

Grupo de Accion por los Derechos Humanos y la Justicia Social. "Mexico Es El Primer Lugar En Violencia Sexual En El Mundo." https://www.facebook.com/GrupoDeAccionDDHH/videos/vb.309601285896447/479491132240794/?type=2&theater, 2016.

Henry, Nicola. *War and Rape: Law, Memory, and Justice*. Abingdon, Oxon and New York: Routledge, 2011.

Inal, Tuba. *Looting and Rape in Wartime: Law and Change in International Relations*. Philadelphia, PA: University of Pennsylvania Press, 2013.

International Initiative for Justice. "Centrality of Sexual Violence and Sexuality to the Hindutva Project." In Swati Bhattacharjee (ed.), *A Unique Crime: Understanding Rape in India*. New York: Ganghchil, 2008.

Iran Human Rights Documentation Center. "Surviving Rape in Iran's Prisons." http://www.iranhrdc.org/english/publications/reports/3401-surviving-rape-in-iran-s-prisons.html, 2011.

Joachim, Jutta. "Framing Issues and Seizing Opportunities: The UN, NGOs, and Women's Rights." *International Studies Quarterly* **47** (2), 2003, 247–74.

Keck, Margaret E. and Kathryn Sikkink. *Activists Beyond Borders: Advocacy Networks in International Politics*. Ithaca, NY: Cornell University Press, 1998.

Langohr, Vickie. "Why Egyptians Have Mobilized Against Public Sexual Violence." *Washington Post*, 6 April 2016.

McGinn, Therese and Sara E. Casey. "Why Don't Humanitarian Organizations Provide Safe Abortion Services?" *Conflict and Health* **10** (03/24/12/21/received 02/26/accepted 2016), 8.

Machado, Amanda. "Two Thirds of Mexican Women Over the Age of 15 Have Experienced Gendered Violence." Matadornetwork. http://matadornetwork.com/pulse/two-thirds-mexican-women-age-15-experienced-gendered-violence-notecalles-campaign-making-sure-changes/, 2016.

Paullier, Juan. "Estoy Harta, Harta, Harta Y Frustrada: El Drama De Imparable Hostigamiento Sexual En México." BBC Mundo. http://www.animalpolitico.com/2016/04/harta-harta-harta-y-frustrada-el-drama-del-imparable-hostigamiento-sexual-en-mexico/, 2016.

Raina, Pamposh. "Muzaffarnagar Gang Rape Cases Languish in Police Files." *New York Times*, 23 October 2013.

Rajesh, Anuradha Saibaba. "Women in India: Abysmal Protection, Peripheral Rights and Subservient Citizenship." *New England Journal of International and Comparative Law* **16**, 2010), 32.

Roiz, Jessica Lucia. "Women in Mexico Fight Street Harassment in Most Creative Way." http://www.latintimes.com/pulse/women-mexico-fight-street-harassment-most-creative-way-video-366674, 2016.

Schlanger, Zoe. "Libya Set to Pay Reparations to Victims of Rape as a War Crimes." Newsweek, 12 June 2014.

Spees, Pam. "Women's Advocacy in the Creation of the International Criminal Court: Changing the Landscapes of Justice and Power." *Signs* **28** (4), 2003, 21.

Tekchandani, Bharti India, Wing Scheduled Caste Development and Multiple Action Research Group. *Efficacy of the Enforcement System in Delivering Justice to Raped Scheduled Caste Women: A Report Prepared for Scheduled Caste Development Wing, Ministry of Welfare, Government of India*. New Delhi: Multiple Action Research Group, 1995.

UN Security Council. Resolution 2122. 2013.

US State Department. "Egypt 2013 Human Rights Report: Executive Summary." 2013.

6. The human right to water and sanitation: champions and challengers in the fight for new rights acceptance

Madeline Baer

Access to clean water and adequate sanitation are undeniably key components of a healthy life with dignity and the fulfillment of multiple human rights. Yet it took over two decades of pressure from civil society groups for the United Nations (UN) to officially recognize water and sanitation as human rights. A transnational "water justice movement" successfully pushed for this recognition despite opposition from powerful adversaries. Representatives from Canada, the USA, and the UK used their power and influence within the global system to derail and dilute attempts to legalize the human right to water and sanitation at every turn. Despite these obstacles, by 2015 all UN member states had acknowledged the human right to water and sanitation as part of binding international law, either through their votes on resolutions or through their obligations under existing international treaties, and dozens of countries have amended their constitutions to include the human right to water and sanitation. How did the human right to water and sanitation come to be relatively accepted despite strong opposition by powerful global actors? What does the trajectory of the campaign to legalize the human right to water and sanitation tell us about new rights acceptance?

This chapter examines the process of establishing water and sanitation as new human rights, with particular attention to the actors who championed and challenged this acceptance. The chapter builds on and challenges extant theory on new rights emergence, which highlights the role of human rights gatekeeper organizations as facilitators of new rights acceptance. Gatekeepers bring legitimacy and resources to a new rights issue, often by successfully linking new rights to established rights claims. I argue that the path toward acceptance of the human right to water and sanitation (HRtWS) does not fit this pattern; much of the work to gain acceptance of the HRtWS

Table 6.1 Advocacy platforms and outcomes

Platforms	United Nations General Assembly	Human Rights Council	Global Water Policy
Outcomes	UNGA Resolutions	Human Rights Council Resolutions	World Water Forum Meeting Agendas and Ministerial Documents

happens outside of the human rights regime and without the active involvement of traditional rights gatekeepers. The water justice movement's successes are linked to effective collaborations between non-human rights non-governmental organizations (NGOs) and states in the Global South to redefine water in the international system. The findings presented here align with the chapter by Shareen Hertel in this volume, which highlights alternative routes to norm evolution from the "bottom up" and largely in the absence of the mainstream human rights movement. Like the Right to Food campaign in India, the campaign for the right to water and sanitation provides an example of how economic, social, and cultural (ESC) rights advocacy acts as a vehicle for contemporary human rights norm change.

Following brief discussions of the HRtWS and new rights acceptance theories, this chapter examines three of the global advocacy platforms where champions advocate for HRtWS: (1) the United Nations General Assembly (UNGA); (2) the Human Rights Council (HRC); and (3) the global water policy domain: the World Water Forum. I focus on the main outcomes of pressure in each of these platforms (Table 6.1).[1]

THE HUMAN RIGHT TO WATER AND SANITATION

Water and sanitation were not listed in the founding human rights documents, including the Universal Declaration of Human Rights, the International Covenant on Civil and Political Rights, and the International Covenant on Economic, Social and Cultural Rights (ICESCR).[2] In 2002 the Committee

[1] Other platforms not discussed here include the UN World Conference on Sustainable Development (Rio +20) in June 2012 that recognized the "right to safe drinking water and sanitation" and the process to define the Sustainable Development Goals for 2015–30, which also includes human rights language for water and sanitation.

[2] The importance of clean water and/or sanitation is mentioned in other human rights conventions, such as the Convention on the Rights of the Child, the

on Economic Social and Cultural Rights issued General Comment 15 stating that the human right to water is derived from the right to an adequate standard of living listed in Article 11 of the ICESCR. While General Comments are non-binding and non-enforceable soft law instruments, General Comment 15 strengthened the profile of the HRtWS in the global system and sparked international advocacy on the right to water (Nelson, 2009).

In development and water policy circles, for the past several decades water has been defined as an "economic good" or a "human need" that is best treated as a commodity subject to the rules of markets (Conca, 2006; Finger and Allouche, 2002; Langford, 2005). Campaigns to define water and sanitation as human rights emerged in Lain America, Asia, and Africa in the late 1990s and early 2000s as a response to a wave of water privatization that left citizens unable to afford services (Conca, 2006). Claiming water services as a human right is often an attempt to put water resources and services outside the reach of profit-making corporations and within the purview of states and communities.

While definitions of the HRtWS vary across time and actors, the language of General Comment 15 and the various resolutions passed in the HRC since 2010 on the HRtWS coalesce on the following criteria: availability (sufficient water supply for personal and domestic use); quality (safe for consumption and does not pose a threat to human health); acceptability (culturally acceptable sanitation facilities, including gender-specific facilities with privacy and dignity); accessibility (water and sanitation services must be accessible); and affordability (including for those in extreme poverty) (De Albuquerque and Winkler, 2010). Civil society groups also frequently demand transparency, accountability, and citizen participation in water management as a key component of the HRtWS. States are obligated to respect, protect, and fulfill the HRtWS through a comprehensive plan to realize these rights.[3] Together these resolutions establish a set of minimum obligations that states must uphold, which is an essential element to implementing ESC rights particularly in areas where private sector participation is a policy option (Gómez Isa, 2008).

The absence of water and sanitation in the founding human rights documents, a long tradition of viewing water as an economic good, and the work of powerful opponents all posed significant obstacles to the acceptance of water and sanitation as new human rights.

Convention on the Elimination of all forms of Discrimination Against Women, and the Convention on the Rights of Persons with Disabilities, yet these conventions do not establish a binding human right to water or sanitation.

[3] See Winkler (2012) for more details on the content of the right.

NEW RIGHTS ACCEPTANCE

For aggrieved groups with minimal access to global systems of power, there is a strong incentive to reframe grievances as human rights claims in the hopes of gaining attention, resources, and access to remedy. Human rights have become a modern lingua franca – a frame that provides an "emancipatory script" that resonates with powerful global actors (Brysk, 2013, p. 32). However, there is also resistance to expanding the human rights repertoire, and particularly strong resistance to empowering and legitimizing ESC rights claims in a human rights regime that focuses primarily on civil/political rights.

New rights claims have an advantage in the battle for recognition when they are framed in terms of pre-existing norms or values that are already widely supported (Finnemore and Sikkink, 1998; Florini, 1996). As Alison Brysk's chapter in this volume details (Chapter 5), the process of expanding the rights repertoire requires new forms of framing to link existing wrongs to established human rights frames. Campaigns for the HRtWS focus heavily on redefining water and sanitation services, long framed as economic goods to be provided by markets, as legitimate human rights necessary for survival and a life with dignity.

The role of human rights gatekeepers is crucial in this process of norm linkage and in placing new rights claims on the global agenda (Bob, 2009). Clifford Bob's theory of new rights acceptance posits that human rights gatekeepers, for example, Amnesty International and Human Rights Watch, have the power to "certify" new rights as worthy of international response (Bob, 2009, p. 4). Local aggrieved groups reach out to gatekeepers hoping their support will unlock access to international organizations, media attention, and increased political pressure from above on violators. In addition to their organizational attributes, such as resources and professional staff, gatekeepers occupy a place within networks of advocates, which gives them the power to influence the entire network agenda (Carpenter, 2011).

While gatekeepers have the power to open doors for new rights claimants, powerful challengers also work to keep those doors firmly closed, thwarting attempts by new rights champions to legitimize their new rights claim. Analysis of new rights acceptance therefore must focus not only on new rights champions but also the challengers who oppose the expansion of the human rights repertoire (Bob, 2009).

The HRtWS is an interesting case in light of these theories of norm change and new rights acceptance. Water is a new rights claim that is relatively successful in terms of gaining international recognition, even in the face of powerful opposition. Yet the traditional human rights gatekeepers have not been at the forefront of campaigns to recognize the HRtWS. Furthermore, although the right to water can be linked to pre-existing norms about the right to life, defining water as a human right directly contrasts with an already deeply entrenched definition of water as an economic good.

The campaign for the HRtWS is a prime example of how human rights advocacy has changed with the onset of globalization. While human rights advocacy on civil/political rights focuses mainly on targeting violating states from above and below with the help of global actors to shame state offenders, a recent wave of "new rights advocacy" seeks to strengthen the role of the state to fulfill ESC rights (Nelson and Dorsey, 2007). New rights advocacy often targets non-state actors in campaigns for new ESC rights, seeking to highlight the responsibilities of states and to bolster their ability to manage the economy in the face of pressure to implement neoliberal policies. This new rights advocacy emerged when civil society groups from the Global South began framing their social and economic grievances as human rights.

The mainstream human rights organizations have lagged behind this trend toward framing economic grievances as human rights. A reluctance to stray too far from traditional civil/political rights resulted in little work on socioeconomic rights until fairly recently. Furthermore, mainstream human rights organizations do not have a strong history of taking on Global South priorities as their own (Gómez Isa, 2011, pp.46–7). As explained by Executive Director Ken Roth, Human Rights Watch's mode of advocacy is based on publicly shaming violators when the following details of the situation are clear: violation, violator, and remedy (Roth, 2004). These three elements are clearest in cases of discriminatory and arbitrary conduct by states mostly commonly seen with civil/political rights violations. The focus on these behaviors combined with a reluctance to advocate for expenditures or distributive justice has kept ESC rights on the margins of the organization's agenda – although this is changing somewhat in recent years.[4] The HRtWS champions are a loosely connected network of NGOs from the Global South and North that calls itself the water justice movement.

THE CHAMPIONS

The water justice movement is a network of hundreds of organizations including local NGOs battling water policies at the municipal and national levels and regional networks such as The African Water Network and Red

---

[4] See Amnesty's "Demand Dignity" campaign, a campaign dedicated to addressing poverty and ESC rights.

VIDA (the Inter-American Network for the Defense and Right to Water) that link these local struggles. Northern NGOs including the Blue Planet Project (an initiative of the Council of Canadians) and US-based Food & Water Watch[5] work to support local movements against water privatization and to influence global water policy. Blue Planet Project was created specifically to coordinate global efforts to enshrine water as a human right, a public trust, and a part of the global commons. Its co-founder, Maude Barlow, is a Canadian author, former senior advisor to the UN on water, and leader in the global movement for the HRtWS. The Center on Housing Rights and Evictions (COHRE) was a key early advocate of the HRtWS, and successfully lobbied the Committee on Economic, Social and Cultural Rights to develop General Comment 15 (Interview Khalfan). Organizations such as WASH-United and Water Aid also work to promote a rights-based approach to water services.[6]

Human rights are not the primary focus of most of these organizations; the strongest champions for the HRtWS are not necessarily traditional human rights organizations. The self-identified "water justice movement" organizations have an explicit anti-private sector participation stance (Davidson-Harden et al., 2007). According to Barlow: "It is widely understood by the global water justice movement that these rights can only be realized within a system that recognizes water as a public trust and a public service" (Barlow, 2015, p. 8). This puts the movement occasionally at odds with their more moderate partners, including Amnesty International and Human Rights Watch, as will be discussed below.

The following sections examine three of the main platforms where the HRtWS has been introduced, with particular attention to the champions and challengers of acceptance for water and sanitation as legal human rights.

1. UNITED NATIONS GENERAL ASSEMBLY

On 28 July 2010 the United Nations General Assembly (UNGA) adopted Resolution 64/292 recognizing "the right to safe and clean drinking water

---

[5] Food & Water Watch is a consumer rights organization focused on corporate and government accountability on water, food, and fishing. They provide advocacy, lobbying, and research that challenge private sector participation in the water sector.

[6] While development organizations such as CARE and Oxfam have increasingly embraced a "rights-based approach" to development (Nelson, 2015, p. 150), these organizations have not taken any significant actions on the human rights to water and sanitation.

and sanitation as a human right that is essential for the full enjoyment of life and all human rights." The passage of this resolution signifies a major step toward acceptance of the HRtWS in the global system.

Champions

The Bolivian representative to the UN, Pablo Solón, introduced the measure to the General Assembly in June 2010. Solón's bold and seemingly sudden proposal took some members of the water justice movement by surprise, and there was initial skepticism that the resolution would pass (Interview O'Callaghan 2015; Interview Naidoo). However, Solón's proposal was not initiated impulsively; rather it was the result of a multi-year collaboration between the water justice movement and the Bolivian government.

In 2008, Blue Planet Project's Maude Barlow was the senior advisor on water issues to then-President of the UNGA, Miguel D'Escoto Brockmann. Upon taking office, Brockmann expressed his support for the idea of a UNGA resolution to address the impact of the global water crisis on the poor (Barlow, 2013, pp. 27–8). Barlow first called for formal recognition of the HRtWS at a speech to the UNGA on 22 April 2009. This proposal for a water resolution was delayed due to opposition from UN members. Representatives from Barlow's own government (Canada) publicly signaled their opposition by physically leaving the room whenever she spoke about the HRtWS in various UN committees and panels (Barlow, 2013, p. 28).[7] Barlow found a strong ally for the idea of a UNGA resolution in Bolivian President Evo Morales, and she encouraged Morales and Solón to "lead the crusade" to introduce the resolution (Barlow, 2013, p. 30).

Solón's proposal in June 2010 and his steadfast support for the resolution quickly activated the water justice movement (Interview O'Callaghan 2015). The main organizer on the ground, Blue Planet Project's Anil Naidoo, scrambled to reach out to as many UN missions in New York as possible to lobby for their support over the course of the 40 days leading up to the vote (Interview Naidoo). While Naidoo lobbied in New York, water activists all over the world lobbied in their home capitals for their governments to vote in favor of the resolution (Interview O'Callaghan).

Attempts to soften or weaken the language, such as one proposal to drop sanitation altogether, were met with an uncompromising stance from Solón. Solón refused to accept another proposal to replace the words "the

---

[7] According to Barlow, opposition from transnational water corporations with influence within the UN was also a major factor in delaying a resolution on the right to water at that time (Barlow, 2013, p. 28).

human right to water and sanitation" with "the human right to *access to* water and sanitation," citing the change as an attempt to allow states to transfer their obligations to private actors (Barlow, 2013, pp. 30–1). Solón preferred to lose the vote than to dilute the language, and he openly challenged states to vote against the HRtWS in the public forum of the General Assembly (Barlow, 2013, p. 31; Interview Nadoo).

The vote took place 28 July 2010 with 122 countries voting in favor and no votes against; 41 countries with concerns and those in opposition to the resolution opted to abstain. These 41 abstentions included three countries that frequently oppose efforts to legalize the HRtWS: the USA, the UK, and Canada.[8]

Challengers

The US representative to the UNGA signaled its opposition by calling for the vote on the resolution.[9] In public statements, the USA argued that a UNGA resolution could harm the process occurring at that time in the HRC, which was also preparing to vote on a similar resolution on water and sanitation later that year. The USA cited the lack of a pre-existing right to water and sanitation in international law and claimed that the process of drafting the UNGA text was not "transparent" (UNGA, 2010). Food & Water Watch interpreted these criticisms as "delay tactics" rather than a concern for the process at the HRC, and they viewed the US abstention as a political move to avoid voting against the resolution (Interview O'Callaghan 2015).

In the "explanation of the vote" section, the UK representative expressed opposition to both the "substance and procedure" of the resolution, claiming that no legal basis for declaring a human right to water or sanitation exists in the international system (UNGA, 2010). The UK echoed the US concerns that a UNGA resolution would undermine the HRC's work, which the UK representative described as proceeding in a more "careful and consensual" manner. Canada's objections were similar,

---

[8] Abstaining countries: Armenia, Australia, Austria, Bosnia and Herzegovina, Botswana, Bulgaria, Canada, Croatia, Cyprus, Czech Republic, Denmark, Estonia, Ethiopia, Greece, Guyana, Iceland, Ireland, Israel, Japan, Kazakhstan, Kenya, Latvia, Lesotho, Lithuania, Luxembourg, Malta, the Netherlands, New Zealand, Poland, Republic of Korea, Republic of Moldova, Romania, Slovakia, Sweden, Trinidad and Tobago, Turkey, Ukraine, United Kingdom, United Republic of Tanzania, United States, Zambia.

[9] When a country calls for a vote on a UNGA resolution it indicates that consensus could not be reached in the negotiations.

citing a lack of consensus among states on the HRtWS and the lack of sufficient grounding in international human rights law.

Barlow described the public commentary by abstaining countries as "angry," yet she interprets their abstentions rather than "no" votes as "the best signal yet that the debate over these fundamental rights was finally winding down" (Barlow, 2013, p. 32). Despite opposition and abstentions by the USA, UK, and Canada, the UNGA resolution passed and initiated a momentum toward increased recognition of the HRtWS in other international arenas including in the HRC.

2. HUMAN RIGHTS COUNCIL

In 2008 the HRC[10] appointed an independent expert, Portugal's Catarina de Albuquerque, to be the Special Rapporteur on the issue of human rights obligations related to access to safe drinking water and sanitation (hereafter Special Rapporteur). On 15 September 2010, several months after the UNGA resolution passed, de Albuquerque presented her first report to the HRC (De Albuquerque, 2010a). On 30 September 2010 the HRC adopted Resolution A/HRC/15/L.14, solidifying the HRtWS as a legally binding human right derived from the right to an adequate standard of living from Article 11 of the ICESCR. The right to water and sanitation was linked to several other already established human rights, as seen in Point 3: "the human right to safe drinking water and sanitation is derived from the right to an *adequate standard of living* and inextricably related to the right to the *highest attainable standard of physical and mental health*, as well as the right to *life* and *human dignity*" (emphasis added). Therefore, the HRtWS is present in existing human rights law through treaties that include these rights.

The 2010 draft resolution was introduced by Germany and Spain with 55 other nations as co-sponsors; 17 of the co-sponsors were countries that abstained from the UNGA resolution earlier that year. In contrast to the UNGA resolution, which had 41 abstentions, there was no call for a vote and the resolution passed unanimously.

Champions

Brazil was an early champion of a resolution on the HRtWS within the HRC. However, attempts by Brazil to insert the HRtWS into other

---

[10] The Human Rights Council is an inter-governmental body comprised of 47 states elected by the General Assembly on a rotating basis.

resolutions on health and related issues before the HRC were unsuccessful, mainly due to forceful and vocal opposition from Canada (Interview Khalfan). Recognizing that water and sanitation required a separate resolution, Germany's human rights ambassador, Tom Koenigs, took up the issue. Germany found an ally in Spain, a long-time supporter of ESC rights, to embark on a strategy to gain legal recognition for water and sanitation within the HRC. They began by requesting the Office of the High Commissioner on Human Rights (OHCHR) conduct a study on equitable access to drinking water and sanitation. After the study was completed, the OHCHR established the independent expert, later the Special Rapporteur, on water and sanitation. The resolution on the HRtWS was meant to follow the release of the first Special Rapporteur's report in September 2010.

Bolivia's sudden proposal for a UNGA resolution in June 2010 came as a surprise to those engaged in the HRC process, and the passage of the resolution created a strain on the HRC process already underway (Interview Khalfan). Some participants felt the UNGA resolution "pre-empted" the work underway at the HRC, while others worried that the lack of consensus for the UNGA resolution could damage the HRC process (International Service for Human Rights, 2010). Participants in the HRC negotiations were unsure if the Council should merely affirm what the UNGA had already declared, or have its own distinct approach. In her statement to the HRC regarding her report, the Special Rapporteur spoke favorably of the UNGA resolution, calling it a "breakthrough" and a demonstration of "political will of the international community to address the lack of access to water and sanitation" (De Albuquerque, 2010b).

There was minimal advocacy by the water justice movement on the HRC, in part because there was a sense that the resolution was going to pass (Interview O'Callaghan 2015). Furthermore, the HRC is based in Geneva, which was inaccessible to many movement actors, and there was less understanding of how the Council process functioned (Interview Naidoo).

While the water justice movement stepped back from this process, in a parallel initiative, Amnesty International publicly voiced its support for the resolution and shamed states that were attempting to derail or dilute the resolution (Amnesty International, 2010a, 2010b). Amnesty reported: "the USA, the UK and Canada, with some support from a small number of other States, have vocally and consistently attempted to block the affirmation of these rights in the present resolution" (Amnesty, 2010b). Amnesty further accused the USA, UK and Canada of attempting to control the definition and scope of these rights as presented in the resolution by limiting the definition of water to "safe drinking water" – a definition that excludes water for washing clothes, preparing food, and personal and household sanitation and hygiene (Amnesty International, 2012).

In 2013, Amnesty called on its national sections to lobby their home governments to support new resolutions in both the UNGA and the HRC to further affirm and elaborate the content of the rights to water and sanitation. The strategy included writing letters to their governments followed by further lobbying in advance of the HRC and UNGA sessions. Amnesty's representative in Geneva participated in ongoing negotiations over resolution drafts before the HRC (Interview Khalfan). Amnesty worked continually with Spain and Germany in the HRC to continue to advance the legal status of the rights, particularly in the face of continued opposition at each step from the USA, the UK, and Canada (Interview Khalfan).[11]

Challengers

As noted above, Canada blocked initial attempts by Brazil to include the HRtWS in other resolutions. The USA threatened to vote against the 2010 resolution throughout the negotiations prior to the vote. The USA and UK attempted to dilute the resolution by proposing changing language from "human right to water" to "human rights obligations *related to* water" (Interview Khalfan). In the explanation of the vote, the UK dissociated itself from the consensus. The UK objected to the inclusion of the right to sanitation, which the UK representative claimed has no basis in international human rights law and no clear definition (Human Rights Council, 2011).

In a surprising turn, the US representative stated that while the USA abstained from the UNGA resolution the USA was "proud to join consensus" on the HRC resolution. In its explanation of the vote, the US representative emphasized that state parties to the ICESCR are responsible to realize the rights contained and derived from the covenant, including the HRtWS. The USA is one of the few countries in the world that has not ratified the ICESCR; therefore, the USA is not legally bound by the ICESCR or by HRC resolutions, making the cost of supporting the resolution low for the USA.

---

[11] Other countries including Egypt, Argentina, India, China, and Turkey also expressed opposition to the HRtWS language, mainly due to concerns over transboundary water issues. Yet their opposition was less consistent and vocal compared to the USA, UK, and Canada (Interview Khalfan).

The HRC resolution received more support than the UNGA resolution possibly as a result of a growing consensus on the legality of the HRtWS (Winkler, 2012, p. 80), or possibly because the UNGA referred to a general human right to water and sanitation while the HRC resolution language was more specific, defining the HRtWS as derived from an existing right (to an adequate standard of living) (Murthy, 2013; Interview Khalfan).

Along with General Comment 15, the UNGA and HRC resolutions contribute to both the legal scaffolding for the HRtWS and the acceptance of a new definition of water and sanitation as human rights in the international system. Significant advances in establishing the HRtWS are also taking place in the global water policy arena, an advocacy platform that is outside the realm of international law.

3. WORLD WATER FORUM

The World Water Forum (WWF) is the largest international conference devoted to water governance. Every three years multiple stakeholders including multinational water companies, government representatives, UN organizations, and international development organizations meet at the Forum to discuss water policy. The WWF is organized by the World Water Council, a think-tank comprised of over 300 private water corporations, investment banks, and water industry associations.

WWF documents since 1997 consistently define water as an economic good or a need, and stress the importance of private sector participation in water services (Barlow, 2013; Gerlak, Baer, and Lopes, 2013). At the close of each WWF a Ministerial Declaration summarizing the main content of the Forum is signed by participating government representatives and released to the public. At every WWF since 2000, members of the water justice movement and a handful of government representatives have attempted to include the words "the human right to water and sanitation" in these declarations, and every time their efforts were rejected – but we can see recent movement toward including rights-based language in WWF documents.

Champions

The global water justice movement attends every WWF with a multi-pronged strategy to work both inside and outside the Forum. They participate in the Forum as audience members and occasionally panelists on the official program, as organizers of Forum "side events" that are included in the WWF schedule but held outside the official Forum, and they work with friendly government representatives to try to influence the discourse on the HRtWS from inside the Forum. Outside the Forum, they organize and collaborate with local activists to hold an Alternative Water Forum and to publicly protest against the Forum. These efforts are led by NGOs including Blue Planet Project and Food & Water Watch. Amnesty International and Human Rights Watch are not regular or visible participants in the WWF organizing or alternative water forums.

Activists from the water justice movement disrupted the 2003 Kyoto Forum expressing their clear opposition to privatization (Bakker, 2007). Although the 2003 Kyoto Forum took place shortly after the issue of General Comment Number 15 on the HRtWS, attempts to include the HRtWS in the Ministerial Declaration were rejected. By the 2006 WWF in Mexico, the HRtWS begins to appear in the discourse of the Forum. Three official WWF sessions discussed the HRtWS[12] and in the opening speeches to the Forum, then-President of Mexico Vicente Fox stated: "Water is above all a human right which no one can renounce," and World Water Council President Loïc Fauchon said: "The right to water is an indispensable element of human dignity" (Martinez and van Hofwegen, 2006, p. 87). Although the official summary of the 2006 WWF reads: "There was a broad consensus about the existence of a human right to water" (Martinez and van Hofwegen, 2006, p. 89) at the Forum, government representatives once again rejected the inclusion of the HRtWS in the Ministerial Declaration despite attempts by the Bolivian representative and others to mobilize support for its inclusion.

At the 2009 WWF in Istanbul, Food & Water Watch, Blue Planet Project, Red VIDA, and dozens of other groups held panels, workshops, debates, and film screenings billed as "side events" to the official Forum.[13] In several panels on water privatization, water justice movement activists dominated the question and answer period providing critiques and alternative data on the outcomes of privatization. This attendance and participation was part of a carefully planned strategy. Activists from dozens of organizations met each night in the basement of a local hotel to discuss plans for challenging and protesting the Forum.

Nightly meetings also included report-backs from official government delegates from several Latin American countries including Bolivia, Ecuador, and Venezuela. The government representatives reported on

---

[12] These include: "Securing the Right to Water: From the Local to the Global, Civil Society Perspectives," "The Right to Water: What Does it Mean and How to Implement it," and "Human Right to Water."

[13] This section is based on fieldwork at the Istanbul World Water Forum in 2009 and subsequent interviews with members of the movement.

what was happening inside Forum meetings and strategized with activists about pushing for inclusion of the HRtWS in the Ministerial Declaration. Delegates from Venezuela and Uruguay reported that the USA, Egypt, and Brazil were blocking the inclusion of the HRtWS in the official Ministerial Declaration, instead promoting defining water as a "human need" as it had been defined in past declarations. The US delegates told Food & Water Watch staff that declaring a HRtWS was impossible for the USA to support, as it would contradict the US Constitution (Interview O'Callaghan 2010). The final Ministerial Declaration references the debate over the HRtWS while rejecting the language: "We acknowledge the discussion within the UN system regarding human rights and access to safe drinking water and sanitation. We recognize that access to safe drinking water and sanitation is a basic human need" (WWC, 2009). In response, the water ministers of Bolivia, Ecuador, Uruguay, and Venezuela created an alternative Ministerial Declaration that included a definition of water as a human right, and they called on other government representatives to not sign the official Ministerial Declaration – 25 governments[14] signed the alternative statement on the right to water, and 16[15] signed both the right to water statement and a statement calling for future WWF meetings to be convened by the UN rather than the World Water Council.[16]

The 2012 WWF in Marseilles, France, the first meeting after the UNGA and HRC resolutions, was the largest event thus far for the water justice movement. The Alternative Forum hosted thousands of attendants, with participation levels rivaling that of the official Forum (Interview O'Callaghan 2015). In contrast to previous WWF agendas and documents, the term "human right" appears on the Marseilles Forum website over 2000 times, and rather than relegating human rights themes to "side events," there were several official sessions focused on the HRtWS. These included a panel led by then-UN Special Rapporteur Catarina de Albuquerque, a session on human rights-based governance led by the French water company Suez with several NGOs, and a session hosted by the World Bank on the implications of national policies on the HRtWS for practitioners.

[14] Bangladesh, Benin, Bolivia, Cameroon, Chad, Chile, Cuba, Ecuador, Ethiopia, Guatemala, Honduras, Morocco, Namibia, Niger, Nigeria, Panama, Paraguay, Senegal, South Africa, Spain, Sri Lanka, United Arab Emirates, Uruguay, Venezuela.

[15] Benin, Bolivia, Cameroon, Chad, Chile, Cuba, Ecuador, Ethiopia, Honduras, Nigeria, Panama, Paraguay, Senegal, Sri Lanka, United Arab Emirates, Venezuela.

[16] Switzerland and Norway indicated that they would support the right to water statement, but had to obtain official approval after the Forum.

The Ministerial Declaration, signed by 84 government ministers, acknowledges recent UN action on the HRtWS and states: "we commit to accelerate the full implementation of the human rights obligations relating to access to safe and clean drinking water and sanitation" (WWC, 2012). While seemingly a victory for the water justice movement, critics charged that this language stops short of a full recognition of the HRtWS and leaves openings for states to avoid the obligations that the HRtWS entails (Barlow, 2013; Provost, 2012).

Challengers

The water justice movement views the WWF as a global meeting of HRtWS opponents (Barlow, 2013; Interview O'Callaghan 2010, 2015). The consistent and adamant opposition by Canada, the USA, and the UK (among others) to including human rights language in the Ministerial Declaration – a non-binding document – displays the importance of controlling the discourse on water in the global policy space.

Despite strong resistance from WWF participants, human rights language is seeping into all areas of the Forum. This is attributable to the continued pressure by the water justice movement working together with a handful of state representatives from the Global South to place human rights on the agenda of the Forum. The water justice movement prioritizes the WWF as a site for their advocacy not because the WWF has the power to legalize the HRtWS, but because the Forum is a global arena where the discourse on water is shaped and reproduced. While the Ministerial Declarations are mostly symbolic documents, the increasing inclusion of human rights language in these documents is a key element in reframing water and sanitation as human rights rather than economic goods.

HUMAN RIGHTS GATEKEEPERS

Mainstream human rights organizations have been reluctant to take on ESC rights issues for decades, and only recently moved toward "partial acceptance" of these rights in their advocacy (Chong, 2006). Amnesty began working on ESC rights in the early 2000s, although the work focuses somewhat narrowly on demanding that these rights be respected without discrimination (Khalfan and Byrne, 2015). Activist circulation amongst international NGOs could account for the recent increase in attention to ESC rights; for example, Amnesty's advocacy on water increased significantly under the guidance of Dr Ashfaq Khalfan, a human rights lawyer and former director of the Right to Water Programme at COHRE.

Amnesty's main entry point for the HRtWS is its Demand Dignity campaign, which focuses on ESC rights and poverty including equal access to public services for people living in slums (Interview Khalfan).[17] Viewed within the broader scope of the decades-long work to redefine water and sanitation as human rights by members of the water justice movement and organizations like COHRE, Amnesty's work on the HRtWS since 2010 arrives a bit late in the timeline and is focused somewhat narrowly on the realm of international law.[18]

Human Rights Watch only recently joined the ranks of organizations working on the HRtWS. Although water is mentioned in various country reports as far back as 1999, it was not until late 2013 when Human Rights Watch began discussing ways to systematically work on the HRtWS (Interview Klasing). In 2014 Human Rights Watch launched a four-year project to increase collaboration with the water justice movement and the Special Rapporteur on water, and to produce research on water and sanitation issues (Interview Klasing). Human Rights Watch has a more moderate stance on privatization than many water justice movement organizations. This stance is due in part to their interpretation of international law on the HRtWS, which does not prohibit private sector participation in the water sector (Gómez Isa, 2008). Klasing explains that it is very important for the organization to "not get ahead of where the law is" when working on the HRtWS and other socioeconomic rights issues (Interview Klasing).

[17] The Demand Dignity campaign also has a "Make Our Rights Law" component, in which Amnesty advocates for all economic, social, and cultural rights to be made part of national law.

[18] Amnesty has produced four country reports and campaign digests that discuss the rights to water and sanitation: Slovenia, Solomon Islands, Kenya, and Israel/Palestine. Amnesty has also worked with partners to include human rights language in the Rio + 20 and Sustainable Development Goals 2015–30 documents.

DISCUSSION

The HRtWS has achieved an enviable status for a new rights claim: all nations are now bound by at least one resolution or treaty that contains the right, countries across the globe are amending their constitutions to include the right,[19] and even the fiercest opponents are forced to acknowledge that the HRtWS is now part of international law. The campaigns for the HRtWS reveal a case of rights expansion that shows an unexpected advocacy process, which is shaped by the type of rights, the actors and decision-making processes of various advocacy platforms, and the presence and strength of challengers. The findings of this chapter speak to several themes addressed in this volume including the challenges associated with framing rights, the role of advocates and gatekeepers, and the implications for implementation in expanding human rights.

Extant theory tells us that new rights claims are most likely to become accepted if they align with pre-existing norms and values and if human rights gatekeeper organizations become champions of the claim in the global system, yet the HRtWS is gaining acceptance largely in the absence of both these criteria.

The HRtWS case suggests that while gatekeepers can play a significant role in assisting new rights claims acceptance, their adoption of a new rights claim is not a necessary condition for international acceptance. Second, this chapter's findings, along with those of the Hertel chapter in this volume, point us to other actors and platforms outside the mainstream human rights regime. The water justice movement is comprised of non-human rights focused organizations, and one of their main advocacy platforms is a large corporate water meeting rather than the mainstream human rights institutions like the HRC. Bob's theory suggests that rights expand through a process that is *mediated by* gatekeepers – but the global campaign for the HRtWS more closely resembles parallel and complementary strategies by gatekeepers like Amnesty that pursue legalization at the HRC, while the water justice movement pursues the framing work to redefine water from an economic good to a human right in symbolic spaces, such as the UNGA process and the WWF.

This chapter shows that much of the work to legitimize the HRtWS is happening outside the human rights regime and is not led by traditional

---

[19] Countries that refer to the right to water in their constitutions include: Democratic Republic of Congo, South Africa, Philippines, Malawi, Gambia, Uganda, Dominican Republic, Belgium, Maldives, Niger, Tunisia, Kenya, Ecuador, Ethiopia, Zambia, Uruguay, Mexico, Panama, Colombia, Venezuela, Bolivia, and Nicaragua.

human rights advocates and gatekeepers. The NGOs leading the campaign for the HRtWS, such as Blue Planet Project and Food & Water Watch, are not human rights organizations. The water justice movement's relative success in gaining acceptance for the HRtWS is linked to their effective collaborations with states in the Global South, particularly Bolivia, Venezuela, Ecuador, among others. The UNGA resolution was a state-led initiative in conjunction with the water justice movement. The HRC resolution was also a state-led initiative (by Germany and Spain). The human rights gatekeepers are not active in the work to insert human rights language at the WWF. Amnesty International and Human Rights Watch are not core members of the water justice movement and only began focusing on the HRtWS in 2010 and 2013, respectively.

As noted in Chapter 5 on violence against women by Alison Brysk, expanding rights often entails reframing an old problem in new terms. Water was already defined and accepted for decades as an economic good and a human need, not a right. The HRC resolution links the HRtWS to other rights such as the right to life, an adequate standard of living, and the highest attainable standard of physical and mental health. However, these are viewed as socioeconomic rights, which occupy a secondary status within the human rights regime in terms of recognition and enforcement. This suggests that expanding rights is not a matter of merely aligning a new rights issue with an established set of norms, as pre-existing established norms can be in direct conflict with the new, rights-based frame.

This may also relate to the challengers for new rights claims. Opposition to defining water and sanitation by the USA, UK, and Canada has been fierce and sustained in all the venues discussed in this chapter. Their opposition may be attributable simply to an objection to being bound by a legal right to water and sanitation; some advocates attribute their opposition to a general objection to legalizing and legitimizing ESC rights (Interview Khalfan). Another potential explanation is that water-rich countries like Canada oppose attaching human rights language to water out of their own material interest in protecting their large water resources. Yet out of the top ten countries with the most renewable water resources in the world, only the USA and Canada opposed the 2010 UNGA Resolution on the HRtWS, suggesting that other water-rich countries did not see the resolution as a threat. Barlow suggests that opposition by the USA, UK, and Canada is rooted in ideology – both a decades-long commitment to the market-based vision for water services and an aversion to legitimizing socioeconomic grievances as new human rights.

As with all human rights, the issue of enforcement and implementation is key. The UNGA and HRC resolutions will not lead directly to implementation of the HRtWS. However, like the United Nations Declaration on the Rights of Indigenous Peoples discussed in Chapter 4 by Felipe Gómez Isa, these resolutions create the legal footprint and key reference points for international, regional, and national-level changes that can bolster implementation. Like the UNDRIP for indigenous rights, the UNGA and HRC resolutions on water outline the minimum content of the rights to water and sanitation, they provide benchmarks for domestic actors to use in their advocacy, and their passage reflects a growing consensus on these rights and principles.

The campaign for the HRtWS reveals that in the ever-shifting landscape of global politics, traditional human rights norms and gatekeepers are not necessarily on the cutting edge of attempts to revise and update the human rights lexicon. Leadership from the Global South and non-human rights focused NGOs is key to ensuring that the emancipatory script of human rights expands to address new forms of inequality and threats to human dignity.

INTERVIEWS

Darcey O'Callaghan, Food & Water Watch, 11 May 2010 and 27 May 2015.
Amanda Klasing, Human Rights Watch, 28 May 2015.
Anil Naidoo, Blue Planet Project, 27 January 2016.
Ashfaq Khalfan, Amnesty International, 4 April 2016.

REFERENCES

Websites last accessed 17 December 2015.

Amnesty International (2010a). "States urged to support rights to water and sanitation," 29 July. https://www.amnesty.org/en/latest/news/2010/07/estados-deben-apoyar-derecho-agua-saneamiento/.

Amnesty International (2010b). "United Nations: all states must support rights to water and sanitation at the Human Rights Council," 28 September. https://www.amnesty.org/en/documents/ior40/017/2010/en/.

Amnesty International (2012). "United Nations: states must recognise and not undermine the content of the rights to water and sanitation," 29 October. https://www.amnesty.org/en/documents/ior41/020/2012/en/.

Bakker, Karen (2007). "The 'commons' versus the 'commodity': alter-globalization, anti-privatization and the human right to water in the Global South". *Antipode*, **39**(3), 430–55.

Barlow, Maude (2013). *Blue Future: Protecting Water for People and the Planet Forever*. New York: The New Press.

Barlow, Maude (2015). "Our right to water: assessing progress five years after the UN recognition of the human rights to water and sanitation". http://canadians.

org/publications/report-our-right-water-assessing-progress-five-years-after-un-recognition-human-rights.

Bob, Clifford (ed.) (2009). *The International Struggle for New Human Rights*. Philadelphia, PA: University of Pennsylvania Press.

Brysk, Alison (2013). *Speaking Rights to Power: Constructing Political Will*. Oxford: Oxford University Press.

Carpenter, R.C. (2011). "Vetting the advocacy agenda: network centrality and the paradox of weapons norms." *International Organization*, **65**(1), 69–102.

Chong, Daniel (2006) "Subsistence rights: why northern NGOs apply the human rights framework to fight extreme poverty." 2006 ISA Paper.

Conca, K. (2006). *Governing Water: Contentious Transnational Politics and Global Institution Building*. Cambridge, MA: The MIT Press.

Davidson-Harden, Adam, Anil Nadoo, and Andi Harden (2007). "The geopolitics of the water justice movement." *Peace Conflict & Development*, **11**, 1–34.

De Albuquerque, Catarina (2010a). *Report of the Independent Expert on the Issue of Human Rights Obligations Related to Access to Safe Drinking Water and Sanitation, Catarina de Albuquerque*. Human Rights Council, Fifteenth Session, 1 July. http://www2.ohchr.org/english/bodies/hrcouncil/docs/15session/A.HRC.15.31.Add.1_en.pdf.

De Albuquerque, Catarina (2010b). *Independent Expert on the Issue of Human Rights Obligations Related to Safe Drinking Water and Sanitation, Ms. Catarina de Albuquerque*. Human Rights Council, 12th Session, 15 September.

De Albuquerque, Catarina and Inga T. Winkler. (2010). "Neither friend nor foe: why the commercialization of water and sanitation services is not the main issue in the realization of human rights." *Brown Journal of World Affairs*, **XVII**(I), 167–79.

Finger, M. and J. Allouche (2002). *Water Privatisation: Trans-national Corporations and the Re-regulation of the Water Industry*. London: Spon Press.

Finnemore, M. and K. Sikkink (1998). "International norm dynamics and political change." *International Organization*, **52**(4), 887–917.

Florini, Ann (1996). "The evolution of international norms." *International Studies Quarterly*, **40**, 363–89.

Gerlak, A., M. Baer and P. Lopes (2013). "Unpacking the discourse around the human right to water." Paper presented at the International Studies Association Annual Meeting, San Francisco, CA, 3–6 April.

Gómez Isa, F. (2008). "Water and privatization: a human rights approach." In M. Manciscidos and C. Fernandez-Jauregi (eds), *The Human Right to Water: Situation and Future Challenges*. Barcelona: Icaria, pp. 151–63.

Gómez Isa, F. (2011). "Freedom from want revisited from a local perspective: evolution and challenges ahead." In K. de Foeter, S. Parmentier, C. Timmerman, and G. Ulrich (eds), *The Local Relevance of Human Rights*. Cambridge: Cambridge University Press, pp. 40–81.

Human Rights Council (2011). *Report of the Human Rights Council on its Fifteenth Session (A/HRC/15/60)*, 31 October. http://www.ohchr.org/EN/HRBodies/HRC/RegularSessions/Session15/Pages/15RegularSession.aspx.

International Service for Human Rights (2010). "GA pre-empts Council and recognizes the human right to water and sanitation." http://www.ishr.ch/news/ga-pre-empts-council-and-recognises-human-right-water-and-sanitation#sthash.sfST2RDy.dpuf.

Khalfan, Ashfaq and Iain Byrne (2015). "Advancing social justice through human rights at Amnesty International." https://www.opendemocracy.net/openglobalrights/ashfaq-khalfan-iain-byrne/advancing-social-justice-through-human-rights-at-amnesty-.

Langford, M. (2005). "The United Nations concept of water as a human right: a new paradigm for old problems?" *International Journal of Water Resources Development*, **21**(2), 273–82.

Martinez, A.P. and P. van Hofwegen (eds) (2006). *Synthesis of the 4th World Water Forum*. Mexico City: World Water Council.

Murthy, S.L. (2013). "The human right(s) to water and sanitation: history, meaning, and the controversy over privatization." *Berkeley Journal of International Law*, **331**(1), Article 3.

Nelson, P. (2009). "Local claims, international standards, and the human right to water." In Clifford Bob (ed.), *The International Struggle for New Human Rights*. Philadelphia, PA: University of Pennsylvania Press, pp. 130–40.

Nelson, P. (2015). "Social movements and the expansion of economic and social human rights advocacy among international NGOs." In LaDawn Haglund and Robin Stryker (eds), *Closing the Rights Gap: From Human Rights to Social Transformation*. Oakland, CA: University of California Press, pp. 149–70.

Nelson, P. and E. Dorsey (2007). "New rights advocacy in a global public domain." *European Journal of International Relations*, **13**(2), 187–216.

Provost, C. (2012). "World Water Forum declaration falls short on human rights, claim experts." *Guardian*, 14 March. http://www.guardian.co.uk/global-development/2012/mar/14/world-water-forum-declaration-human-rights.

Roth, K. (2004). "Defending economic, social and cultural rights: practical issues faced by an international human rights organization." *Human Rights Quarterly*, **26**(1), 63–73.

UNGA Resolution 64/292. The Human Right to Water and Sanitation. http://www.un.org/waterforlifedecade/human_right_to_water.shtml.

UNGA (United Nations General Assembly) (2010). 108th Plenary Meeting, 28 July. http://www.un.org/en/ga/search/view_doc.asp?symbol=A/64/PV.108.

Winkler, Inga (2012). *The Human Right to Water: Significance, Legal Status and Implications for Water Allocation*. Oxford: Hart Publishing.

WWC (World Water Council) (2009). Ministerial statement – Istanbul, Turkey. http://www.worldwatercouncil.org/fileadmin/world_water_council/documents_old/World_Water_Forum/WWF5/Ministerial_Statement_22_3_09.pdf.

WWC (World Water Council) (2012). Ministerial Declaration – Marseilles, France. http://www.worldwaterforum6.org/en/news/single/article/the-ministerial-declaration-of-the-6th-world-water-forum/.

7. Human rights and corporate social responsibility

Michael Stohl and Cynthia Stohl

INTRODUCTION

The last few decades have witnessed unparalleled accelerations in the processes of globalization, simultaneously increasing the potential efficacy of past models of social activism and social justice and creating new opportunities for actors engaged in the struggle for communities and sustainable development. In this chapter we explore the growing corporate social responsibility movement, and the evolving interrelationships and expectations of states, non-governmental organizations (NGOs), and corporations. We focus specifically on the development of new conceptions of corporate social responsibility (CSR) as an expansion of the concept of human rights across several generations, with special attention to communication rights in the new media environment. Although what comprises CSR has evolved over time it still remains a highly contested concept (May, Cheney, and Roper, 2007). In general, CSR references the expectations and responsibilities of business to society to contribute to the well-being of stockholders, internal and external stakeholders, and the sustainability of our global environment. But what CSR actually means in terms of the scope of corporate behavior and its relationship to human rights, international regulation, and compliance is still evolving. Here we suggest that emerging communication technologies in the digital age are now reshaping concern with employee and stakeholder communication rights. These concerns transcend issues of the workplace and expand the public and scholarly conception of human rights.

In this chapter, we demonstrate strong parallels between the growth of the global human rights regime and the burgeoning international interest in issues of CSR. The connections between CSR and human rights were fueled by corporate outrages such as the notorious 1911 Triangle Shirtwaist Factory in New York City, the 1976 Lockheed bribery scandal, and the tight linkage between the diamond company DeBeers and apartheid in South Africa in the 1970s and 1980s (see Stohl, Stohl, and Townsley, 2007 for a fuller discussion of the historical connections between CSR and human rights). In the 1990s these connections were amplified by the labeling of "conflict diamonds" and the drawn out civil war in Sierra Leone as well as public accusations and formal lawsuits against companies in the petroleum sector. Strong evidentiary arguments alleging that Enron, ExxonMobil, Unocal, and Shell had colluded with several repressive Asian and African regimes (for example, India, Burma, Nigeria) to imprison and execute anti-corporate activists fueled public debate and social protests about the social role and responsibilities of large multinational corporations in the global system. Wettstein (2012) suggests "[W]hat was new about this emerging debate was not per se the connection of human rights and business, but rather that its concern with human rights started to reach decisively beyond labor and employment issues, to which earlier analyses of the topic had traditionally been limited" (p. 742).

In the opening years of the current millennium it was still unusual, however, when addressing the power of national, multinational, and transnational corporations to suggest that CSR and human rights were connected. Such connections were typically beyond the operational purview of national and transnational regulatory agencies, and were not an important linkage for human rights, management, business, or social science scholars. As late as 2003 Scott Pegg (2003, p. 11) argued, "most of the academic work on transnational corporations ignored the subject of human rights . . . This neglect has been reciprocal: most of the academic work on human rights has tended to overlook the role that TNCs can play in promoting or violating human rights." Yet, whether one examines new journals (*Business and Human Rights Journal*, 2015), encyclopedias (*Encyclopedia of Corporate Social Responsibility*, 2013), handbooks (*The Handbook of Communication and Corporate Social Responsibility*, 2011), or collections of essays (*Business and Human Rights in the Global Economy*, 2016) there remains a great theoretical and practical divide between CSR research and practice and the business human rights perspectives.

Even in this decade where the intersection of CSR and human rights has been the subject of increased conversation and debate, in large part because of the groundbreaking work of John Ruggie, the United Nations (UN) Secretary-General's Special Representative on business and human rights (Ruggie, 2008, 2010), the bifurcation continues. Ruggie's well-established tripartite framework includes three major principles: Protect, Respect, and Remedy. Under this rubric, it is a corporation's responsibility to respect human rights, the state's duty to protect human rights, and global society's obligation to develop effective access to mediate and provide remedies when corporate actions abuse human rights.

According to Wettstein (2012), two core issues contribute to the separation of CSR and human rights. First is the "problem of voluntariness" (p. 748). When CSR is considered as a voluntary responsibility, he argues, the fundamental moral nature of human rights claims is excluded. In this perspective, corporations define their own responsibilities without adhering to anything beyond that which is legally mandated within national corporate law (for example, financial reports, bribery, conflicts of interest disclosures). There are no common definitions or global principles of what CSR means, expectations and obligations are not codified, and there are no mechanisms to demand compliance. Thus, Wettstein laments, the legal obligations which are central to human rights frameworks are considered to be outside the boundaries of CSR. Human rights scholars contend that without sanctions any effort to constrain corporate behavior will be limited to NGO and civil campaigns. Bauer (2011, pp. 174, 175) notes

> the business and human rights movement distinctively claims that international rights law provides a hard legal benchmark against which companies can be judged and will improve corporation reputation . . . standards should be legally obligatory rather than voluntary – and end in itself not a path to profit making . . . The aim is to shift focus from needs to the rights of affected community – and from acts of charity toward accountability to international law.

Another concern that adds to the constraining features of the voluntary context for CSR comes from traditional social movement literature. Empirical findings suggest that when there is overreliance on citizen activism rather than regulatory mechanisms, the investigatory topics and the activities which are monitored tend to privilege middle and upper class stakeholder interests who have the economic freedom to take part in social protest and greater economic buying power (Jenkins, 1983). Thus, within a voluntary framework, the pressures to act when CSR is demanded are in those domains that most directly affect middle and upper class consumers – and not necessarily those which address universal human rights.

The second problem Wettstein (2012) articulates is "the problem of non-political responsibility" (p. 570). He argues that human rights have traditionally been deemed the responsibility of governments whereas corporations are generally conceived as private institutions without political reference. States, not corporations, are explicit subjects of international human rights laws. In this view, corporations are economic actors, driven and rationalized through economic models – not political, social, or ethical concerns. Although today we find many cases in the CSR literature which move beyond the constraining economic role of corporations (Stohl, Stohl, and Townlsey, 2007), the fundamental framing of CSR is predominantly within the business case (Carroll and Shabana, 2010) in which doing what is right for society is shaped by doing what it takes for a company to do well. In this view, human rights are neither the fundamental responsibility nor a necessary obligation of a corporation that they are for a nation state.

However, we suggest that in the emerging digital environment, the disjuncture between CSR and human rights is becoming increasingly less distinct and less defensible. The ubiquity and affordances of digital communication and social media (including visibility, persistence, editability, and association, Treem and Leonardi, 2012)[1] not only make boundaries across different spheres of experience more permeable, they blur distinctions between private and public realms, social and instrumental contexts, and personal and political fields (Bimber, Flanagin, and Stohl, 2012). In today's media environment, corporate human rights violations are more likely to become known and public demands for accountability and remedy more widespread. The visibility affordance of social media, for example, enables greater, easier, and timelier access regarding information about corporate interactions with employees and other stakeholder groups to all citizens regardless of socioeconomic status (SES). This visibility provides meta-knowledge about what groups of employees and stakeholders know (Treem and Leonardi, 2012, p. 153), thus increasing public knowledge about employee and community experiences vis-à-vis private organizations that heretofore had remained hidden. Persistence enables curation and the creation of repositories for corporate messages, creating a robust context of traceable communicative patterns that can have consequences beyond initial transmission (Boyd, 2010). When cumulative records of past corporate activity transcend corporate control and evidence of alleged transgressions can easily be curated and disseminated publicly, it becomes more difficult for state authorities to ignore demands for accountability and the linkage between CSR and human rights is strengthened. Furthermore, editability captures the ease of creating and editing information about organizations on social media, enabling unofficial and non-technical individuals to participate in information gathering and sharing. Association refers to the possible connectivity afforded by social media that not only supplements existing relationships and shared experiences and attitudes but enables emergent connections to larger communities that create new support networks, build social capital, and develop a greater sense of community that can work together to connect corporate responsibility and human rights.

In other words, the affordances of the contemporary media environment enable knowledge and demands accountability of corporate activity in ways never possible before, generating a sense of community and a trove of information that can be used by the human rights activist community to connect issues of CSR with human rights. But social media has not only brought new possibilities for identifying, documenting, and communicating about corporate human rights abuses. *Additionally, social media has broadened the landscape under which corporate activity itself directly falls under the domain of human rights – and we suggest this may be even more transformative.* As we demonstrate below, the communication landscape occasioned by the rapid permeability of private/public, work/personal boundaries associated with new information technologies makes the voluntary and apolitical nature of CSR unsustainable in the global environment.

Specifically, corporate actions to develop standards for users' digital access and to create policies for regulating employee communication and social media use have both become part of an emerging third generation CSR communication regime that no longer can stand outside the domain of human rights and international law. For example, when technology companies like Facebook and Google have to decide whether they will assist regimes that want to monitor and thwart dissident activity by providing access to personal accounts, to deny the sale of technology to authoritarian regimes that can be used to track, target, jail, or execute dissidents (see Anderson and Rainie, 2012) and/or provide open access to all information on the world wide web, Facebook and other platforms, or censor or produce limited search engines (see Baker and Tang, 2015 for a discussion of Google); decisions can no longer be seen or justified as purely business decisions. They are framed as issues of CSR because the decisions impact communication rights of free expression, privacy, and the right to organize – all human rights enshrined in the Declaration of Human Rights (Articles 19–21) as well as the UN Global Compact. Today, after public outrage and protests, many corporations – including Google – have signed on to the Global Network Initiative, a multi-stakeholder CSR project through which they not only make a commitment to core principles of free expression and privacy for their employees and the community, but also agree to be accountable and evaluated independently on the extent to which they actually protect the global public from violations of communication rights (Brown and Korff, 2012).

It is this potential development of norms and laws governing communicative CSR that we argue is an important and expanding human rights frontier, where CSR is closely aligned not just with respect for human rights of all stakeholders, but the protection of established rights and access to remedy as well. In 2012 the Pew Research Center's Internet and American Life Project (Anderson and Rainie, 2012) found that 51 percent of their sample agreed with the statement, "By 2020 technology firms with their headquarters in democratic countries will be expected to abide by a set of norms – for instance the Responsibility to Protect (R2P) citizens attacked or challenged by their governments." According to the Pew report, respondents stated that,

> a Western telecommunications firm would not be able to selectively monitor or block the internet activity of protestors at the behest of an authoritarian government without significant penalties in other markets.

Thus, we see the beginning of a communicative regime and a third generation of CSR that is enmeshed with human rights concerns, sanctions, and international legislation. Moreover, this is not just happening with issues associated with large telecommunication firms and global political challenges. On the interpersonal and local levels, small and large companies throughout the world are attempting to mediate and control employee communication on social media, regulating messaging on employee work accounts *and* on their private accounts, addressing communicative activity when employees are using corporate technology *as well as* on their own devices, not just when employees are speaking as representatives of the organization where they work but *also* as private citizens. These policies address CSR and, as found by Stohl, Etter, Banghart, and Woo (2015), represent an expanding domain of employee human rights. Indeed, social media policies that are focused on regulating employee communication across multiple contexts are now being contested in courts throughout the world, often under the grounds that these policies violate employees' communication rights, for example, "Everyone has the right to freedom of opinion and expression; this right includes freedom to hold opinions without interference and to seek, receive and impart information and ideas through any media and regardless of frontiers (Article 19, Declaration of Human Rights).

Our central arguments are explicated below. First, attention to the dynamic processes associated with the development of the international human rights regime provides important insights for the future development of a global CSR/human rights regime. Second, the connection between CSR and human rights is not merely about material working conditions under which workers' human rights are constrained (for example, anti-sweat shop legislation) or enabled (for example, fair wages and reasonable working hours, safe working conditions), but about the communicative conditions within which organizational and interorganizational interactions take place. Third, because of the ever-increasing rate of social connectedness associated with globalization and emerging technologies, the continuing development of the CSR regime is likely to occur at a faster pace than that which was witnessed in the development of the human rights regime.

THE HUMAN RIGHTS REGIME

To place the development of a CSR regime in context, we first briefly rehearse the establishment of the human rights regime. Global regimes are defined as "sets of implicit or explicit principles, norms, rules, and decision-making procedures around which actors' expectations converge in a given area of international relations" (Krasner, 1983, p. 2). They embody the rules and conventions adopted by states to structure their relations (Rittberger, 1993). Regimes also "constitute frames of reference to new processes of rule formation and rule making" (Arts, 2000, p. 516). These norms, rules, and decision-making procedures are, of course, not as dramatic as the wars, terrorist attacks, or natural and man-made disasters that feature on the front pages of our daily newspapers or the lead story on the television news, but they are at the heart of the billions of everyday interactions that in fact compose global relations and corporate behavior on a daily basis.

Most scholars of human rights would argue that the establishment of the United Nations and the adoption of the Universal Declaration of Human Rights on 10 December 1948 have been the two most significant contemporary events for the provision, protection, and promotion of human rights within and among states and the creation of a global human rights regime as they provide the foundation upon which all subsequent human rights activity has been based (Donnelly, 1993; Farer, 1992; Forsythe, 2000). Within the charter, there are two contending themes (Alger, 2002). First, the charter is anchored in the clearest language in the protection of Westphalian sovereignty. Article 7 states that:

> Nothing contained in the present Charter shall authorize the United Nations to intervene in matters which are essentially within the domestic jurisdiction of any state or shall require Members to submit such matters to settlement under the present Charter.

Second, in the second paragraph of the Charter's preamble members "reaffirm [their] faith in fundamental human rights, in the dignity and worth of the human person, in the equal rights of men and women." The subsequent adoption of the Universal Declaration of Human Rights established the standards upon which human rights performance was subsequently judged and further legitimated the importance of human rights as a concern both within and across state boundaries.

Since the adoption of the Charter 68 years ago, the world community has come far in the development of both a comprehensive body of law and institutions to protect and promote human rights and, importantly, a discourse that supports those rights. The emergent set of rules, resources, norms, standards, protocols, institutional frameworks, and communication practices that now constitute the "structure" of the human rights regime and thereby facilitate and constrain state action, has become far more extensive and detailed.

The evolutionary process of legitimation of the human rights regime sheds light on several features that we argue are necessary for a CSR regime to develop. First, the unfolding narrative shows the ways in which the formal articulation of norms and expectations is a necessary, although insufficient, condition for the establishment of an international regime. Second, we see the increasing role that NGOs can play when rights or sustainability discourse becomes an accepted frame of discussion. Third, the process illustrates how power relations among NGOs, governments, and other international actors (including corporations) can shift over time. Fourth, as power relations shift, networks are reconfigured, giving space to new voices and processes. And finally, as more actors gain legitimacy in the conversations, sectors blur and new possibilities, both positive and negative, emerge.

AN EMERGING CSR REGIME

Most contemporary accounts of the development of CSR begin with a discussion of the early twentieth century ideas of business magnates like Andrew Carnegie who argued that for capitalism to thrive, organizations must behave in ways that are consistent with a charity principle (helping the unfortunate) and a stewardship principle (taking care of the local environment in which the corporation is situated) (see Carrrol and Shabana, 2010). As Jennifer Bair (2015) reminds us, discussions about corporate codes of conduct and their connection to human rights emerged out of the discussions of the G77 for a New International Economic Order (NIEO) in the 1970s and discussions were formally initiated in 1975. Those discussions were concluded in 1992 without a formal positive result. But at the same time that the UN talks commenced the OECD issued a Ministerial Declaration on International Investment and Multinational Enterprises which was designed to promote standards for MNCs within the member states. "Multinationals were advised to comply with national laws, encouraged to make a positive contribution to economic and social progress in their countries of operation, contribute to technology transfer, and not harm the environment" (Ruggie and Nelson, 2015, p. 5). The issues that gave rise to the UN discussions, the overwhelming power wielded by MNCs against weak states and the need for international organizations to protect the exploited states, did not of course disappear. During the next decade, global discussions of the need for corporate ethical guidelines and standard setting intensified as newly formed states joined the UNs and the European Union (EU) expanded. While promoting voluntary actions, paralleling the formal articulation of rights and human values within the Declaration of Human Rights, Kofi Annan announced the Global Compact in January 1999 at the World Economic Forum in Davos, Switzerland and appealed to corporations to help save the open market (www.un.org/News/Press/docs/1999/19990201.sgsm6881.html):

> Specifically, I call on you – individually through your firms, and collectively through your business associations – to embrace, support and enact a set of core values in the areas of human rights, labour standards, and environmental practices.

Setting voluntary standards was the cornerstone of Annan's proposal. He contrasted two ways of promoting CSR: one through the international policy arena in which states ceded authority to multinational institutions or the other, through promoting the values through action within the corporate sphere. He noted:

> Many of you are big investors, employers and producers in dozens of different countries across the world. That power brings with it great opportunities – and great responsibilities. You can uphold human rights and decent labour and environmental standards directly, by your own conduct of your own business.

Moreover, given the scope and connectedness of global problems to organizational action, international policies, treaties, and conventions began to address corporations and ethical issues (Schwartz, 2002). International governmental organizations (IGOs) such as the International Labor Organization (ILO) and NGOs including the Global Reporting Initiative established broad initiatives to encourage and promote the development of, and compliance with, ethical codes. The UN urged corporations and nations to embrace the Global Compact:

> a voluntary international corporate citizenship network initiated to support the participation of both the private sector and other social actors to advance responsible corporate citizenship and universal social and environmental principles to meet the challenges of globalization. (www.un.org/Depts/ptd/global.htm)

The ten principles of the Global Compact were drawn from the Universal Declaration of Human Rights (1948) and represent all three generations of CSR (Stohl, Stohl, and Townsley, 2007). These rights closely parallel the development of the first three generations of human rights development. First generation human rights began with the Magna Carta and extend through the English Bill of Rights in 1689, the Declaration of Independence, and the Declaration of the Rights of Man in 1789. They first arose to protect the individual from the power of the state and generally were conceived as negative rights, freedoms from interference. First generation rights are seen as belonging to the individual and often favor the abstention from, rather than the intervention of, governments and institutions. These include, for example, the freedom from arbitrary execution, the freedom from unreasonable detention, the prohibition against torture and inhumane treatment, and the right to freedoms of thought and expression. The parallel first generation rights of the CSR movement are captured in the words of the economist Milton Friedman (1970):

> The social responsibility of business is to increase its profits . . . to make the most money as possible while conforming to the basic rules of the society, both those embodied in law and those embodied in ethical culture.

In the 1970s, the definition of what is or is not responsible corporate behavior was conceptualized through a narrow definition of the law and its associated coercive mechanisms. The Lockheed Scandals of 1976 – in which high-ranking Japanese political and business officials, including members of the then Prime Minister Tanaka's office, were paid more than $3 million in bribes and Prince Bernhard (husband of the queen of the Netherlands) was charged with receiving bribes to ensure that Lockheed would win a contract over a French firm – led directly to the 1977 passage of the Foreign Corrupt Practices Act (FCPA) by the US Congress. The act explicitly forbids US firms from paying bribes anywhere, even if they are legal in the external jurisdiction in which they may be operating.

Over the next 40 years first generation corporate responsibility was extended through parallel treaties, agreements, and legislation around the globe modeled upon the FCPA principles (for example, the 1996 Inter-American Convention Against Corruption, the OECD convention of 1997, and further Council of Europe, EU and African Union treaties, as well as the 2003 UN Convention against Transnational Organized Crime and the 2003 UN Convention against Corruption). Significantly this first generation approach to CSR has also led to the establishment of civil society organizations to help monitor corporate activity, a crucial role NGOs also played in the establishment of the human rights regime. Monitoring and protecting first generation responsibilities have also resulted in changing the relationships among NGOs, corporations, and governments. Thus, Transparency International publishes a yearly report on the state of corruption within societies, which includes adherence to the FCPA. The index also spotlights government's role in CSR.

The case of former Saudi Ambassador to the USA Prince Bandar illustrates the changing role of NGOs in the network of corporate responsibility. Bandar was reportedly paid $30 million a year for at least ten years to secure the continuation of an arms deal first brokered by Margaret Thatcher on behalf of BAE systems, the UK's largest arms manufacturer. The disclosure that Britain had shut down its probe of BAE, and would thus not prosecute, led Transparency International to request that the United States Department of Justice fraud prosecutors investigate BAE and pressure the UK government into reopening its review. US concerns were then discussed at two subsequent OECD meetings expanding the conversation on the role of governments in CSR (Meyer, 2007).

The second generation of rights developed in the context of the nineteenth century development of capitalism, industrialization, and class struggle in which workers demanded more humane conditions of employment and compensation. Whereas first generation rights emphasize restraint and legal foundations, second generation rights demand state intervention on behalf of claimants. These rights include the right to fair and equitable wages; the right to rest and leisure, including reasonable limitation of working hours and periodic holidays with pay; the right to basic health care; and the right to a safe working environment. The parallel second generation CSR rights are captured in the words of Nigel Griffiths, the UK Minister for Corporate and Social Responsibility, a position that in and of itself signifies the institutionalization of CSR within government beyond first generation thinking:

> CR is not new. When Robert Owen joined David Dale in 1800 at his spinning mill in New Lanark he created a school and workers' housing and he provided medical services. In short, he ploughed business profits into improving the lives of employees and their families. And over the course of the next century the Cadburys, Frys, Rowantrees [sic], William Lever and others followed suit. And so it has continued to the present day.

Principles 3–6 of the Global Compact also represent the development and instantiation of second generation corporate responsibility in the global arena. Principle 5, for example, addresses the abolition of child labor, and Principle 6 is concerned with the elimination of discrimination in respect of employment and occupation. The interventionist role of the state in assuring CSR is clearly articulated.

The Global Compact also represents the evolution of the international human rights regime to what is described as the "third generation." The third generation focuses on the rights of "humankind," or our collective humanity. These rights are markedly different from those addressed in the first two generations insofar as they are collective rather than individual rights, and can only be realized through global participation, cooperation, and agreement. Unlike the rights of the first and second generation, third generation rights are positive rather than zero-sum rights. The right to live in peace and the right to share a healthy and balanced environment through responsible management are examples of third generation rights. Sir Geoffrey Chandler, Founder-Chair of Amnesty International UK Business Group 1991–2001 and former senior executive of the Royal Dutch/Shell Group argues:

> At its best, CSR is defined as the responsibility of a company for the totality of its impact, with a need to embed society's values into its core operations as well as into its treatment of its social and physical environment. Responsibility is accepted as encompassing a spectrum – from the running of a profitable business to the health and safety of staff and the impact on the societies in which a company operates.

Third generation CSR represents the dynamics of globalization and a dramatic shift in the expectations for the global corporation (Stohl, Stohl, and Townsley, 2007). It goes beyond Ruggie's principles, which situate corporate responsibility in terms of negative obligations to refrain from behavior that does not respect human rights, while leaving positive and proactive engagement in the promotion of human rights to the nation state. Rather, the third generation of CSR expands responsibilities to a large set of stakeholders within a context of intensifying global connectedness, aspirational discourse, and collaboration among corporate, non-governmental, and governmental organizations (Ihlen and Roper, 2014). In this new conception, CSR is no longer a top-down communication process (Stohl, Etter, Banghart, and Woo, 2015) and communication dynamics have become an essential linking mechanism between human rights and CSR. In third generation rights what it means for a corporation to be socially responsible is derived from mutually defined responsibilities that are negotiated and agreed upon through a process of stakeholder dialogue (Black, 2005). As a consequence, there is no longer separation between activities associated with the political system and activities of the corporate sphere (Harman and Porter, 1997). Thus, in third generation CSR it is no longer acceptable for Google to justify its complicity in internet censorship in China as a socially responsible business as it did in 2006 (Amnesty International Report, 2006). Corporations are no longer depoliticized, private business actors, but entities responsible for setting, implementing, and developing the norms and values of contemporary society (Crane et al., 2008). From a third generation CSR perspective, then, communication is not simply a mechanism through which organizations and their employees are expected to convey objectives, intentions, and avowedly good deeds (that is, including their various CSR activities), nor merely the process by which organizational CSR strategies are enacted. Rather, employee/employer communication is a continuous practice "through which social actors explore, construct, negotiate, and modify what it means to be a socially responsible organization" (Christensen and Cheney, 2011 p.491).

GLOBAL DEVELOPMENTS

As suggested above, social media has the potential to become a powerful communicative mechanism for transparency, stakeholder dialogue, and forging employee and community connections, thus creating new and expanding contexts that link human rights and the third generation of CSR. This connection, however, is not only based on the fact that social media space may be a place where corporate activities and human rights violations and remedies can be identified, discussed, and debated (Whelan, Moon, and Grant, 2013), but also because social media space is a contentious location in which employee/citizen rights are being regulated and sometimes denied. In other words, social media policies, designed to regulate employees' use of social media, are quickly becoming a catalyst for expanding human rights discussions and sensibilities into discussions of CSR. Stohl, Etter, Banghart, and Woo (2015), for example, identify five central communicative tenets embedded in contemporary notions of CSR that instantiate human rights and are enshrined in the Universal Declaration of Human Rights, the Global Compact, and the ILO's Declaration on Fundamental Principles and Rights at Work: (a) freedom of speech; (b) collective information sharing; (c) respecting differences; (d) engagement and stakeholder dialogue; and (e) transparency. Using these foundation principles (Table 7.1) they examined the degree to which the social media policies of 152 major corporations that appear on the Global 500 index embodied communicative human rights principles. Their findings suggest that social media is most often conceived within a business frame, not a human rights frame, and that more than two-thirds of companies' policies violate internationally agreed upon CSR communicative/human rights norms to some degree. One-third of the most recent policies did incorporate human rights concerns in their regulations.

What is most critical for our emerging normative argument, however, is that recent rulings by courts throughout the world are linking social

Table 7.1 Five communicative tenets of second and third generation corporate social responsibility

Communicative tenet	Foundational principle	Sources	Examples from CSR-related documents
Freedom of speech	Businesses should support and respect the protection of internationally proclaimed human rights including freedoms of speech, expression, and association regardless of the region of the world in which they operate and the position of the stakeholder	Article 19 of the Universal Declaration of Human Rights (United Nations, 2015b)	Article 7 of the EU Charter of Fundamental Rights states that "Everyone has the right to respect for his or her private and family life, home and communications" (European Commission, 2010)
Collective information sharing	The responsibility of organizations is to explicitly permit employees to engage in concerted activities (e.g., sharing information about work conditions) for the purpose of mutual aid or protection	Principle 3 of the United Nations, (2015a) Global Compact; European Commission's, (2010) Policies on Worker's Rights; Articles 20 and 23 of the Universal Declaration of Human Rights (United Nations, 2015b)	The U.S. (National Labor Relations Board, 2015) "protects the rights of employees to act together to address conditions at work, with or without a union. This protection extends to certain work-related conversations conducted on social media, such as Facebook and Twitter"
Respecting differences	Respect different values, opinions, beliefs, and attitudes of stakeholders that engage with an organization.	International Convention on the Elimination of All Forms of Racial Discrimination; Convention on	The International Labor Organization's, (2015) Declaration makes it clear that the "elimination of discrimination in respect of employment

Table 7.1 (continued)

Communicative tenet	Foundational principle	Sources	Examples from CSR-related documents
	Discrimination in any form is unwarranted	the Elimination of All Forms of Discrimination Against Women (United Nations, 2015b)	and occupation" is a Universal right and that these rights apply to all people in all States – regardless of the level of economic development
Engaging with stakeholders	Through dialogic engagement, stakeholders' views and perspectives need to be taken into account in the negotiation of the responsibilities and expectations of organizations	The European Business Network for Corporate Social Responsibility; Principle 10 of the Rio Declaration On Environment And Development	"Environmental issues are best handled with the participation of all concerned citizens, at the relevant level" (United Nations, 1992)
Transparency	Transparent communication not only inhibits deception and corruption but enables the fair negotiation of corporations' and employees' responsibilities	Principle 10 of the United Nations, (2015a) Global Compact	"For companies, the benefits of transparency include building trust from stakeholders and creating a positive brand image, which can help to reduce reputational risks in the event of a crisis. Open and honest reporting on policies, procedures and operations also forces companies to take responsibility for the impact of their business" (Woods, 2013)

media policies to CSR and communication human rights. Decisions by the National Labor Relations Board in the USA (Proskauer, 2014) have ruled against many of the corporate restrictions on employee social media use, arguing that they are violating employee's rights including rights of privacy, freedom of thought, freedom of opinion and expression, and the right to engage in "concerted activities" for the "mutual aid and protection" of their co-workers. Rulings in the European Court of Justice, the Australian Works Councils, among many other national and international court systems, are also beginning to address corporate responsibility in regulating employee social media use in terms of human rights and the collapsing contexts between work and non-work communication, public and private communication.

And it is not just the rulings that are expanding human rights into the CSR domain. In a recent survey of US companies, 18 percent report having dismissed employees because of something they posted on social media (CareerBuilder, 2016). The news coverage and public outrage regarding some of these corporate actions – such as when *The Times of India* developed a social media policy which demanded that employees provide the company access to their private social media accounts (Kahn, 2014), and city fire fighters were fired because of comments they made about non-work related civic issues on their personal Facebook pages in Orange County Florida (Herbert, 2013) – have heightened perceptions regarding the link between CSR and human rights. The dismissals have prompted public discussion and a developing consensus that CSR extends beyond an organization's obligations to its stockholders and that corporations are ethically responsible for upholding and protecting communication human rights. In other words, social media has transformed the corporate landscape in which *corporate activities and communicative relationships with their employees have been incorporated into the human rights regime.*

CONCLUSION

In this chapter we have explored the development of new conceptions of CSR as an expansion of the concept of human rights and focused especially on corporate behaviors with respect to social media and communication rights in the new media environment that have emerged in the past two decades. Although there is still tension between those that view CSR as voluntary and private and those who approach the question in terms of business and human rights through compulsory actions, we have argued that conceptions of CSR have evolved over time. While CSR still remains a highly contested concept, there have nonetheless been advances in the development of not only voluntary actions but international regulation and compliance and the space has been opened for greater advances in human rights.

As with the emergence of the global human rights regime, the communicative processes associated with the UN Global Compact have produced much greater attention to, and consideration of, CSR as a norm of global behavior. The interactions of corporations, states, NGOs, and an engaged citizenry are compelling significant changes in the expectations concerning CSR through the development of networks that embrace multiple segments of society. We would argue that CSR is now firmly embedded within evolving patterns of global relations that help communicatively constitute a new global CSR regime that will advance human rights. Evidence for this may be seen in the UN Guiding Principles on Business and Human Rights, endorsed by the Human Rights Council in Resolution 17/4 of 16 June 2011. The Framework rests on three pillars (Ruggie and Nelson, 2015, p. 3):

1. The state duty to protect against human rights abuses by third parties, including business, through appropriate policies, regulation, and adjudication.
2. An independent corporate responsibility to respect human rights, which means that business enterprises should act with due diligence to avoid infringing the rights of others and to address adverse impacts with which they are involved.
3. Greater access by victims to effective remedy, judicial and non-judicial.

What is still uncertain at this point is (1) whether the business risk frame will overpower CSR considerations across the globe; (2) what international regulations and mechanisms will become institutionalized (and when); and (3) who will provide the protections necessary to maintain these rights and the dialogue necessary to promote CSR from within as well as without the corporation. As Baer (this volume) in her discussion of water rights notes, "Human rights have become a modern lingua franca – a frame that provides an 'emancipatory script' that resonates with powerful global actors (Brysk, 2013, p. 32). However, there is also resistance to expanding the human rights repertoire, and particularly strong resistance to empowering and legitimizing ESC [economic, social, and cultural] rights claims in a human rights regime that focuses primarily on civil/political rights." Finally, as with the development of the human rights regime, this growth and development of this emerging regime will be characterized by periods of threats to roll back advances – and these threats will come from both states that have been historical proponents of the expansion of rights as well as states that have been historical opponents.

In the context of CSR, the evolution of the question of business and human rights is still more positive than negative. While Thornthwaite (2013) cautions that in "creating a murky middle ground" between what is public and private expression, personal content and work and employment-related communication "online technologies have also opened new windows through which employers may view and potentially regulate employees' off–duty conduct. This could enable a re–emergence of employer control over employees' lives resembling that associated with the traditional master–servant relationship, but without concomitant reciprocity," the findings of Stohl, Etter, Banghart, and Woo (2015) suggest that almost a third of social media guidelines embrace – at least to some extent – a third generation CSR perspective. In these cases, employees are explicitly encouraged to express their own opinions and to engage and share information with various internal and external stakeholders. Moreover, while social media legislation is in its early stage of development throughout the globe and some legal rulings continue to back (and even expand) the power of employers to constrain speech, some legal rulings have protected the communication rights of workers. Clearly, the CSR regime has not yet been fully developed.

At present, it is still too early to determine if the protect, respect, remedy framework authored by Ruggie will dramatically alter the development of the CSR regime. However, it is clear that it has boosted the standard setting, promotion, and protection mechanisms that foster successful regimes and that another step has been taken on the path to securing the legitimacy and institutionalization of the CSR regime. Further, it has not only served to explicate the connection between the study of CSR and human rights much more clearly but also connected the development of both the CSR and human rights regimes such that the state is no longer the only legitimate locus for human rights within the contemporary global system. In future, it is not too far-fetched to suggest that not only will the corporation have a responsibility to respect human rights, but also a duty to protect human rights. At the same time, it remains the obligation of both states and global society to develop effective access to mediate and provide remedies when corporate actions abuse human rights. All of this affirms the clear advance of both the expansion of human rights and corporate responsibilities for that expansion.

NOTE

1. Affordances are the qualities or properties of an object that define its possible uses or make clear how it can or should be used.

REFERENCES

Alger, C.F. (2002), "Identifying opportunities for coping with 'failed states' in emerging global governance," Paper presented at the Failed States Workshop V, University of California, Santa Barbara, CA, September.

Amnesty International (2006), "China: Amnesty accuses Yahoo!, Microsoft, and Google of hypocrisy in China and urges users to take action against them," Press release. http://www.amnesty.org.uk/press-releases/china-amnesty-accuses-yahoo-microsoft-and-google-hypocrisy-china-and-urges-users-take (accessed 12 October 2016).

Anderson, J. and L. Rainie (2012), "The future of corporate responsibility," Pew Research Center for Internet, Science, Tech, 5 July. http://www.pewinternet.org/2012/07/05/the-future-of-corporate-responsibility/.

Arts, B. (2000), "Regimes, non-state actors, and the state system: a 'structurational' regime model," *European Journal of International Relations*, **6**, 515–44.

Bair, J. (2015). "Corporations at the United Nations: echoes of the New International Economic Order?" *Humanity: An International Journal of Human Rights, Humanitarianism, and Development*, **6**(1), Spring, 159–71.

Baker, Jane Stuart and Lu Tang (2015), "Exploring dialectical tensions for institutional maintenance: a case of Google and its censored Chinese search engine," *International Journal of Communication*, **SI**(9), September, 20. http://ijoc.org/index.php/ijoc/article/view/2955/1466 (accessed 12 October 2016).

Bauer, J. (2011), "Business and human rights: a new approach to advancing environmental justice in the United States," in S. Hertel and K. Libal (eds), *Human Rights in the United States: Beyond Exceptionalism*, Cambridge: Cambridge University Press, pp. 175–96.

Bimber, B., A.J. Flanagin, and C. Stohl (2012), *Collective Action in Organizations: Interaction and Engagement in an Era of Technological Change*, Cambridge: Cambridge University Press.

Black, L. (2005), "Contested meanings of corporate social responsibility: The social responsibility of company directors," Paper presented at the Ministerial Council for Corporations, Melbourne, Australia. http://www.buseco.monash.edu.au/mgt/research/governance/pdf-downloads/hellicar.pdf (accessed 12 October 2016).

Boyd, D. (2010), "Social network sites as networked publics: affordances, dynamics, and implications," in Zizi Papacharissi (ed.), *Networked Self: Identity, Community, and Culture on Social Network Sites*, New York: Routledge, pp. 39–58.

Brown, I. and D. Korff (2012), "Digital freedoms in international law. Practical steps to protect human rights online," 17 May. http://ifap-is-observatory.ittk.hu/taxonomy/term/651/0.

Brysk, A. (2013), *Speaking Rights to Power: Constructing Political Will*, Oxford: Oxford University Press.

CareerBuilder (2016), *Annual CareerBuilder Survey*. http://www.careerbuilder.com/share/aboutus/pressreleasesdetail.aspx?id=pr923&sd=11/24/2015&ed=11/24/2015 (accessed 12 October 2016).

Carroll, A.B. and K.M. Shabana (2010), "The business case for corporate social responsibility: a review of concepts, research and practice," *International Journal of Management Reviews*, **12**(1), 85–105. doi: 10.1111/J.1468-2370.2009.00275.X.

Christensen, L.T. and G. Cheney (2011), "Interrogating the communicative dimensions of corporate social responsibility," in Ø. Ihlen, J. Bartlett, and S. May (eds), *Handbook of Communication and Corporate Social Responsibility*, Malden, MA: Wiley-Blackwell, pp. 491–504.

Crane, A., D. Matten, and J. Moon (2008), "Ecological citizenship and the corporation politicizing the new corporate environmentalism," *Organization & Environment*, **21**(4), 371–89. doi:10.1177/1086026608326075.

Donnelly, J. (1993), *International Human Rights*, Boulder, CO: Westview Press.

European Commission (2010), *Charter of Fundamental Rights of the European Union*. http://eur-lex.europa.eu/LexUriServ/LexUriServ.do?uri=OJ:C:2010:083:0389:0403:en:PDF (accessed 12 October 2016).

Farer, T. (1992), "The United Nations and human rights: more than a whimper, less than a roar," in R. Claude and B. Weston (eds), *Human Rights in the World Community*, Philadelphia, PA: University of Pennsylvania Press, pp. 227–40.

Forsythe, D. (2000), *Human Rights in International Relations*, Cambridge: Cambridge University Press.

Friedman, M. (1970), "The social responsibility of business is to increase its profits," *The New York Times Magazine*, 13 September. http://select.nytimes.com/ gst/abstract.html?res¼F10F11FB3E5810718EDDAA0994D1405B808BF1D3 (accessed 15 October 2006).

Harman, W. and M. Porter (eds) (1997), *The New Business of Business: Sharing Responsibility for a Positive Global Future*, San Francisco, CA: Berrett-Koehler.

Herbert, W.A. (2013), "Can't escape from the memory: social media and public sector labor law," Paper presented at the ABA Technology in the Practice and Workplace Committee National Symposium on Technology in the Practice and Workplace, Berkeley, CA. http://www.americanbar.org/content/dam/aba/events/labor_law/2013/04/aba_national_symposiumontechnologyinlaboremploymentlaw/12_herbertpanel.authcheckdam.pdf (accessed 30 May 2016).

Ihlen, Ø. And J. Roper (2014), "Corporate reports on sustainability and sustainable development: 'We have arrived'," *Sustainable Development*, **22**(1), 42–51. doi:10.1002/Sd.524.

International Labour Organization (2015), "Labour standards." http://ilo.org/global/standards/lang–en/index.htm (accessed 12 October 2016).

Jenkins, J.C. (1983), "Resource mobilization theory and the study of social movements," *Annual Review of Sociology*, **9**, 527–53.

Kahn, A. (2014), "Times of India's bizarre social media policy treats employees as bonded labors!" http://dazeinfo.com/2014/08/27/times-indias-bizzare-social-media-policy-treats-employees-bonded-labors/.

Krasner, S. (ed.) (1983), *International Regimes*, Ithaca, NY: Cornell University Press.

May, S., G. Cheney and J. Roper (eds) (2007), *The Debate Over Corporate Social Responsibility*, New York: Oxford University Press.

Meyer, J. (2007), "US investigating BAE payoff allegations," *Los Angeles Times*, 15 June. http://www.latimes.com/news/nationworld/nation/la-na-bae15jun15,1,318780.story?coll¼la-headlines-nation&ctrack¼1&cset¼true (accessed 12 July 2007).

National Labor Relations Board (2015), "Rights we protect," 1 March. http://www.nlrb.gov/rights-we-protect (accessed 12 October 2016).

Pegg, S. (2003), "An emerging market for the new millennium: transnational

corporations and human rights," in Jedrzej George Frynas and Scott Pegg (eds), *Transnational Corporations and Human Rights*, London: Palgrave Macmillan.
Proskauer (2014), "Social media in the workplace around the world 3.0," Data file. http://www.proskauer.com/files/uploads/social-media-in-the-workplace-2014.pdf (accessed 12 October 2016).
Rittberger, V. (ed.) (1993), *Regime Theory and International Relations*, Oxford: Clarendon Press.
Ruggie, John (2008), *Protect, Respect and Remedy: A Framework for Business and Human Rights: Report of the Special Representative of the Secretary-General on the Issue of Human Rights and Transnational Corporations and Other Business Enterprises*, 7 April 2008, UN Human Rights Council A/HRC/8/5. http://www.refworld.org/docid/484d2d5f2.html (accessed 12 October 2016).
Ruggie, J.G., (2010), "Protect, Respect, and Remedy: the UN Framework for Business and Human Rights," in Mashood A. Baderin and Manisuli Ssenyonjo (eds), *International Human Rights Law: Six Decades after the UDHR and Beyond*, Burlington: Ashgate, pp. 519–38.
Ruggie, J.G. and T. Nelson (2015), "Human rights and the OECD Guidelines for Multinational Enterprises: normative innovations and implementation challenges" Corporate Social Responsibility Initiative Working Paper No. 66. John F. Kennedy School of Government, Harvard University, Cambridge, MA.
Schwartz, M.S. (2002), "A code of ethics for corporate code of ethics," *Journal of Business Ethics*, **41**, 27–43.
Stohl, C., M. Stohl, and N. Townsley (2007), "A new generation of global corporate social responsibility," in S. May, G. Cheney, and J. Roper (eds), *The Debate Over Corporate Social Responsibility*, Oxford: Oxford University Press, pp. 30–44.
Stohl, C., M. Etter, S. Banghart, and D.J. Woo (2015), "Social media policies: implications for contemporary notions of corporate social responsibility," *Journal of Business Ethics Online First*, 1–24 July.
Thornthwaite, L. (2013), "Social media, unfair dismissal and the regulation of employees' conduct outside . . . conduct outside work," *Australian Journal of Labour Law*, **26**(2), 164–84.
Treem, J.W and P.M. Leonardi (2012), "Social media use in organizations: exploring the affordances of visibility, editability, persistence, and association," *Communication Yearbook*, **36**, 143–89.
United Nations (1992), *Report of the United Nations Conference on Environment and Development*. http://www.un.org.proxy.library.ucsb.edu:2048/documents/ga/conf151/aconf15126-1annex1.htm (accessed 12 October 2016).
United Nations (2015a), *The Ten Principles*. https://www.unglobalcompact.org/AbouttheGC/TheTENPrinciples/ (accessed 12 October 2016).
United Nations (2015b), *The Universal Declaration of Human Rights*. http://www.un.org.proxy.library.ucsb.edu:2048/en/documents/udhr/ (accessed 12 October 2016).
Wettstein, F. (2012), "CSR and the debate on business and human rights: bridging the great divide," *Business Ethics Quarterly*, **22**(4), 739–70. doi: 10.5840/beq201222446.
Whelan, G., J. Moon, and B. Grant (2013), "Corporations and citizenship arenas in the age of social media," *Journal of Business Ethics*, **118**(4). 777?790. doi: 10.1007/S10551-013-1960-3.

Wood, D.J. (2000), "Theory and integrity in business and society," *Business & Society*, **39**(4), 359–78. http://www.ethicaltrade.org/blog/protect-respect-and-remedy-what-does-ruggies-framework-mean-ethical-trade.

Woods, S. (2013), "The importance of transparency," *CSR Asia*, **9**(25). http://www.csr-asia.com/weekly_news_detail.php?id=12273 (accessed 12 October 2016).

PART IV

Expanding mechanisms

8. Forging alternative routes to norms change: economic rights protagonists

Shareen Hertel

Civil and political rights have dominated the formal human rights system for much of the past half-century, shaping not only the politics between states but often within them. They have cast a long shadow over the emergence of the modern human rights movement (Moyn, 2010; Neier, 2013) and the development of corresponding theories of norms evolution. But economic rights – defined as the rights to subsistence, to work, and to income guarantees for those who cannot provide for themselves – are newly resurgent, in part because of the efforts of actors on the margins of the mainstream human rights movement. The chapter explores alternative routes to norms evolution from the bottom up, drawing insights from contemporary right to food rights advocacy in India. It aims at deepening the current within the international relations (IR) literature that recognizes the neglected Southern roots of norms change and institutional creation (see 2014 special issue of *Global Governance*; Nelson and Dorsey (2008) and Chong (2010).

It complicates an emerging literature on the politics of "backlash" (Hopgood, Snyder, and Vinjamuri, 2017) that has tended to focus on the negative impact of outsiders' responses to the promotion of human rights, by instead analysing conditions under which action on the margins deepens and enhances the promotion of human rights. Empirically, this chapter demonstrates that some of the most creative advocacy on economic rights has emerged through advocacy campaigns that dismiss, ignore, or supersede (in the Indian case) the prevailing international interpretation of human rights norms.

Economic rights protagonists like those discussed in this chapter often operate outside the well-trod pathway of transnational advocacy networks (which often privilege civil and political rights). Yet their actions yield sharpened accountability, claim-making and more robust legal protections that stand to enrich the human rights canon and expand protections for structurally marginalized people more generally. The nuanced interpretation of the right to food that simultaneously seeks to prevent hunger deaths while also enforcing bureaucratic responsibility for improved access to food over time is but one example of expanding rights emerging from beyond the mainstream human rights movement (Hertel, 2017).

A VIEW FROM THE TRENCHES

Since the 1980s, Indian activists have fought to transform hunger from an everyday occurrence to a source of national shame. Despite its status as the world's largest democracy and a rising regional power in both economic and geopolitical terms, India has a seemingly intractable hunger problem. One-third of all malnourished children worldwide are Indian and upwards of half the country's population is undernourished despite strong legal entitlements for the right to food, a steadily growing economy, and a relatively high level of government spending on subsidized food for the poor. The federal government of India spends upwards of 2 percent of gross domestic product (GDP) on social programs including subsidized feeding programs administered at the state level nationwide, but people (especially children) remain hungry (Hertel, 2015).

Playing the classic human rights "shame-and-blame" game on a largely domestic level, activists involved in what has become known as the Right to Food (RTF) campaign have pointed to the paradox of state-subsidized food rotting in public warehouses just kilometers from where people have died for want of distribution. They have charged the Indian government with failing in its duty to enforce the country's constitutional protection of the right to life by linking lack of access to grain (especially in drought-prone areas) to "hunger deaths."[1] And they have shamed individual bureaucrats for their lack of willingness or ability to staunch inefficiency and corruption in public feeding programs at the state and local levels, nationwide (Srinivasan and Narayanan, 2007).

In the process, the RTF campaign has marshaled the largest case of public interest litigation (PIL) in Indian history in defense of the right to food. Filed in 2001 by one of India's foremost human rights organizations (the People's Union for Civil Liberties), this landmark "PUCL case" is ongoing (Birchfield and Corsi, 2010; Hertel, 2015). The RTF campaign has also pushed for legislative action on hunger since 2011, lobbying during the drafting of a National Food Security Act that eventually passed in 2013 but has yet to be fully implemented across India.

All of these efforts have taken place without the impetus of outside actors. Indian activists have driven the process of social mobilization, legal advocacy, lobbying, and policy reform – without seeking the support, consent, or insights of groups in the broader human rights movement beyond India. Individual activists may be (and often are) members of transnational epistemic communities (professors, public interest lawyers, non-governmental organization (NGO) leaders and so on) but the Right to Food Campaign is not animated from outside. It is not translating international human rights norms on the right to food into Indian parlance. Nor is it seeking to pressure the Indian state with incentives or sanctions wielded through transnational coalitions.

Rather, contemporary human rights advocacy on the right to food in India is largely a home-grown phenomenon, with the Indian Constitution (not international treaty law) serving as the normative anchor and the network of groups involved in pressing for reform largely based within the country itself. The domestic arena has remained the arena of choice for the RTF campaign in part because the benefits of doing so (and the constraints internal to the campaign) have made this a pragmatic choice. But the mode of advocacy and the substance of the claim-making in this campaign have implications far beyond India. As I argue in this chapter, the case of the RTF campaign serves as a focal point for theorizing both new routes to norms evolution and expanded interpretations of the content of rights.

SIGNPOSTS IN THE LITERATURE

The interpretation of norms evolution developed in this chapter builds upon anthropologist Sally Engle Merry's concept of vernacularization (1997, 2006), a process through which non-dominant actors translate and adapt outside human rights norms in order to render them acceptable and effective at the local level. Koen De Feyter and other legal scholars have similarly explored the localization of human rights norms (De Feyter, Parmentier, Timmerman, and Ulrich, 2011) aimed at enhancing both the practicability and impact of such norms. I also draw on IR theory by Amitav Acharya, who highlights the role that non-dominant actors have played in transforming contemporary norms of state sovereignty through processes of localization (2004) and subsidiarity (2011). Risse, Ropp, and Sikkink (1999, 2013), Keck and Sikkink (1998), Finnemore and Sikkink (1998), Bob (2005), and others within IR theory have offered nuanced accounts that explicitly involve non-state actors (often from within non-dominant states or on the margins of wealthy societies) in the process of human rights norms evolution. But the bulk of this work has focused on civil and political rights advocacy rather than economic and social rights advocacy, with the exception of Brysk (2002, 2013).[2]

Social movement scholars, by contrast, have long been preoccupied with popular responses to class-based, racial, gendered, and other forms of inequality. A strong strain of social movement theory focuses explicitly on the forces driving the internationalization of social movement protest (Chabot, 2010; Tarrow, 2001, 2005a [2011], 2005b). Major journals such as *Social Movement Studies*, or *Mobilization*, have featured articles that explain the conditions under which particular movements employ human rights frames domestically and/or internationally in defense of human rights (for example, Tazreiter, 2011), while other scholarship in the social movement tradition has focused on the transnationalization of economic justice protests, in particular (Bandy and Smith, 2005; Smith, 2007).

But social movement theory has tended not to intersect with the broader literature on human rights norms evolution – with important exceptions such as Keck and Sikkink (1998) or Compa (2010). And when such intersection has taken place, the resulting scholarship has tended to focus less on the emergence of alternative norms from below than on explaining the conditions under which protest transnationalizes and dominant norms spread across borders. Social movement theory's touchstones such as van Stekelenburg, Roggeband, and Klandermans's landmark volume *The Future of Social Movement Research* (2013) include only a few passing references to human rights, while the editors of the major reference work in the field, the *Blackwell Companion to Social Movements*, pointedly note the absence of a chapter on the human rights movement in their own anthology (Snow, Soule, and Kriesi, 2004).

This chapter bridges the gaps between key literatures in anthropology, IR, and social movement theory in an effort to explain why and how economic rights advocacy functions as a vehicle for contemporary human rights norms change. As the case of the RTF campaign reveals and my earlier work on norms change in Mexico and Bangladesh has demonstrated (Hertel, 2006), activists based in the "Global South" have tended not to look to their counterparts in the "North" (or to the governments of Northern states) for advice or support on economic rights protection and promotion. Critical historians of human rights would agree that when the mainstream movement has taken up economic rights at all, it has tended to do so in extremely constrained ways (Marks, 2014; Moyn, forthcoming).

Conversely, some of the most creative approaches to promoting economic rights come from activists and scholars in the Global South and are circulating through South/South exchanges and reverberating from South to North. The constitutions of states such as India, Mexico, Brazil, or South Africa include stronger provisions for economic rights than do those of many industrialized states (Law and Versteeg, 2010). A vibrant current of legal and social science scholarship explores the contours of evolving jurisprudence and related institutional reforms and corresponding social struggles in defense of constitutionally guaranteed and/or internationally guaranteed economic rights (Albisa, Scott, and Tissington, 2013; Biehl and Petryna, 2013; Gauri and Brinks, 2008, 2014; Yamin and Gloppen, 2011).[3] Newer scholarly work on human rights advocacy in the United States such as that included in volumes edited by Armaline, Glasberg, and Purkayastha (2011), Hertel and Libal (2011), and Blau, Brunsma, Moncada, and Zimmer (2009) explores why and how a hegemonic state has projected civil and political human rights enforcement internationally, yet has resisted it at home while also refusing to accept economic rights as rights. Grassroots activists within the United States have responded to this state of affairs by challenging American hegemony from within, occasionally through transnationalized protests (see Bauer, 2011) that build upon advocacy efforts outside the United States to delineate the normative and practical frontiers of economic rights and their limits.

A THEORETICAL ROADMAP

Myriad forms of protest occur in defense of economic rights – from bread riots in the context of structural adjustment, to demonstrations by members of communities demanding respect for their right to free, prior, and informed consent before large dam projects are sited on their land or minerals are extracted from it. In some cases, protesters may invoke international law in defense of their rights to land, employment, education, or livelihood. In others, activists concentrate their efforts instead on implementation of constitutional guarantees or other domestic legal remedies, as in the RTF campaign. This chapter develops a framework for understanding why actors opt to operate at differing levels of action and with reference to differing normative frameworks, using the case of the RTF as a plausibility probe to explore the framework's implications in practice.

Social movement theorists (particularly scholars working within the framework of the political process model)[4] explain social mobilization as a function of material, ideational, and institutional conditions. Such constraints and opportunities affect the choice of whether or not to act domestically or internationally – including the extent to which activists accept, dismiss, ignore, or supersede outside norms. Human rights activists, like all social actors, are opportunists to some extent. Even normatively motivated actors are also compelled by material interests and take action mindful of achieving maximal gains in both the normative and material domains (Bob, 2005; Hertel, 2006).

This chapter employs a political process model to explain the evolution of three alternative routes to human rights norms evolution: the first, in which activists dismiss outside norms; the second, in which they ignore them; and the third, in which they supersede outside norms. These forms are not hierarchical or sequential. Rather, each is triggered by a differing combination of normative and material factors explained below.

Activists can dismiss outside norms in a number of ways and under differing conditions. In other work (Hertel, 2006), I have referred to outright dismissal of a norm in the context of human rights advocacy as "blocking." Blocking entails action by people on the receiving end of advocacy efforts who seek to halt or at least significantly stall a campaign's progress "in order to pressure senders to change their frame" (Hertel, 2006, pp. 6, 15, 24–9). Dismissing norms this way is inherently conflictual. In contrast to Merry's notion of vernacularization as well as Acharya's of localization, blocking does not center on a process of normative translation. It is more akin to Acharya's concept of subsidiarization, which he describes as an explicit rejection of certain outside norms and the substitution of alternative ones in order to justify the creation of new international institutions.

The second alternative route to norms evolution involves ignoring norms and can occur in several ways. In some instances, as illustrated in my previous work on the emergence of norms around women's labor rights in Mexico (Hertel, 2006), activists can employ the subtle mechanism of "backdoor moves" in an effort to augment a campaign's normative frame by stealth. They may appear to accept the dominant frame but instead insert alternative normative understandings covertly. By contrast, activists may entirely ignore outside efforts at norms promotion. Activists who simply ignore outside norms opt not to register them intellectually or in practice. There is no attempt at translation. There is no direct conflict. For an outside observer, this route to norms evolution presents the hermeneutical challenge of distinguishing between an actor who is aware but ignores a norm, and one who is simply ignorant of it entirely.

The decision about whether to "dismiss" or "ignore" outside norms depends upon a range of material and ideational factors including: the level of conflict that actors are willing to take on in defense of norms, and whether local activists launch the campaign themselves, or perceive it as being thrust upon them from outside the local context. If outside advocacy efforts involve minimal to no local consultation, they can be blocked or dismissed entirely by the people such campaigns ostensibly aim to help. Cultural clashes, not surprisingly, provoke dismissal of outside norms in a manner that Merry has richly illustrated. But her theory does not create a framework for determining the tipping point at which actors opt to adopt or vernacularize rather than block or ignore outside norms.

Another factor that influences whether actors dismiss or ignore international norms and/or advocacy linkages is the level of potential funding available to participants in any given human rights campaign. If there is the potential for shared resources (from foundations, individual donors, or other sources) then activists outside the mainstream human rights movement are less likely to overtly dismiss outside advocacy efforts because doing so could compromise their access to such resources. Similarly, weighing the potential for increased media attention can tip the balance toward accepting outside normative frames and networks. Like financial resources, media attention is a resource that activists can employ to increase their leverage over targets through classic shame-and-blame techniques, or to increase membership in social movement organizations.

A relational factor that can affect the degree to which outside norms and related advocacy efforts are dismissed or not is the degree of potential audience receptivity to a campaign's claims. Like financial and media resources, audience receptivity has material roots. A receptive audience can channel resources – including new participants – into a movement, so dismissal of an outside norm or the campaign it animates is less likely if audience receptivity to the claim (or central frame) is high. By contrast, an oppositional audience can create negative incentives. Rather than dismiss outside norms, activists can play a key role in shaping the frame and/or repertoire of organizing tactics in order to render them compatible with a given audience they seek to influence.[5] Similarly, the level of inter- and intra-group rivalry within campaigns can influence norm change and coalition-building. If individual activists are personal rivals or if the campaign evolves in a manner that reinscribes broader social divides (such as class or ethnic or postcolonial divisions) then local activists may be more inclined to dismiss outside advocacy efforts and the normative frames that animate them.

A final factor to consider is the nature of domestic, regional, and international institutions as potential channels for protest. Certain institutions have public review mechanisms and are more open to public requests for information than others. Campaigns that aim to influence receptive institutions are less likely to dismiss outside norms compatible with those institutions than the norms central to less penetrable institutions.

Beyond dismissing or ignoring outside norms, there is a third alternative route to norms evolution that involves superseding the dominant interpretation of human rights both in theory and in practice, emphasizing local normative frameworks that are more expansive or complex than global ones and centering mobilization at the national or local level. Risse, Ropp, and Sikkink warn in their recent collective project, *The Persistent Power of Human Rights* (2013), the transnationalized power of international human rights advocacy around Western/Northern norms is generating a backlash that stands to undercut the protection of international human rights norms. This chapter offers an alternative perspective, in which actors on the margins of the mainstream human rights movement ultimately enhance the scope of human rights protection around economic rights by animating their campaigns in spaces outside it and with reference to alternative normative understandings. When local institutions trump the capacity of international ones in protecting particular types of rights – for example, when local institutions are better equipped to benchmark progressive implementation of economic rights or when local norms are strong and complementary – actors may deem it better to "opt out of" internationalized contention on human rights until international actors catch up to them.

Campaigns that supersede outside norms and advocacy networks do not operate from a position of weakness. Relative weakness predisposes actors either to dismiss or ignore outside norms and advocacy efforts if they are engaging in negative forms of backlash. Actors who are in a position of relative weakness, for example, may have domestic institutional frameworks that are too debilitated or resource constraints that are so pronounced that they cannot enforce even their own local norms – let alone outside ones. So they opt to dismiss or ignore the outsiders. When the localized risk of making international connections is too steep (that is, when it could provoke internal reprisals), actors are even more likely to dismiss or ignore outside norms than to rise above them. By contrast, the choice to organize a campaign in a manner that supersedes outside norms leaves more options on the table than dismissing or ignoring them does.

This third route to norms evolution leaves activists open to circling back (at some point) to consider building international connections, both functionally and normatively. Many of the activists involved in India's RTF campaign, for example, have focused their efforts on reforming the implementation of national law and shoring up domestic institutions rather than international ones.[6] Participants in the RTF campaign have found it preferable to bind the hands of Indian politicians and to make appeals for more effective food distribution in the name of citizenship rights rather than seeking to influence international policymakers or making claims on economic resources at the international level. In the process, their domestically driven advocacy has caught the attention of outsiders such as the former United Nations (UN) Special Rapporteur on Food, Olivier DeSchutter, who has highlighted the creative interpretation of economic rights and the multifaceted strategy for implementation central to the RTF campaign (DeSchutter, 2013). The RTF campaign thus offers a useful vehicle for studying creative new routes to the evolution of human rights norms – specifically, the mechanism of superseding the dominant normative fray in the promotion of economic rights.

PROBING THE CASE

Given the theoretical framework for alternative routes to human rights norms evolution developed in this chapter, we can now explore the "fit" between the RTF campaign case and the framework itself. This should be viewed as a plausibility probe – not as definitive "proof" of the validity of the framework – and an invitation to other scholars to explore advocacy at the margins of the human rights movement using this framework as a starting point. In the case of the RTF campaign:

1. *No international advocacy campaign was "launched"* to remedy hunger in India; this is a home-grown effort. Hence, the RTF campaign has not opted either to dismiss or ignore outside efforts – because there haven't been any.
2. *Funding for the campaign has been entirely local*; the campaign's own website and those of key NGOs involved have pointedly noted that they do not accept "outside" funding for right to food advocacy. Hence, there was no purchase in internationalizing contention in order to tap outside resources.[7]
3. *Indian media attention to the campaign, when it has arisen at all, has tended to focus on the campaign in relation to domestic law and policy reform debates.* Many of the Indian activists and observers of the RTF campaign who I interviewed commented on the middle-class bias of the Indian press and characterized the coverage of hunger-related issues as episodic (at best) and sensationalized or one-dimensional (at worst).[8] Based on analysis of my original dataset of 2100 news articles published in four major Indian daily newspapers from 1990 to 2015, I find that when the Indian print media covers food, it does so disproportionately by framing related issues in terms of national obligations under constitutional law and national implementation strategies (Hertel, 2015; Hertel, Tagliarina, and Buerger, forthcoming).[9]
4. *Audience receptivity to hunger issues in general in India is low* (see Dreze, 2002) *but when discussed at all, they are framed in national terms as an Indian problem with Indian solutions.* This, in turn, is linked to a

postcolonial cultural orientation that renders India a norms-maker, not a norms-maker, on economic rights (that is, a country that creates new interpretations of rights from within rather than adapting norms from outside). India has a human rights-based constitution. The constitutional drafting process in India took place simultaneously with the drafting in New York of the Universal Declaration of Human Rights by the-then fledgling UN (1948) and involved some of the same intellectual architects (Waltz, 2001). And fealty to the Indian Constitution as the principal source of norms persists, even among activists who are aware of international normative frameworks. As one Bangalore-based grassroots activist explained: "I think for most of us, even when we are students or we are just beginning our work as activists, the UN Declaration of Human Rights, or the UN [Charter], or the Beijing Declaration – all those things are reference points for us . . . But when it comes to saying that this is my right, then I'll say that this is in my constitution."[10]

Public protest is part of daily life; the scope and frequency of public street protests and the variety of tactics is a hallmark of India's noisy democracy (Guha, 2008), creating a strong base from which Indian activists can mobilize and a social expectation of protest as part of public life. As the world's largest democracy, India is also the progenitor of the Gandhian norm of non-violent social protest, which as Chabot (2010) argues, has influenced significantly the evolution of other social movements outside India (including the US Civil Rights movement). Taken together, all of these factors contribute to the role of Indian actors as protagonists in developing new interpretations of the right to food and corresponding strategies for enforcement through the courts and popular protest.

5. *Inter-group rivalries in the RTF campaign are complex, rooted in differences over the purpose and process of advocacy.* As a staffer of the Supreme Court-appointed Commissioner on the Right to Food noted to me, "there are many people in the campaign who will say, 'Look, we're very happy that this is happening and that [people in] one of the most vulnerable sections of India . . . are getting justice. But we're wondering if it's at the cost of other issues?'"[11] The campaign's decision to seize political opportunities in the domestic policy sphere was a pragmatic choice. The right-leaning coalition that had governed India in the 1990s on the crest of rising prosperity was ousted in 2004, in part, as a result of its inability to curb rising inequality. The coalition government that assumed office in 2004 – namely, the United Progressive Alliance (UPA), dominated by the Congress Party – rhetorically championed a politics of "everyman," in which food

policy reform became a pet program of then Congress Party leader, Sonia Gandhi (Hertel, Tagliarina, and Buerger, forthcoming).

The UPA, in turn, invited several of the left-leaning intellectuals who had been active in promoting social mobilization on economic rights to take part in its internal deliberations on public policy reform as members of the National Advisory Council to the UPA. Thus, the RTF campaign's own evolution became intertwined with that of the evolving national food policy reform effort under Gandhi's coalition. But as it became clear that the scope of national food policy reform driven by the UPA would fall far short of the campaign's goals, these proponents resigned from the Council. The campaign subsequently issued pointed critiques of the National Food Security Act (FNSA) that passed in 2013. In the years since the election of right-leaning Prime Minister Narendra Modi, the RTF campaign has criticized the halting implementation of NFSA as emblematic of failed food policy reform writ large and has continued to advocate for broader and deeper policy reforms.

6. *Institutional channels for protest are strongest domestically.* At the outset of the campaign with the Indian government already directing major resources toward public feeding programs, members of the RTF campaign reasoned they had greater likelihood of affecting reform of these programs than pushing for change in international food policy (Hertel and Randolph, 2013). But focusing on the National Food Security Act came at a high cost to the campaign: the bill that ultimately became law in September 2013 laid out minimum criteria for subsidized food policies less robust that those already in existence at the state level in multiple states across India. A campaign that opened with radical claim-making on the right to food in 2001 eventually found itself just over a decade later confronted by the limits of realizing those claims in practice at the national level – structural limits on economic rights fulfillment echoed in other postcolonial struggles, but not even acknowledged by most mainstream human rights advocates in the West (Moyn, forthcoming).

IMPLICATIONS OF NEW FORMS OF NORMS EVOLUTION

Activists central to the RTF campaign moved beyond the "violations approach" to monitoring economic shortfalls dominant in the mainstream human rights movement outside India by developing a hybrid approach that simultaneously demanded prevention of hunger deaths (that is, guarantee of the right to life) and progressive implementation of economic rights (that is, improved food distribution through ongoing reform of public feeding programs). The RTF campaign's main contribution to broader economic rights discourse has been this creative melding of non-derogable and progressively realized rights demands (Hertel, 2015, p.76).

Stepping back to consider how this campaign's experience may contribute to a broader rethinking of norms evolution and advocacy strategies, we see that national institutions in countries outside the West in some instances have stronger track records on economic rights interpretation and implementation than do governments or institutions in industrialized countries (including the United States). India's Supreme Court and National Human Rights Commission created an enabling context in which the RTF campaign could play the role of norms protagonist on the right to food. Activists involved in the campaign deftly used Indian law and the robust and expanding interpretation of the right to food in the ongoing PUCL case to push the boundaries on interpreting and implementing economic rights. The legacy of Gandhian social protest and the deep mobilization networks on economic rights issues already present in India meant that activists in this case certainly didn't need to look "outside" for inspiration, tools, or strategies for promoting economic rights. And their struggles continue to inform broader discussion of economic rights – well beyond India – as evidenced by DeSchutter's invocation of the campaign as an example of cutting-edge advocacy.

The case of the RTF campaign should thus lead to a rethinking of the dominant routes to norms evolution. Economic rights protagonists in this case have been much more than translators. They are not solely reactive to outside forces. They are often highly proactive proponents of new normative frameworks that supersede the limits of outside discourses and chart a new course for evolving struggles to expand the interpretation and enjoyment of human rights.

NOTES

1. Interview by the author with the former Special Rapporteur for the Indian Human Rights Commission responsible for inquiry into hunger deaths in the state of Orissa, 11 January 2012, New Delhi. (This and other interview data were collected in conformance with University of Connecticut Institutional Review Board (IRB) Protocol No. H11-116.) For a report on related activity of the National HR Commission, see the NHRC/Civil Society newsletter, 17 August 2002, available at http://www.isidelhi.org.in/hrnews/isidownload/Nhrc/NHRC-2002.pdf. For full reports from the National HR Commission on right to food-related issues, see http://nhrc.nic.in/library/rightofood/mainfood.htm.

2. Stachursky (2013, p. 5) refers to this as an "analytical bias" in the IR literature on human rights, toward physical integrity rights (for example, freedom from torture, disappearance, extrajudicial killing, arbitrary arrest, detention).
3. Osiatynski (2009) sounds a cautionary note on the promise of economic rights constitutionalism in *Human Rights and Their Limits.*
4. See Zirakzadeh (2011) for a comprehensive discussion.
5. Audiences' receptivity can serve as both a positive and negative incentive: McAdam (1999) explains why key actors in the US-based civil rights movement chose to make African-American churches central to the movement's mobilization structure, while Anderson (2003) and Goluboff (2010) explain the same movement's decision to frame claims around civil rights rather than economic rights in the wake of anti-communist threats throughout the 1960s.
6. The author has conducted interviews with activists, policymakers, government actors, and academics in Bangalore and New Delhi, India (from December 2011 through January 2012) and via Skype from June 2012 to the present, in conformance with IRB Protocol H11-116 (see endnote 1).
7. Interview with a staff member of the Office of the Supreme Court Commissioner on the Right to Food, 9 April 2013, via Skype. This interviewee noted that at least one NGO involved in the campaign – the Human Rights Law Network – did accept foreign funding for its more general work. But other interview data points to the relative independence of the RTF campaign from foreign funding – including interviews with several academics involved in the campaign (that is, one on 10 June 2012, via Skype; another on 12 January 2012, in New Delhi). See also Hertel (2016, fn.18 and fn.19) for RTF campaign budget analysis.
8. Examples include an interview by the author with a scholar-activist based in rural Karnataka, 7 January 2012; with a human rights lawyer based in Bangalore, 3 January 2012; with a Bangalore-based academic, 3 January 2012; and with a staff member at a Delhi-based development NGO, 11 January 2012.
9. Newspapers coded include: *The Times of India*, *Press Trust of India*, *Hindustan Times*, and *The Deccan Herald*. Coding terms for both datasets are available upon request from the author.
10. Interview by the author with Bangalore-based human rights activist, 2 January 2012. For discussion of the normative foundations of the Indian Constitution, see Jain (2000).
11. Interview by the author with Delhi-based staff member of the Supreme Court-appointed Commissioner on the Right to Food (via Skype), 20 July 2012.

REFERENCES

Acharya, Amitav (2004), "How Ideas Spread: Whose Norms Matter? Norm Localization and Institutional Change in Asian Regionalization," *International Organization* **58** (2), 239–75.

Acharya, Amitav (2011), "Norm Subsidiarity and Regional Orders: Sovereignty, Regionalism, and Rule-making in the Third World," *International Studies Quarterly* **55** (1), 95–123.

Albisa, Cathy, Brittany Scott, and Kate Tissington (2013), "Demolishing Housing Rights in the Name of Market Fundamentalism: The Dynamics of Displacement in the United States, South Africa, and India," in Lanse Minkler (ed.), *The State of Economic and Social Human Rights: A Global Overview*, Cambridge and New York: Cambridge University Press, pp. 86–116.

Anderson, Carol (2003), *Eyes Off the Prize: The United Nations and the African*

American Struggle for Human Rights, 1944–1955, Cambridge and New York: Cambridge University Press.

Armaline, William T., Davita Silfen Glasberg, and Bandana Purkayastha (eds) (2011), *Human Rights in Our Own Backyard: Injustice and Resistance in the United States*, Philadelphia, PA: University of Pennsylvania Press.

Bandy, Joe and Jackie Smith (eds) (2005), *Coalitions Across Borders: Transnational Protest and the Neoliberal Order*, Lanham, MD: Rowman and Littlefield.

Bauer, Joanne (2011), "Business and Human Rights: A New Approach to Advancing Environmental Justice in the United States," in Shareen Hertel and Kathryn Libal (eds), *Human Rights in the United States: Beyond Exceptionalism*, Cambridge and New York: Cambridge University Press, pp. 175–98.

Biehl, João and Adriana Petryna (eds) (2013), *When People Come First: Critical Studies in Global Health*, Princeton, NJ: Princeton University Press.

Birchfield, Lauren and Jessica Corsi (2010), 'Between Starvation and Globalization: Realizing the Right to Food in India," *Michigan Journal of International Law* **31** (4), 691–764.

Blau, Judith, David L. Brunsma, Alberto Moncada, and Katherine Zimmer (eds) (2009), *The Leading Rogue State: The US and Human Rights*, Boulder, CO: Paradigm Publishers.

Bob, Clifford (2005), *The Marketing of Rebellion: Insurgents, Media, and International Activism*, Cambridge and New York: Cambridge University Press.

Brysk, Alison (ed.) (2002), *The Globalization of Human Rights*, Berkeley, CA: University of California Press.

Brysk, Alison (2013), *Speaking Rights to Power: Constructing Political Will*, Oxford and New York: Oxford University Press.

Chabot, Sean (2010), "Dialogue Matters: Beyond the Transmission Model of Transnational Diffusion Between Social Movements," in Rebecca Kolins Givan, Kenneth M. Roberts, and Sarah A. Soule (eds), *The Diffusion of Social Movements: Actors, Mechanisms, and Political Effects*, Cambridge and New York: Cambridge University Press, pp. 99–124.

Chong, Daniel (2010), *Freedom from Poverty: NGOs and Human Rights Praxis*, Philadelphia, PA: University of Pennsylvania Press.

Compa, Lance (2010), "Framing Labor's New Human Rights Movement," in Rebecca Kolins Givan, Kenneth M. Roberts, and Sarah A. Soule (eds), *The Diffusion of Social Movements: Actors, Mechanisms, and Political Effects*, Cambridge and New York: Cambridge University Press, pp. 56–77.

De Feyter, Koen, Stephan Parmentier, Christiane Timmerman, and George Ulrich (eds) (2011), *The Local Relevance of Human Rights*, Cambridge and New York: Cambridge University Press.

DeSchutter, Olivier (2013), "Empowering Women to Improve Food Security: What Works and Why," *The Guardian Professional*, 13 March, accessed 6 January 2016 at http://www.theguardian.com/global-development-professionals-network/2013/mar/12/empowering-women-food-security.

Dreze, Jean (2002), "On Research and Action," *Economic and Political Weekly* **37** (9), 817–19.

Finnemore, Martha and Kathryn Sikkink (1998), "International Norm Dynamics and Political Change," *International Organization* **52** (4), 887–917.

Gauri, Varun and Daniel M. Brinks (eds) (2008). *Courting Social Justice: Judicial Enforcement of Social and Economic Rights in the Developing World*, Cambridge and New York: Cambridge University Press.

Gauri, Varun and Daniel M. Brinks (2014), "The Law's Majestic Equality? The Distributive Model and the Postcolonial State," *Perspectives on Politics* **12** (2), 375–93.

Goluboff, Risa L. (2010), *The Lost Promise of Civil Rights*, Cambridge, MA: Harvard University Press.

Guha, Ramachandra (2008), *India After Gandhi: The History of the World's Largest Democracy*, New York: Harper Perennial.

Hertel, Shareen (2006), *Unexpected Power: Conflict and Change Among Transnational Activists*, Ithaca, NY: Cornell University Press.

Hertel, Shareen (2015), "Hungry for Justice: Social Mobilization on the Right to Food in India," *Development and Change* **46** (1), 72–94.

Hertel, Shareen (2016), "A New Route to Norms Evolution: Insights from India," *Social Movement Studies* **15** (6), 610–21.

Hertel, Shareen (2017), "Re-framing Human Rights Advocacy: The Rise of Economic Rights," in Stephen Hopgood, Jack Snyder, and Leslie Vinjamuri (eds), *Human Rights Futures*, Cambridge and New York: Cambridge University Press.

Hertel, Shareen and Kathyrn Libal (eds) (2011), *Human Rights in the United States: Beyond Exceptionalism*, Cambridge and New York: Cambridge University Press.

Hertel, Shareen and Susan Randolph (2013), "The Right to Food: A Global Overview," in Lanse Minkler (ed.), *The State of Economic and Social Rights*, Cambridge and New York: Cambridge University Press, pp. 21–60.

Hertel, Shareen, Corinne Tagliarina, and Catherine Buerger (forthcoming), "Cheap Talk on Food: Party Politics in India and the Challenge of Implementing the Right to Food," *Human Rights Quarterly*.

Hopgood, Stephen, Jack Snyder, and Leslie Vinjamuri (eds) (2017), *Human Rights Futures*, Cambridge and New York: Cambridge University Press.

Human Rights Law Network (n.d.), "Analysis of the Application of the International Human Rights Standards from the Perspective of Human Rights Practitioners: The Right to Food in India," accessed 6 January 2016 at http://www.hrln.org/hrln/right-to-food/reports/296-analysis-of-the-application-of-the-international-human-rights-standards-from-the-perspective-of-human-rights-practitioners-the-right-to-food-in-india.html.

Jain, M.P. (2000), "The Supreme Court and Fundamental Rights," in S.K. Verma and Kusum Kumar (eds), *Fifty Years of the Supreme Court of India: Its Grasp and Reach*, Oxford and New Dehli: Oxford University Press, pp. 1–100.

Keck, Margaret and Kathryn Sikkinnk (1998), *Activists Beyond Borders: Advocacy Networks in International Politics*, Ithaca, NY: Cornell University Press.

Law, David and Mila Versteeg (2010), "The Evolution of Global Constitutionalism," Washington University in St. Louis School of Law – Legal Studies Research Paper Series No. 10-10-01, accessed 6 January 2016 at http://papers.ssrn.com/sol3/JELJOUR_Results.cfm?form_name=Pip_jrl&journal_id=382963&Network=no&SortOrder=numHits&stype=desc.

Marks, Susan (2014), "Four Human Rights Myths," in David Kinley, Wojciech Sadurski, and Kevin Walton (eds), *Human Rights: Old Problems, New Possibilities*, Cheltenham, UK and Northampton, MA, USA: Edward Elgar, pp. 217–35.

McAdam, Douglas (1999), *Political Process and the Development of Black Insurgency, 1930–1970*, Chicago, IL: University of Chicago Press.

Merry, Sally Engle (1997), "Legal Pluralism and Transnational Culture: The Ka Ho'okolokolonui Kanaka Maoli Tribunal, Hawai'i, 1993," in Richard A. Wilson (ed.), *Human Rights, Culture and Context: Anthropological Perspectives*, London: Pluto Press, pp. 28–48.

Merry, Sally Engle (2006), "Transnational Human Rights and Local Activism: Mapping the Middle," *American Anthropologist* **108** (1), 38–51.

Moyn, Samuel (2010), *The Last Utopia: Human Rights in History*, Cambridge, MA: Harvard University Press.

Moyn, Samuel (forthcoming), *The Powerless Companion: Human Rights in the Age of Global Inequality*, Cambridge, MA: Harvard University Press.

Neier, Aryeh (2013), *The International Human Rights Movement: A History*, Princeton, NJ: Princeton University Press.

Nelson, Paul J. and Ellen Dorsey (2008), *New Rights Advocacy: Changing Strategies of Development and Human Rights NGOs*, Washington, DC: Georgetown University Press.

Osiatynski, Wiktor (2009), *Human Rights and Their Limits*, Cambridge and New York: Cambridge University Press.

Risse, Thomas, Stephen C. Ropp, and Kathryn Sikkink (eds) (1999), *The Power of Human Rights: International Norms and Domestic Change*, Cambridge and New York: Cambridge University Press.

Risse, Thomas, Stephen C. Ropp, and Kathryn Sikkink (eds) (2013), *The Persistent Power of Human Rights: From Commitment to Compliance*, Cambridge and New York: Cambridge University Press.

Smith, Jackie (2004), "Transnational Movements and Processes," in David A. Snow, Sarah A. Soule, and Hanspeter Kriesi (eds), *The Blackwell Companion to Social Movements*, Oxford: Wiley-Blackwell.

Smith, Jackie (2007), *Social Movements for Global Democracy*, Baltimore, MD: Johns Hopkins University Press.

Snow, David A., Sarah A. Soule, and Hanspeter Kriesi (eds) (2004), *The Blackwell Companion to Social Movements*, Oxford: Wiley-Blackwell.

Srinivasan, Vivek and Sudha Narayanan (2007), "Food Policy and Social Movements: Reflections on the Right to Food Campaign in India," Case Study 11-1 of the program Food Policy for Developing Countries: The Role of Government in the Global Food System, Ithaca, NY: Cornell University, accessed 6 January 2016 at http://www.academia.edu/1166069/Food_Policy_and_Social_Movements_Reflections_on_the_Right_to_Food_Campaign_in_India.

Stachursky, Benjamin (2013), *The Promise and Perils of Transnationalism: NGO Activism and the Socialization of Women's Human Rights in Egypt and Iran*, Oxon, UK and New York: Routledge.

Tarrow, Sidney (2001), "Transnational Politics: Contention and Institutions in International Politics," *American Review of Political Science* **4**, 1–20.

Tarrow, Sidney (2005a), "The Dualities of Transnational Contention: 'Two Activist Solitudes' or a New World Altogether?" *Mobilization: An International Journal* **10** (1), 53–72, reprinted with permission in Cyrus E. Zirakzadeh (ed.) (2011), *Social and Political Movements, Volume 4: Components, Local Conditions, and International Context*, Los Angeles, CA: Sage.

Tarrow, Sidney (2005b), *The New Transnational Activism*, Cambridge and New York: Cambridge University Press.

Tazreiter, Claudia (2011), "Local to Global Activism: The Movement to Protect the Rights of Refugees and Asylum Seekers," *Social Movement Studies* **9** (2), 201–14.

van Stekelenburg, Jacqueline, Conny Roggeband, and Bert Klandermans (eds) (2013), *The Future of Social Movement Research: Dynamics, Mechanisms, and Processes*, Minneapolis, MN: University of Minnesota Press.

Waltz, Susan (2001), "Universalizing Human Rights: The Role of Small States in the Construction of the Universal Declaration of Human Rights," *Human Rights Quarterly* **23** (1), 44–72.

Yamin, Alicia Ely and Siri Gloppen (eds) (2011), *Litigating Health Rights: Can Courts Bring More Justice to Health?*, Cambridge, MA: Harvard University Press.

Zirakzadeh, Cyrus Ernesto (ed.) (2011), *Social and Political Movements, Volume 2: Emergence and Evolution of Political Process Theory*, Los Angeles, CA: Sage.

9. Expanding rights: norm innovation in the European and Inter-American courts

Wayne Sandholtz

This chapter explores how regional courts have produced innovations that have expanded the reach of human rights norms. The stability of human rights norms is a necessary illusion. For rules to guide behavior, actors need to see them as establishing fixed standards of conduct. But rules are necessarily general and incomplete, and conduct is relentlessly particular. The collision between the two constantly triggers disputes, and disputes end up modifying the rules (Sandholtz, 2007, ch. 1). International courts are increasingly important sites for such disputes and the resulting development of norms.

The proliferation of international courts and their increasing activity are leading toward a judicialization of world politics (Alter, 2014). Three world regions – Africa, the Americas, and Europe – now have functioning courts dedicated to the fulfillment of rights for the people of their respective member states. The African Court for Human and Peoples' Rights, the newest of the three regional human rights courts, has not yet made its stamp on human rights norms and practices in Africa. But the other two courts, the European Court of Human Rights (ECtHR) and the Inter-American Court of Human Rights (IACtHR), have in recent decades produced important innovations in human rights norms. By interpreting and applying human rights norms, the courts fill in gaps in the law or extend it to cover new situations.

The volume as a whole takes rights to be political constructions, and this chapter examines the regional human rights courts as protagonists in the struggle over defining and fulfilling rights. The ECtHR and the IACtHR offer insights into several of the book's main themes: these courts provide an *institutional* arena in which new kinds of *claims* can be advanced and recognized. At times, the human rights courts have *empowered* previously marginalized groups, for example, women, gays and lesbians, indigenous communities, and the families of those silenced by forced disappearance.

The ECtHR and the IACtHR have contributed not just to *consolidating* their respective regional human rights regimes but also to developing human rights law.

I suggest that the courts' strategies for extending rights depend on (1) the level of human rights fulfillment in the member states (their politico-legal contexts); and (2) as emphasized by multiple contributions to this volume, the type or status of the rights concerned, distinguishing between qualified and non-derogable rights. In response to these conditions, a characteristic strategy of the ECtHR has been to trim the leeway granted to states in restricting individual rights (their "margin of appreciation") for the sake of broader public purposes. The IACtHR has frequently advanced rights by recognizing positive obligations on the part of states. The conclusion returns to some of the volume's core concerns regarding barriers to the expansion of rights and the sources of resistance or even backlash.

NORM EXPANSION AND THE ROLE OF COURTS

Students of international norms and institutions have devoted more attention to how new norms come into being than to what happens to norms after they are created. Research on international norms has tended to focus on processes of norm creation, whether they are seen as driven by norm entrepreneurs and activist networks (Brysk, 1993, 2000; Finnemore and Sikkink, 1998; Keck and Sikkink, 1998; Risse and Sikkink, 1999; Risse et al., 2013) or as endpoints in a process of rational institutional design (Koremenos, 2008, n.d.; Koremenos et al., 2001). But once norms exist, they trigger dispute-driven processes that end up modifying the norms themselves.

The inherent dynamism of normative systems is fueled by two kinds of tensions. The first tension is between rules that are inevitably more general than the infinitely varied circumstances in which they are supposed to guide behavior. The second tension is between different norms that could apply to the same action or problem (Krook and True, 2012, pp. 109–11; Sandholtz, 2007, 2009). People's (and states') conduct constantly activates both kinds of tensions, and actors inevitably disagree about how rules should be interpreted and applied. Such disputes launch practical arguments – contestation – that modify the rules (Sandholtz, 2007; Wiener, 2004). The rules can become clearer or less clear, more or less subject to exceptions, broader or narrower, stronger or weaker – but they cannot remain unchanged. The modified rules then create the context for subsequent disputes, and the cycle repeats (Sandholtz, 2007, ch. 1, 2009).

Courts are created specifically to resolve disputes over norms, establishing authoritative interpretations and argumentation frameworks that shape subsequent disputes. They are therefore sites where the progressive expansion of human rights can occur. By "norm expansion" I mean changes that extend the scope or reach of norms. It includes both the creation of new norms and the reinterpretation of existing rules. Expansive norm development implies that a rule changes in one or more of the following ways:

1. Higher norm status. A rule, or set of rules, rises in the norm hierarchy, or becomes a higher order rule. For example, when the European Court of Justice (ECJ) created the doctrines of direct effect and supremacy, it elevated certain European Community treaty provisions to constitutional status (Stein, 1981).
2. Application to additional subjects. An existing rule expands in scope by being applied to new categories of actors. For instance, the ECtHR extended the non-discrimination norm in Article 14 (European Convention on Human Rights) to a new group, namely, homosexuals.[1] The move to extend certain international human rights norms to apply to private companies (Brysk, 2005; Kinley and Tadaki, 2003–04; Ratner, 2001; Weissbrodt and Kruger, 2003) offers another example.
3. Application to additional categories of behavior. An existing rule also expands in scope by application to new kinds of action or behavior. For example, the ECtHR and the IACtHR have both extended general anti-discrimination norms to recognize violence against women as a form of discrimination.[2]
4. Creating new positive duties. Even when the rights of persons remain unchanged, the duties of states relative to those rights can expand. The regional human rights conventions identify general positive duties of states. For instance, the American Convention on Human Rights obligates states to "undertake to adopt . . . such legislative or other measures as may be necessary to give effect" to Convention rights (Article 2). Based on this and other Convention provisions, the IACtHR has established a duty of states to investigate and prosecute serious human rights violations.[3]

---

[1] *Kozak v. Poland*, European Court of Human Rights (2010).

[2] *Opuz v. Turkey*, European Court of Human Rights (2009); *González et al. ("Cotton Field") v. Mexico*, Inter-American Court of Human Rights (2009).

[3] *Velásquez Rodríguez v. Honduras*, Inter-American Court of Human Rights (1988).

COURTS AND THEIR CONTEXTS

The political and human rights contexts within which courts operate shape the judicial strategies that they are likely to deploy to expand rights.

Human Rights Contexts

How courts can deploy their capacity for expanding the scope of rights norms depends in part on their human rights context, that is, on the degree of rights fulfillment among the states subject to their jurisdiction. The human rights context determines not whether courts can expand rights, but the strategies of rights expansion that are available to them. If member states are mostly rights respecting, the court can expand the scope of the international rights regime by following the rights leaders. Thus, when a majority of states has expanded a given right, the court can extend that right to the laggards. In this way the court can rule expansively but with a degree of political cover. If states are mostly rights laggards, the court must lead. It cannot follow the majority because doing so would mean abandoning its mission, losing legitimacy, and becoming irrelevant.

Each approach – following the rights leaders or being the rights leader – implies a different strategy for the court in grounding and justifying its expansive decision-making. Where the level of rights fulfillment is high, and a majority of states has enacted domestic rules that are more protective of rights than the practice being challenged in litigation, the international court (IC) can expand rights by aligning its rulings with the more advanced majority. This strategy of "majoritarian activism" (Maduro, 1998) protects the court from generalized backlash because a majority of the states would support the court's interpretation. The ECtHR has employed this strategy in a number of rights domains, grounding expansive interpretations of rights in a "European consensus" (Dzehtsiarou, 2011a, 2011b; Letsas, 2013). Where the rights context is less favorable, that is, where the majority of states does not protect rights, the IC must lead. If the court is unwilling to move ahead of the states in upholding rights, it will be seen as tolerating violations and will lose credibility. What each strategy means in practice depends in part on the type of right in question.

Non-derogable and Qualified Rights

What it means for a court to follow the leaders or take the lead in rights expansion will differ between non-derogable and qualified rights. Rights in the first category do not permit limitations or exceptions. Non-derogable rights include the core physical integrity rights, for example, the rights to be free from torture, forced disappearance, and extrajudicial killing. With non-derogable rights, the scope of the right is not open to interpretation. Such rights cannot be expanded to new actors or categories of behavior because they are universal and permit no exceptions. The court's decision on the merits of the claim (that is, whether or not a violation of Convention rights occurred) turns on the facts, not on an interpretation of the law. But the court can engage in expansive norm development in other ways, by:

1. establishing new procedural rights
2. establishing new positive duties on the part of states.

Qualified rights include all rights that can be limited or restricted by law when necessary to realize legitimate public purposes. This category includes, for instance, freedom of expression, the right to personal liberty, the right to privacy, and the right to property. These rights are not unlimited. For instance, the right to freedom of expression can be limited by a prohibition on incitement to violence, based on the legitimate interest in public order and security. Courts can expand qualified rights by narrowing the kinds of state actions that constitute acceptable restrictions on those rights. In practice, courts can:

1. find that the state restrictions on a right are not necessary in a democratic society
2. find that the means employed by the state infringe on a right more than is necessary to achieve the public aim.

EXPANDING RIGHTS: THE ECTHR AND THE IACTHR

Both the ECtHR and the IACtHR have produced rights-expanding jurisprudence. The European Court is widely seen as the most influential human rights court in the world. Its greater prestige is built on its longer history of adjudicating rights, its extensive case law, and the influence its judgments have had on law and policy in its member states (Keller and Stone Sweet, 2008). The ECtHR has largely achieved what the Inter-American Court aspires to, namely, establishing "logics of collective, transnational rights protection, and . . . enlisting participation in the Convention's expansionary dynamics" (Stone Sweet and Keller, 2008, p. 6). The IACtHR may be the younger sister, but it has also generated innovative rights jurisprudence.

Indeed, both courts have adopted a "living instrument" approach to

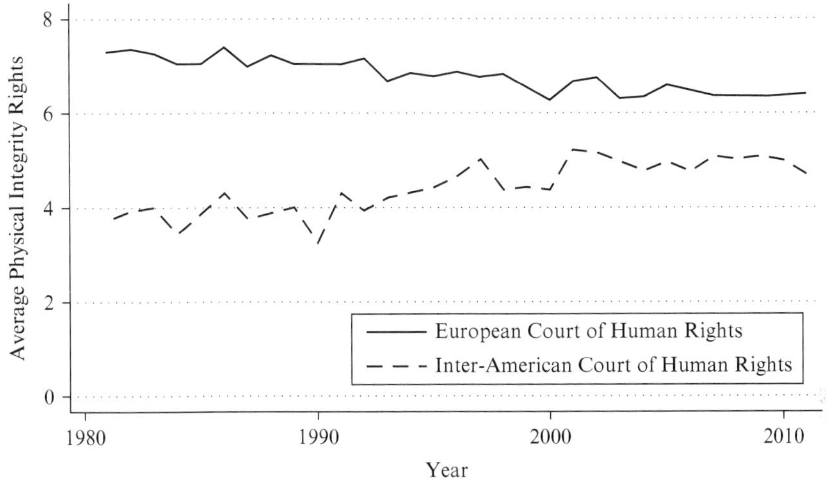

Figure 9.1 Average physical integrity rights scores, ECtHR and IACtHR countries, 1981–2011

their respective basic laws, the European Convention on Human Rights[4] and the American Convention on Human Rights.[5] A living instrument approach means that the underlying convention should be interpreted in light of the evolving needs and standards of current society (Letsas, 2013). Both courts have thus been willing to move beyond a minimum standard interpretation of convention rights and to interpret rights progressively.

Where the two courts differ is in their contexts and their approaches to expanding rights. The arguments set out in the previous section, on human rights contexts and on the types of rights in question, help to explain the courts' varying approaches. Figures 9.1 and 9.2 depict the average level of respect for rights among ECtHR and IACtHR countries, for both non-derogable rights (physical integrity rights)[6] and an important set of qualified rights (civil rights).[7] Both types of rights have been better protected in Europe than in Latin America. Also noteworthy is the gradual narrowing of the gap between the two regions, as the Council of Europe

---

4 *Tyrer v. United Kingdom*, European Court of Human Rights (1978).

5 *The Right to Information on Consular Assistance in the Framework of the Guarantee of the Due Process of Law*, Inter-American Court of Human Rights (1999).

6 As measured by CIRI; Cingranelli, Richards, and Clay (2014).

7 As measured by Freedom House; Freedom House (2014).

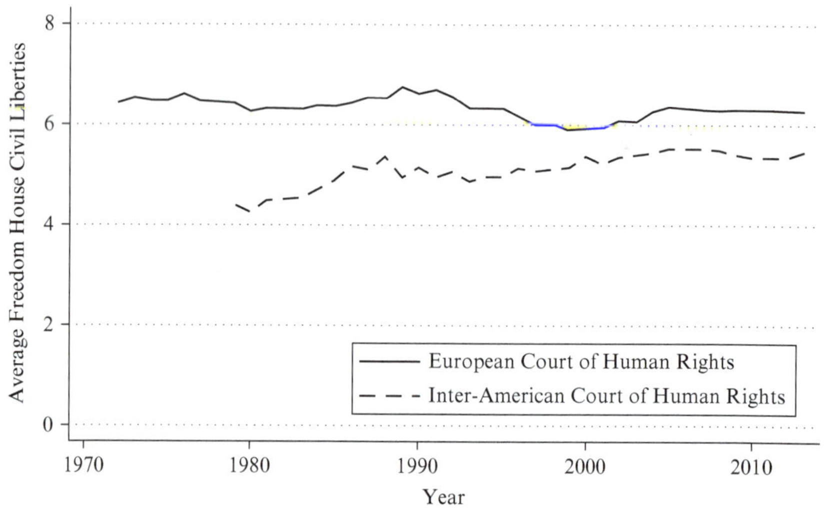

Figure 9.2 Average civil liberties scores, ECtHR and IACtHR countries, 1972–2012

has added countries with more serious rights failures and democratic transitions have stabilized in Latin America.

During its first decades, when the ECtHR developed its progressive approach to rights interpretation, it operated in a context in which the level of states' respect for human rights was high. Moreover, the violations that the ECtHR was asked to adjudicate overwhelmingly concerned civil rights, like privacy and property rights, not core physical integrity rights like torture (though those kinds of violations would reach the Court later). In other words, during its formative years, the ECtHR dealt mainly with qualified rights, in which the central task was to balance individual rights with legitimate public purposes.

The entry into the Council of Europe of states from Eastern and Central Europe and the former Soviet Union after 1990 meant that the Court's membership embraced countries with poor rights records, including abuses of core physical integrity rights. But by then the ECtHR's approach to expansive development of rights was in place. That approach has been one of expanding rights where a group of leading states has extended a right beyond the current interpretation of the European Convention (emerging consensus). The Court grounds its expansive interpretations in its own case law and in the practice of progressive rights-leading states.

In contrast, the IACtHR has operated in a context of low levels of respect for human rights across most of the region, often under brutal authoritarian regimes or in civil wars. The types of abuses brought to the Commission and the Court included massive violations of core physical integrity rights: torture, forced disappearances, and extrajudicial killings. Beginning in the 1980s, dictatorship gave way to democratic transitions. By the first decade of the new century, democracy was consolidating but still a work in progress in much of the region. Systematic repression had mostly ceased, but the Court was presented with claims arising out of the authoritarian period, as well as with ongoing violations of core physical integrity rights. In other words, the work of the IACtHR has been dominated by cases involving non-derogable rights. In this human rights context, the strategy of majoritarian activism was not available because following the practice of the majority of states would not advance rights. Furthermore, because the Court was dealing with violations of non-derogable rights, it could not innovate by shifting the balance point between individual rights and legitimate state purposes. So the IACtHR has expanded rights, as suggested above, by asserting new procedural rights and new positive duties of states.

ECtHR: From European Majority to Emerging International Trend

The ECtHR regularly expands Convention rights by interpreting them "in a progressive manner" (Stone Sweet and Keller, 2008, p. 6). In its early years, the Court was widely seen as establishing "minimum, and largely minimal, standards for basic rights" (Stone Sweet and Keller, 2008, p. 6). In the late 1970s, however, the Court started to shift to a different approach, in which a state's limitation on a qualified right could be found to violate the Convention if a majority of states in the Council of Europe had adopted a more expansive interpretation of the right in question. In a landmark decision, the ECtHR announced that the relevant standards were those of the broader community of European states: "The Court must also recall that the Convention is a living instrument which . . . must be interpreted in the light of present-day conditions. In the case now before it the Court cannot but be influenced by the developments and commonly accepted standards in the penal policy of the member States of the Council of Europe in this field."[8]

In a growing number of cases and for a growing range of rights, the ECtHR narrowed the margin of appreciation by looking to the majority practice of member states (European consensus). If a majority of states adhered to a more progressive norm than the one being challenged, the Court could ground a more expansive interpretation of the right in that majoritarian

---

8 *Tyrer v. United Kingdom*, European Court of Human Rights (1978, para. 31).

position. For example, the ECtHR found that laws that criminalized homosexuality in Northern Ireland violated the Convention right to respect for private life (Article 8). The Court invoked a majoritarian logic: "there is now a better understanding, and in consequence an increased tolerance, of homosexual behaviour to the extent that *in the great majority of the member States of the Council of Europe* it is no longer considered to be necessary or appropriate to treat homosexual practices of the kind now in question as in themselves a matter to which the sanctions of the criminal law should be applied."[9] The ECtHR quoted that passage, and its majoritarian logic, in determining that a similar Irish law violated the Convention.[10] Conversely, when the Court has not been able to identify a majority of European states in favor of an expanded right, it has been willing to defer to states. In a challenge to Austria's denial of same-sex marriages or legal recognition of such unions, the ECtHR did not find a violation of the European Convention right to marriage and family life (Article 12), noting that only six of 47 states parties to the Convention permitted same-sex marriages.[11]

The ECtHR built on a majoritarian logic even more assertively in the *Soering* case, regarding extradition. The issue arose in a claim by Jens Soering that his extradition to the United States, where he faced a potential death sentence, would violate the Convention's prohibition of torture and "inhuman or degrading treatment or punishment" (Article 3). The clear European consensus abolishing capital punishment did not necessarily mean that the death penalty per se violated Article 3. However, the Court declared that "the manner in which [the death penalty] is imposed or executed . . . as well as the conditions of detention awaiting execution" could violate Article 3. And the majoritarian logic applied to those factors: "Present-day attitudes in the Contracting States to capital punishment are relevant for the assessment [of] whether the acceptable threshold of suffering or degradation has been exceeded."[12] In the end, the Court judged that Soering could not be extradited because there was a real risk that he would suffer the "death row phenomenon," which would violate his Article 3 right to be free from inhuman or degrading treatment or punishment. In later cases the Court extended that logic, ruling that states could not deport[13] or expel[14] persons who would face a real risk of ill-treatment, even where the risk would arise from non-state actors.

---

9 *Dudgeon v. The United Kingdom*, European Court of Human Rights (1981).
10 *Norris v. Ireland*, European Court of Human Rights (1988).
11 *Schalk and Kopf v. Austria*, European Court of Human Rights (2010).
12 *Soering v. The United Kingdom*, European Court of Human Rights (1989).
13 *Cruz Varas and others v. Sweden*, European Court of Human Rights (1991).
14 *D. v. The United Kingdom*, European Court of Justice (1997).

In subsequent cases, the Court would show itself willing to expand rights based not on European consensus but on emerging international trends. In fact, in *Hirst v. The United Kingdom*, the Court declared that the lack of European consensus was not in itself determinative.[15] Regarding the rights of persons who have undergone gender reassignment surgery, the ECtHR initially followed a majoritarian approach. In early cases, the Court declined to find an obligation on states to allow post-operative persons to alter their official gender identity because no European majority position had yet emerged.[16] But in *Goodwin v. The United Kingdom*, the Court reversed that jurisprudence. It grounded its reasoning not in the presence of a European consensus, but rather in the existence of a "continuing international trend" of recognizing transsexual rights.[17]

The Court went a bit further in *Demir and Baykara v. Turkey* (2008). The case involved the state's prohibition of a public sector trade union, which the Court found to violate Article 11 (freedom of association). The Court noted that in interpreting the Convention, it "can and must take into account elements of international law other than the Convention, the interpretation of such elements by competent organs, and the practice of European States reflecting their common values," and it identified "common ground in modern societies."[18] The Court's willingness to shift to a broader, international normative frame of reference for interpreting regional human rights norms was clear (Letsas, 2013, p. 122).

IACtHR: Creating Positive Obligations

The Inter-American Court, in contrast, has from the beginning looked outward to support its interpretations of the American Convention (Contreras, 2012, p. 56; Neuman, 2008, pp. 101–2). The IACtHR could hardly rely on a regional consensus on expanding rights when for most of its history the member states have been plagued by weak or non-existent democratic institutions and poorly functioning judicial systems. Consequently, the IACtHR has only rarely even referred to a margin of appreciation or deference to states' choices in implementing Convention rights (Contreras, 2012).

---

[15] *Hirst v. The United Kingdom (No. 2)*, European Court of Human Rights (2005).

[16] *Rees v. The United Kingdom*, European Court of Human Rights (1986); *Cossey v. The United Kingdom*, European Court of Human Rights (1990); *Sheffield and Horsham v. The United Kingdom*, European Court of Human Rights (1998).

[17] *Goodwin v. The United Kingdom*, European Court of Human Rights (2002).

[18] *Demir and Baykara v. Turkey*, European Court of Human Rights (2008).

Because violations of core physical integrity rights – torture, extrajudicial killings, and disappearances – constituted the bulk of its docket, the IACtHR was faced with a different interpretive task than was the ECtHR. With non-derogable rights, finding a violation of the Convention depends on the facts, not on a determination of the appropriate balance between individual rights and state purposes. A primary avenue for the Inter-American Court to expand rights has been through establishing new positive obligations for states. The Convention basis for positive state obligations is based on four provisions. First, Article 1 requires states "to ensure to all persons . . . the free and full exercise" of Convention rights and freedoms. Second, Article 2 obligates states "to adopt . . . such legislative or other measures as may be necessary to give effect to those rights and freedoms." Third, Article 8 defines the right of every person to a fair trial, and fourth, Article 25 enunciates "the right to simple and prompt recourse" (judicial protection).

One of the most important obligations established by the Court is the duty of the state to investigate, prosecute, and punish serious violations of basic rights. Disappearances and extrajudicial killings, of course, violate the rights of the immediate victims. But the Court has found that the lack of investigation, prosecution, and punishment of the perpetrators of such crimes also constitutes a violation of the right of the next of kin to clarification of the fate of those who have been subject to disappearance or extrajudicial killing. The Court has not created a new right but rather expanded the right to a fair trial (Article 8) and the right to judicial protection (Article 25) to include clarification of the fate of the disappeared (Burgorgue-Larsen and Úbeda de Torres, 2011, pp. 699–709). In a disappearance case brought against Guatemala, the Court explained that the state's failure to determine the whereabouts of the disappeared, Efraín Bámaca Velásquez, and its obstruction of efforts to do so, violated "the right of the victim or his next of kin to obtain clarification of the facts relating to the violations."[19] And in a subsequent decision the Court declared that "for more than 18 years, the next of kin" had been "unable to obtain judicial determination of the facts and those responsible," constituting a violation by Peru of "their right to judicial protection and judicial guarantees" under the American Convention.[20]

The Court announced the obligation to investigate and prosecute in its first judgment in a contentious case, involving a forced disappearance in

---

[19] *Bámaca Velásquez v. Guatemala*, Inter-American Court of Human Rights (2000).

[20] *Cantoral Huamaní and García Santa Cruz v. Peru*, Inter-American Court of Human Rights (2007).

Honduras. The state, the Court ruled, had a duty "to use the means at its disposal to carry out a serious investigation of the violations committed within its jurisdiction."[21] The Court later confirmed and elaborated this obligation, notably in *Goiburú*, where it explained that the investigation must be "prompt, serious, [and] impartial" and that the obligation had *jus cogens* status.[22] The investigation must be effected by competent authorities who are genuinely independent "from the officials involved in the facts of the case"[23] and must possess "all the means necessary to promptly carry out all those actions and inquiries essential to clarifying the fate of the victims and identifying those responsible."[24]

The duty to investigate and prosecute gross violations of human rights undergirds one of the Court's more assertive expansions of regional human rights norms: judging amnesty laws incompatible with the American Convention. As Latin America emerged from an era of brutal dictatorships and civil wars in the 1980s and 1990s, the transitions frequently included amnesty laws. The laws were created to shield state actors from prosecution and punishment for the gravest violations of basic rights, generally involving torture, disappearances, and extrajudicial killings. Among the states that had enacted amnesties of this sort were Argentina, Brazil, Chile, El Salvador, Guatemala, Peru, and Uruguay. The amnesty laws undermined the edifice of regional human rights because they precluded what the IACtHR was created to do, namely, holding states accountable for violations. In its first amnesty judgment, the Court not only ruled that Peru's amnesty laws violated the Convention but also declared that they lacked legal effect.[25] In subsequent rulings, the Court reaffirmed the incompatibility of amnesties with the Convention and ordered that states not allow them, or similar barriers, to obstruct the investigation, prosecution, and punishment of gross violations.[26]

The IACtHR also created a positive obligation for states to prevent serious abuses of basic rights. One of the Court's most striking moves in

---

21 *Velásquez Rodríguez v. Honduras*, Inter-American Court of Human Rights (1988, para. 174).

22 *Goiburú et al. v. Paraguay*, Inter-American Court of Human Rights (2006).

23 *Zambrano Vélez v. Ecuador*, Inter-American Court of Human Rights (2007).

24 *Tiu Tojín v. Guatemala*, Inter-American Court of Human Rights (2008).

25 *Barrios Altos v. Peru*, Inter-American Court of Human Rights (2001).

26 See *Serrano Cruz Sisters v. El Salvador*, Inter-American Court of Human Rights (2005); *Almonacid Arellano et al. v. Chile*, Inter-American Court of Human Rights (2006); *"Las Dos Erres" Massacre v. Guatemala*, Inter-American Court of Human Rights (2009); *Gomes Lund et al. ("Guerrilha do Araguaia") v. Brazil*, Inter-American Court of Human Rights (2010); *Gelman v. Uruguay*, Inter-American Court of Human Rights (2011).

this direction came in its decision in the "*Cotton Field*" case, which arose out of the disappearance or murder of hundreds, and probably thousands, of women in Juarez, Mexico. The judgment held that the state had not taken sufficient measures to halt and prevent violence against women, and that the failure constituted a violation of the Convention. The state was under an obligation that "encompasses all those measures of a legal, political, administrative and cultural nature that ensure the safeguard of human rights."[27] The state must not only prevent violations by agents of the state but also "adopt the necessary measures, not only at the legislative, administrative and judicial level . . . to prevent and protect individuals from the criminal acts of other individuals."[28]

Finally, the IACtHR has established positive obligations for states with regard to marginalized groups, like indigenous communities. For instance, the Court has recognized a duty for states to recognize and guarantee the right of indigenous groups to communal ancestral lands.[29] The obligation applies even to states that do not recognize indigenous communal property rights in their domestic law.[30]

INTERNATIONAL COURTS AND POTENTIAL OBSTACLES TO EXPANDING RIGHTS

The primary constraint facing any international court is the willingness of states and other actors to accept its decisions and adjust their conduct to the court's interpretations of regional and international norms. In this section, I assess some potential obstacles as human rights courts seek to expand human rights norms: non-compliance, state withdrawal, and the curtailing of courts' authority.

---

[27] *González et al. ("Cotton Field") v. Mexico*, Inter-American Court of Human Rights (2009, para. 252).

[28] *Pueblo Bello Massacre v. Colombia*, Inter-American Court of Human Rights (2006); see also *Baldeón-García v. Peru*, Inter-American Court of Human Rights (2006).

[29] *Mayagna (Sumo) Awas Tingni Community v. Nicaragua*, Inter-American Court of Human Rights (2001); *Sawhoyamaxa Indigenous Community v. Paraguay*, Inter-American Court of Human Rights (2006).

[30] *Saramaka People v. Suriname*, Inter-American Court of Human Rights (2007).

Non-compliance

Non-compliance could constrain ICs in two ways, *ex ante* (as a threat, leading courts to anticipate non-compliance and shape their judgments to conform with state preferences (Carrubba et al., 2008)) and *ex post* (as a punishment, with states refusing to carry out IC judgments). Evidence from the ECJ shows convincingly that the *ex ante* threat is not credible (Stone Sweet and Brunell, 2012, 2013). In any case, the threat of non-compliance will have a limited effect on human rights courts' willingness to rule expansively. States are not the only, and not necessarily the most important, constituencies of human rights courts. Compliance coalitions (Hillebrecht, 2014) or compliance constituencies (Alter, 2014), including multiple branches and levels of government as well as a range of non-state actors, can also be decisive members of pro-compliance coalitions.

Ex post non-compliance is also unlikely systematically to constrain international courts. Rather than constraining ICs, non-compliance tends to activate them (Stone Sweet and Brunell, 2012, 2013), as violations give rise to new claims. In any case, compliance has generally been high among ECtHR states (Hawkins and Jacoby, 2010, p. 66); about half of the Court's orders receive full compliance (Hillebrecht, 2014, pp. 48–51). Compliance with ECtHR orders for pecuniary awards and interim measures has been "quite high," but the failure to carry out orders to investigate and prosecute has been "widespread" (Baluarte and De Vos, 2010, p. 16).

For the IACtHR, partial compliance occurs in 83 percent of the cases (Hawkins and Jacoby, 2010, p. 37). Using a different measure, Hillebrecht finds full compliance with about 34 percent of the remedies ordered by the IACtHR, though the rate varies widely across states and across types of mandates (Hillebrecht, 2014, pp. 48–51). For orders of the IACtHR, compliance with pecuniary awards has been "quite high" and with symbolic remedies about 50 percent. But only about 25 percent of orders for "measures of non-repetition" have been implemented, and in only one instance has an order to investigate, prosecute, and punish been carried out completely (Baluarte and De Vos, 2010, pp. 20–1). And supreme courts in Argentina, Chile, and Venezuela have openly refused to implement IACtHR orders (Huneeus, 2011). Still, despite substantial non-compliance with its judgments, the IACtHR continues to engage in the progressive development of human rights law.

Withdrawal

The threat of withdrawal from a court's jurisdiction might also be seen as the most drastic means of constraining its decision-making. For the

ECtHR, the threat of exit from the regime is not credible, largely because acceptance of the Court's jurisdiction is mandatory for membership in the Council of Europe (COE). The most serious threats of withdrawal have come in recent years from the United Kingdom and Russia (Madsen, forthcoming). Russia, which has been one of the countries most frequently brought before the ECtHR and found in violation of the Convention in the vast majority of cases, has been suspended from voting in key COE organs and threatened with expulsion. Russia has also threatened to exit the COE on several occasions since 2000 (Provost, 2015). The ECtHR does not appear to have retreated from its expansionary, living instrument approach to interpreting the European Convention, though it may have allowed the United Kingdom a greater margin of appreciation in some recent cases (see Madsen, forthcoming). On the Inter-American side, two states have withdrawn (Trinidad and Tobago and Venezuela), though only Venezuela's withdrawal was motivated by displeasure with the Court's decisions. The IACtHR has shown little sign of abandoning its assertive approach to expanding rights.

Curtailing Courts' Competences

In practice, cutting back an IC's powers is virtually impossible. In the Inter-American System, states could revise the Court's rules of procedure or curtail its jurisdiction only by a two-thirds majority vote of the states parties, a threshold that could be reached only if displeasure with the IACtHR were extremely broad. In Europe, the barriers are even higher. Amending the European Convention to cut back the Court's powers or jurisdiction would require unanimity among the 47 member states.

States, nevertheless, occasionally indicate their displeasure with the courts by threatening to rein in their powers. Bolivia recently called for the Inter-American Commission to be shut down (Picq, 2012). In 2015 Ecuador's President Correa proposed the creation of a new Latin American Court of Human Rights (Cerqueira, 2015) and Brazil reacted against a Commission decision by withholding its Organization of American States (OAS) dues (Cerqueira, 2015). In Europe, COE member states have signaled to the European Court their desire for the Court to be less assertive in expanding Convention rights. The 2012 Brighton Declaration affirms the principle of subsidiarity, that states have the primary role in safeguarding rights and freedoms, with the ECtHR exercising a secondary, supervisory function, and the margin of appreciation (Council of Europe, 2012, para. 11). The member states subsequently signed Protocol 15, which (when ratified by all of the member states) will amend the preamble to the Convention by including references to the principle of subsidiarity and the "doctrine" of the margin of appreciation (Council of Europe, 2013). Still, Protocol 15 does not curtail the competences of the ECtHR.

CONCLUSION

The ECtHR and the IACtHR have both actively expanded the scope of international human rights norms in their respective regions, within political contexts that shaped their available options. This chapter thus resonates with the book's underlying premise that rights construction is a political process. The ECtHR and the IACtHR must constantly balance their desire to expand the scope of human rights norms with the necessity of maintaining acceptance and support among their compliance constituencies, including states. The ECtHR's main strategy for expanding rights has been to steadily reduce the scope allowed to states to restrict individual rights for the sake of public purposes, first by finding a European consensus and later by identifying emerging international trends. The Inter-American Court's favored approach has been to expand rights by establishing positive duties for states to ensure respect for rights, prevent violations, and investigate and prosecute serious abuses.

Explaining the difference in strategies reinforces a theme common to many of the chapters in this volume, namely, that the type of right involved affects the process of rights expansion. In Europe, as a majority of states narrowed the scope for public purposes to justify limitations on qualified rights, the ECtHR could follow the rights leaders. In contrast, for most of its history the IACtHR confronted grave violations of non-derogable physical integrity rights. The option of following the states was foreclosed and the court had to lead.

Finally, a common concern in the volume is how actors and institutions engaged in expanding rights inevitably confront resistance and the potential for backlash. For example, the widespread failure to implement some kinds of remedies (notably, to investigate and prosecute) constitutes an obstacle to greater fulfillment of rights in both regions. Still, significant levels of non-compliance with its decisions have not appeared to restrain the rights-expanding impulses of the Inter-American Court. And recent state resistance to the ECtHR has not reduced the Court's formal authority, though it may well show greater deference to states in some cases or on some issues. On balance, the regional human rights courts seem likely to remain important sources of rights innovation and expansion.

CASES CITED

Almonacid Arellano et al. v. Chile (2006), Preliminary Objections, Merits, Reparations and Costs, Inter-American Court of Human Rights, Series C No. 154, decided 26 September 2006, IHRL 1538 (IACHR 2006).

Baldeón-García v. Peru (2006), Merits, Reparations and Costs, Inter-American Court of Human Rights, decided 6 April 2006.

Bámaca Velásquez v. Guatemala (2000), Merits, Inter-American Court of Human Rights, Series C No. 70, decided 25 November 2000.

Barrios Altos v. Peru (2001), Merits, Inter-American Court of Human Rights, Series C No. 75, decided 14 March 2001.

Cantoral Huamaní and García Santa Cruz v. Peru (2007), Merits, Reparations and Costs, Inter-American Court of Human Rights, Series C No. 167, decided 10 July 2007.

Cossey v. The United Kingdom (1990), Judgment, European Court of Human Rights, App. No. 10843/84, decided 27 September 1990.

Cruz Varas and others v. Sweden (1991), Judgment, European Court of Human Rights, App. No. 15576/89, decided 20 March 1991.

D. v. The United Kingdom (1997), Judgment, European Court of Justice, App. No. 30240/96, decided 2 May 1997.

Demir and Baykara v. Turkey (2008), Judgment, European Court of Human Rights, App. No. 34503/97, decided 12 November 2008.

Dudgeon v. The United Kingdom (1981), Judgment (Merits), European Court of Human Rights, App. No. 7525/76, decided 22 October 1981.

Gelman v. Uruguay (2011), Merits and Reparations, Inter-American Court of Human Rights, Series C No. 221, decided 24 February 2011.

Goiburú et al. v. Paraguay (2006), Merits, Reparations and Costs, Inter-American Court of Human Rights, Series C No. 153, decided 22 September 2006.

Gomes Lund et al. ("Guerrilha do Araguaia") v. Brazil (2010), Preliminary Objections, Merits, Reparations and Costs, Inter-American Court of Human Rights, Series C No. 219, decided 24 November 2010.

González et al. ("Cotton Field") v. Mexico (2009), Preliminary Objection, Merits, Reparations and Costs, Inter-American Court of Human Rights, Series C No. 205, decided 16 November 2009.

Goodwin v. The United Kingdom, Judgment (Merits and Just Satisfaction), European Court of Human Rights, App. No. 28957/95, decided 11 July 2002.

Hirst v. The United Kingdom (No. 2) (2005), Judgment, European Court of Human Rights, App. No. 74025/01, decided 6 October 2005.

Kozak v. Poland (2010), Judgment, European Court of Human Rights, App. No. 13102/02, decided 2 March 2010.

"Las Dos Erres" Massacre v. Guatemala (2009), Preliminary Objection, Merits, Reparations and Costs, Inter-American Court of Human Rights, Series C No. 211, decided 24 November 2009.

Mayagna (Sumo) Awas Tingni Community v. Nicaragua (2001), Merits, Reparations and Costs, Inter-American Court of Human Rights, Series C No. 79, decided 31 August 2001.

Norris v. Ireland (1988), Judgment (Merits and Just Satisfaction), European Court of Human Rights, App. No. 10581/83, decided 26 October 1988.

Opuz v. Turkey (2009), Judgment, European Court of Human Rights, App. No. 33401/02, decided 9 June 2009.

Pueblo Bello Massacre v. Colombia (2006), Merits, Reparations and Costs, Inter-American Court of Human Rights, Series C No. 140, decided 31 January 2006.

Rees v. The United Kingdom (1986), Judgment, European Court of Human Rights, App. No. 9532/81, decided 17 October 1986.

Saramaka People v. Suriname (2007), Preliminary Objections, Merits, Reparations and Costs, Inter-American Court of Human Rights, Series C No. 172, decided 28 November 2007.

Sawhoyamaxa Indigenous Community v. Paraguay (2006), Merits, Reparations and Costs, Inter-American Court of Human Rights, Series C No. 146, decided 29 March 2006.

Schalk and Kopf v. Austria (2010), Judgment, European Court of Human Rights, App. No. 30141/04, decided 24 June 2010.

Serrano Cruz Sisters v. El Salvador (2005), Merits, Reparations and Costs, Inter-American Court of Human Rights, Series C No. 120, decided 1 March 2005.

Sheffield and Horsham v. The United Kingdom (1998), Judgment, European Court of Human Rights, App. No. 31-32/1997/815-816/1018-1019, decided 30 July 1998.

Soering v. The United Kingdom (1989), Judgment, European Court of Human Rights, App. No. 14038/88, decided 7 July 1989.

The Right to Information on Consular Assistance in the Framework of the Guarantee of the Due Process of Law (1999), Advisory Opinion OC-16/99, Inter-American Court of Human Rights, Series A No. 16, decided 1 October 1999.

Tiu Tojín v. Guatemala (2008), Merits, Reparations and Costs, Inter-American Court of Human Rights, Series C No. 190, decided 26 November 2008.

Tyrer v. United Kingdom (1978), Judgment, European Court of Human Rights, Series A No. 26, Application No. 5856/72, decided 25 April 1978.

Velásquez Rodríguez v. Honduras (1988), Merits, Inter-American Court of Human Rights, Series C No. 4, decided 29 July 1988.

Zambrano Vélez v. Ecuador (2007), Merits, Reparations and Costs, Inter-American Court of Human Rights, Series C No. 16, decided 4 July 2007.

REFERENCES

Alter, Karen J. (2014), *The New Terrain of International Law: Courts, Politics, Rights*, Princeton, NJ: Princeton University Press.

Baluarte, David C. and Christian M. De Vos (2010), *From Judgment to Justice: Implementing International and Regional Human Rights Decisions*, Open Society Justice Initiative, 204 pp., accessed 8 April 2016 at https://http://www.opensocietyfoundations.org/reports/judgment-justice-implementing-international-and-regional-human-rights-decisions.

Brysk, Alison (1993), "From Above and Below: Social Movements, the International System and Human Rights in Argentina," *Comparative Political Studies*, **26** (3), 259–85.

Brysk, Alison (2000), *From Tribal Village to Global Village: International Relations and Indian Rights in Latin America*, Stanford, CA: Stanford University Press.

Brysk, Alison (2005), *Human Rights and Private Wrongs*, New York: Routledge.

Burgorgue-Larsen, Laurence and Amaya Úbeda de Torres (2011), *The Inter-American Court of Human Rights: Case Law and Commentary*, Oxford: Oxford University Press.

Carrubba, Clifford J., Matthew Gabel, and Charles Hankla (2008), "Judicial Behavior Under Political Constraints: Evidence from the European Court of Justice," *American Political Science Review*, **102** (4), 435–52.

Cerqueira, Daniel (2015), "Brazil, Ecuador, and the Inter-American Human Rights System," Americas Quarterly, accessed 8 April 2016 at http://www.americas-quarterly.org/content/brazil-ecuador-and-inter-american-human-rights-system.

Cingranelli, David L., David L. Richards, and K. Chad Clay (2014), *The Cingranelli-Richards (CIRI) Human Rights Dataset*, Version 2014.04.14, http://www.humanrightsdata.org.

Contreras, Pablo (2012), "National Discretion and International Deference in the Restriction of Human Rights: A Comparison Between the Jurisprudence of the European and the Inter-American Court of Human Rights," *Northwestern University Journal of International Human Rights*, **11** (1), i–27.

Council of Europe (2012), *High Level Conference on the Future of the European Court of Human Rights: Brighton Declaration*, accessed 8 April 2016 at http://www.echr.coe.int/Documents/2012_Brighton_FinalDeclaration_ENG.pdf.

Council of Europe (2013), *Protocol No. 15 Amending the Convention for the Protection of Human Rights and Fundamental Freedoms: Explanatory Report*, accessed 8 April 2016 at http://www.echr.coe.int/Documents/Protocol_15_explanatory_report_ENG.pdf.

Dzehtsiarou, Kanstantsin (2011a), "Does Consensus Matter? Legitimacy of European Consensus in the Case Law of the European Court of Human Rights," *Public Law*, **3** (3), 534–53.

Dzehtsiarou, Kanstantsin (2011b), "European Consensus and the Evolutive Interpretation of the European Convention on Human Rights Legitimacy and the Future of the European Court of Human Rights," *German Law Journal*, **12** (10), 1730–45.

Finnemore, Martha and Kathryn Sikkink (1998), "International Norm Dynamics and Political Change," *International Organization*, **52** (4), 887–917.

Freedom House (2014), *Country Ratings and Status, 1973–2014*, accessed 8 April 2016 at https://freedomhouse.org/report-types/freedom-world.

Hawkins, Darren and Wade Jacoby (2010), "Partial Compliance: A Comparison of the European and Inter-American Courts of Human Rights," *Journal of International Law and International Relations*, **6** (1), 35–85.

Hillebrecht, Courtney (2014), *Domestic Politics and International Human Rights Tribunals: The Problem of Compliance*, Cambridge: Cambridge University Press.

Huneeus, Alexandra (2011), "Courts Resisting Courts: Lessons from the Inter-American Court's Struggle to Enforce Human Rights," *Cornell International Law Journal*, **44** (3), 493–534.

Keck, Margaret E. and Kathryn Sikkink (1998), *Activists Beyond Borders: Advocacy Networks in International Politics*, Ithaca, NY: Cornell University Press.

Keller, Helen and Alec Stone Sweet (eds) (2008), *A Europe of Rights*, Oxford: Oxford University Press.

Kinley, David and Junko Tadaki (2003–04), "From Talk to Walk: The Emergence

of Human Rights Responsibilities for Corporations in International Law," *Virginia Journal of International Law*, **44** (4), 931–1024.
Koremenos, Barbara (2008), "When, What, and Why Do States Choose to Delegate?," *Law and Contemporary Problems*, **71** (1), 151–92.
Koremenos, Barbara (n.d.). "An Economic Analysis of International Rulemaking," Department of Political Science, University of Michigan, 19 pp.
Koremenos, Barbara, Charles Lipson, and Duncan Snidalma (2001), "The Rational Design of International Institutions," *International Organization*, **55** (4), 761–99.
Krook, Mona Lena and Jacqui True (2012), "Rethinking the Life Cycles of International Norms: The United Nations and the Global Promotion of Gender Equality," *European Journal of International Relations*, **18** (1), 103–27.
Letsas, George (2013), "The ECHR as a Living Instrument: Its Meaning and Legitimacy," in Andreas Føllesdal, Birgit Peters, and Geir Ulfstein (eds), *Constituting Europe: The European Court of Human Rights in a National, European and Global Context*, Cambridge: Cambridge University Press, pp. 106–41.
Madsen, Mikael Rask (forthcoming), "The European Court of Human Rights and the Politics of International Law," in Wayne Sandholtz and Christopher A. Whytock (eds), *Handbook on the Politics of International Law*, Cheltenham, UK and Northampton, MA, USA: Edward Elgar.
Maduro, Miguel Poiares (1998), *We, the Court: The European Court of Justice and the European Economic Constitution*, Oxford: Hart.
Neuman, Gerald L. (2008), "Import, Export, and Regional Consent in the Inter-American Court of Human Rights," *European Journal of International Law*, **19** (1), 101–23.
Picq, Manuela (2012), *Is the Inter-American Commission too Progressive?*, Al Jazeera, accessed 8 April 2016 at http://www.aljazeera.com/indepth/opinion/2012/06/2012658344220937.html.
Provost, René (2015), "Teetering on the Edge of Legal Nihilism: Russia and the Evolving European Human Rights Regime," *Human Rights Quarterly*, **37** (2), 289–340.
Ratner, Steven R. (2001), "Corporations and Human Rights: A Theory of Legal Responsibility," *Yale Law Journal*, **111** (3), 443–545.
Risse, Thomas and Kathryn Sikkink (1999), "The Socialization of Human Rights into Domestic Practices: Introduction," in Thomas Risse, Stephen C. Ropp, and Kathryn Sikkink (eds), *The Power of Principles: International Human Rights Norms and Domestic Change*, Cambridge: Cambridge University Press, pp. 1–38.
Risse, Thomas, Stephen C. Ropp, and Kathryn Sikkink (eds) (2013), *The Persistent Power of Human Rights: From Commitment to Compliance*, Cambridge: Cambridge University Press.
Sandholtz, Wayne (2007), *Prohibiting Plunder: How Norms Change*, New York: Oxford University Press.
Sandholtz, Wayne (2009), "Explaining International Norm Change," in Wayne Sandholtz and Kendall Stiles (eds), *International Norms and Cycles of Change*, Oxford: Oxford University Press, pp. 1–26.
Stein, Eric (1981), "Lawyers, Judges, and the Making of a Transnational Constitution," *American Journal of International Law*, **75** (1), 1–27.
Stone Sweet, Alec and Thomas Brunell (2012), "The European Court of Justice,

State Noncompliance, and the Politics of Override," *American Political Science Review*, **106** (1), 204–13.
Stone Sweet, Alec and Thomas L. Brunell (2013), "Trustee Courts and the Judicialization of International Regimes: The Politics of Majoritarian Activism in the European Convention on Human Rights, the European Union, and the World Trade Organization," *Journal of Law and Courts*, **1** (1), 61–88.
Stone Sweet, Alec and Helen Keller (2008), "The Reception of the ECHR in National Legal Orders," in Helen Keller and Alec Stone Sweet (eds), *A Europe of Rights*, Oxford: Oxford University Press, pp. 3–28.
Weissbrodt, David and Muria Kruger (2003), "Norms on the Responsibilities of Transnational Corporations and Other Business Enterprises with Regard to Human Rights," *American Journal of International Law*, **97** (4), 901–22.
Wiener, Antje (2004), "Contested Compliance: Interventions on the Normative Structure of World Politics," *European Journal of International Relations*, **10** (2), 189–234.

10. Feminist foreign policy as state-led expansion of human rights

Valerie M. Hudson

INTRODUCTION

The world of foreign and security policy has traditionally been seen as gendered male. The world of arms, war, and high stakes diplomacy is still a fairly woman-less world, and the same can be said of the academic field of security studies and the interstitial world of policy think tanks. And yet inroads are being made, slowly but surely.

The purpose of this chapter is to trace the arc of the idea that there could be a "feminist" state foreign/security policy, and then to assess both the promise and the pitfalls of such a stance. In this case, the *state* would become the main agent promoting this human rights expansion. A feminist foreign/security policy (FFSP) would embrace the idea that human rights and national security are not contradictory goals of state policy unless we choose to see them as such. However, an FFSP would go further and also propose that women's empowerment, women's voice, and women's security constitute the great bridge between the two aspirations.

HOW THE WOMANLESS WORLD WAS UNMADE

For as long as warfare has been gendered male, there have been women warriors, women casualties, and women peace advocates. In other words, women have always been involved in a system they could neither define nor, ultimately, reshape. What interests us here is a turn that arguably gathered momentum in the early 1990s; the idea that national security must include women's security, that human rights must include women's rights, and that the councils of human decision-making on these matters must include women in more than token numbers. This conceptual move was, I would argue, of tremendous import in redefining both "security" and the state obligations that attend that objective. Treating women as beings with full human rights could not but lead to a reconceptualization of security, for most violations of women's rights included openly normalized insecurity. The chapter by Alison Brysk (Chapter 5) covers in admirable detail the struggle to see femicide, female genital cutting, and wartime rape as important human rights issues. Rather, the present chapter is focused more on how the conduct of state foreign/security policy has been transformed by new international understanding of the linkages between "women, peace, and security," and how certain states have taken up the call and become agents of its promulgation.

While there was surely much groundwork undertaken by the international women's movement that preceded this turn in the early 1990s, in June 1993, at the United Nations (UN) World Conference on Human Rights in Vienna, the international community for the very first time explicitly condemned human rights violations perpetrated against women, such as female genital cutting, female infanticide, and sex tourism. What was striking is that state rhetoric began to change as a result.

The US delegation, which included high-profile figures such as Arvonne Fraser and Geraldine Ferraro, championed this new emphasis on women's rights. Indeed, non-governmental organizations (NGOs) such as the Global Campaign for Women's Human Rights and its spokeswoman Charlotte Bunch had been pressuring US administrations for years to act. By the end of the conference, delegates declared that women's rights are "an inalienable, integral, and indivisible part of universal human rights" (Ferraro, 1993; Riding, 1993; Wikipedia, 2013). Indeed, as historian Karen Garner (2013, p. 111) relates, the Global Campaign went even further, and

> convened a "Global Tribunal on Violations of Women's Human Rights" that took place at the NGO forum held just prior to the opening of the UN government conference. At the Tribunal, 33 women from 24 countries gave emotional and powerful testimony documenting widespread instances of domestic violence, female genital mutilation, torture, terrorism and war crimes specifically directed at women. [T]he public tribunal [was] presided over by a panel of international judges who connected these abuses to violations of existing international human rights treaties and attended by government delegates.

This conceptual turn had real effects on state rhetoric. For example, in his summary to Congress of the Human Rights Conference, John Shattuck, the Assistant Secretary of State for Human Rights and Humanitarian Affairs at the time, pronounced, "The Clinton Administration regards promoting the cause of women's rights as a key element of our overall human rights policy" (Garner, 2013, p. 114). And in 1994 the Office of International Women's Issues, or OIWI, was created and placed in the portfolio of the Undersecretary of State for Global Affairs in the US State

Department. This institutionalization of state commitment was to lay the groundwork for a more sweeping expansion in later years, as we will see.

The September 1995 Fourth World Conference of Women in Beijing was arguably the next benchmark in this narrative. The conference attracted an unprecedented number of attendees. Estimates put the number of participants at the official government-sponsored conference at 17,000 with more than another 30,000 attending the associated "shadow" NGO Forum (Garner, 2013, pp. 144–5). But in retrospect, the most important moment of that conference was when the First Lady of the "global hegemon" came to the podium and uttered words which are memorized to this day. Kate Grant (2013), a member of the US delegation that day, remembers,

> While citing ways that women's lives across cultures and continents had similar challenges, [Clinton] then proceeded to address a litany of abuses, framing them each not simply as "women's problems," but as profound violations of human rights . . . Hillary Clinton stood there and proclaimed eleven earth shaking words: "Women's rights are human rights and human rights are women's rights." The normally staid crowd erupted in applause. That simple powerful phrase became the battle cry of a global movement.

A second reconceptualization – one that explicitly obligated states to action – was also needed. In this very abridged history, I'd suggest that this second movement came at the very turn of the century, with the October 2000 UN Security Council Resolution 1325. This declaration represented yet another step forward for women – a major one – for it defined women not only as passive recipients of aid or justice, but also as *agents* integral to peace, stability, and security. United Nations Security Council Resolution (UNSCR) 1325 represents a critical intellectual turning point concerning how women are perceived with respect to foreign/security policy, for if women are agents, then they have a right to be "at the table" where decisions on these matters are made. In addition, if women are agents, then two conclusions follow: (1) women can be state agents, engendering state obligation to actively include women in state activities, and (2) women can be objects of state programming designed to further empower their agency, and not simply secure their safety.

Chief among the commitments outlined in the declaration is that member states should "ensure increased representation of women at all decision-making levels in national, regional, and international institutions and mechanisms for the prevention, management, and resolution of conflict" (United Nations Security Council, 2000). Further measures include incorporating more women into field operations personnel, including military peacekeepers, assessing peace proposals based in part on their impact on women and girls, and prosecuting sex crimes in war without the possibility of granting amnesty. Indeed, while momentum had been gathering since 1996, when the Rwanda Tribunal first called for rape to be prosecuted as a war crime, Brysk points out that the idea that wartime rape was a "real" war crime was only codified by the International Criminal Court in 2001, after the passage of 1325 (Brysk, this volume).

It is difficult to overstate the symbolic significance of UNSCR 1325. For the first time in history, humanity had declared that the male monopoly over issues of war and peace was unwarranted and unjustifiable. Furthermore, state promotion of this human rights expansion was now formally obligated. The potential ripple effects could not then be calculated, and, indeed, the full effects have yet to be fully understood. UNSCR 1325 was followed by numerous related or add-on Security Council resolutions, such as 1327, 1820, 1888, 1889, 1960, 2106, 2122, and 2242, approximately one every 18 months. While some have suggested that these subsequent resolutions may have had the effect of siloing "women's issues" (Meger, 2012), the uninterrupted cadence of resolutions, not to mention the high level review of 1325 at its 15-year anniversary (UNWomen, 2015), the creation of UNWomen in 2010 that concentrated organizational competence on these issues, and DPKO's 2014 announcement of its Gender Strategy (United Nations DPKO/DFS, 2014) suggest that at least at the international level, this reconceptualization will endure.

THE TRANSLATION TO STATE FOREIGN/ SECURITY POLICY

While the world would have to wait until 2015 to hear a foreign minister announce their government would follow an explicitly "feminist foreign policy" (Government Offices of Sweden, 2015), since 2000, women have been chosen as defense ministers and foreign ministers across several regions. Even pre-dating UNSCR 1325, foreign aid agencies adopted gender lenses through successive waves of development planning paradigms, such as WID (Women in Development), WAD (Women and Development), and GAD (Gender and Development), with many programs designed to empower women as agents. Many militaries had effected the integration of women soldiers to a greater or lesser degree as well. Even so, a coordinated state effort to formally and explicitly put women near the top of the foreign/security policy gender had arguably not yet been attempted.

That would change in 2009. The selection of Hillary Clinton as US Secretary of State in 2009, and her tenure until early 2013, provides a rich case study of how the "women, peace, and security" standpoint articulated by the UN could be translated into a state agenda. As the US State Department also oversees the United States Agency for International Development (USAID), Clinton held two of three of the levers of US foreign/security policy in her hands: diplomacy and development. And as a statutory member of the National Security Council, Clinton had a prominent seat at the table where all foreign/security policy matters of import would be decided during the first term of the Obama Administration.

As part of Clinton's start-up package, Obama elevated the Office of International Women's Issues, which became the OGWI, the Office of Global Women's Issues, increasing its budget ten-fold (Garner, 2013, p. 418). Obama also granted that the head of OGWI hold the rank of ambassador and stipulated they would report directly to the Secretary of State. In this way, Clinton could ensure the institutional memory necessary to emphasize the security and socio-economic well-being of women well into the future. An OGWI representative also joined the State Department's Policy Planning staff, the strategic think tank for State, and OGWI moved from a little office on G Street to the top floor of the main State Department building. In bureaucratic terms, there could have been no clearer signal that the State Department was taking gender issues seriously.

Clinton initiated the first ever Quadrennial Diplomacy and Development Review (QDDR), published in 2010, to outline a four-year plan for the State Department and USAID; women and girls are mentioned a total of 133 times in its 242 pages. The QDDR asserts that American foreign policy will "focus our development efforts in six specific areas that build on our strengths: sustainable economic growth, food security, global health, climate change, democracy and governance, and humanitarian assistance. In each area, we will invest in women and girls at every turn, with the goal of empowering them" (US Department of State, 2010, p. x). This document lays out a rationale for supporting women that is rooted not only within a human rights discourse, but also involving realism:

> The protection and empowerment of women and girls is key to the foreign policy and security of the United States. As President Obama's National Security Strategy recognizes, "countries are more peaceful and prosperous when women are accorded full and equal rights and opportunity. When those rights and opportunities are denied, countries lag behind."
>
> And as Secretary Clinton has emphasized repeatedly and consistently, "women are critical to solving virtually every challenge we face as individual nations and as a community of nations . . . when women have equal rights, nations are more stable, peaceful, and secure." The status of the world's women is not simply an issue of morality – it is a matter of national security.

> To that end, women are at the center of our diplomacy and development efforts – not simply as beneficiaries, but also as agents of peace, reconciliation, development, growth, and stability.
>
> To foster and maximize the diplomatic and development outcomes we seek, we will integrate gender issues into policies and practices at State and USAID. We will ensure that gender is effectively addressed throughout all bureaus and missions, include gender in strategic planning and budget allocation, and develop indicators and evaluation systems to measure the impact of our programs and policies on women and girls. (US Department of State, 2010, p. 23)

The programming associated with this new emphasis on women and girls was remarkable. Clinton's Feed the Future Initiative and Global Health Initiative prioritized programs for women. Clinton created the Secretary's International Fund for Women and Girls to channel private donations in this area. She partnered with the UN to disseminate 100 million cookstoves to mitigate the endless respiratory and eye infections that women suffered from by laboring over traditional hearths that usually burned dung or wood; she made sure the State Department's budget figures highlighted how much money was devoted to programs for women and girls; she put forward the Data 2X Initiative to improve the collection of statistics about the situation of women and girls to serve as benchmarks for policy evaluation. She supported the creation of UNWomen and promoted UN Security Council resolutions that forwarded the aims of 1325, such as UNSCR 1820, 1888, 1889, and 1960,[1] which addressed several related issues, including reporting and accountability for sexual violence in war.

Clinton was also instrumental in establishing the US National Action Plan (NAP) for Women, Peace, and Security in 2011, detailing the actions to be implemented by the US government in fulfillment of UNSCR 1325.[2] These governmental frameworks were comprehensive and cumulative. For example, in just one year – her last full year as Secretary, 2012 – the US government put forth a Counter-Trafficking in Persons Strategy in February, a Policy on Gender Equality and Female Empowerment in March, an Implementation Plan for the NAP in August, a Strategy to Prevent and Respond to Gender-based Violence Globally also in August, the Equal Futures Partnership in September, and a Vision for Ending Child Marriage and Meeting the Needs of Married Children in October (Steinberg, 2013b).

---

1 Followed by 2106 and 2122 in the year 2013, after she had stepped down from being Secretary of State.

2 In addition, she added the United States as one of the countries covered in the TIP (Trafficking in Persons) Report.

Clinton also attempted to change attitudes within the State Department. During March of 2012 she issued a Policy Guidance Advancing Gender Equality and Promoting the Status of Women and Girls (US Department of State Office of Global Women's Issues, 2012). This was an internal document that went out to every bureau and embassy, asking each to gather information and perform a gender analysis on the situation of women within their area of expertise. The integration of women would also be incorporated into the State Department's three-year strategic plans in the areas of planning/budgeting, programming, monitoring/evaluation, and management/training. A three-day course on gender integration was developed in order to incorporate it into the Foreign Service Institute (FSI) training curriculum, while gender modules will soon be integrated into FSI courses (Klein, 2013).

Clinton also creatively implemented a "women's track" to various annual diplomatic bilateral strategic dialogues that took place with India, Pakistan, China, Indonesia, Australia, and other countries. This enabled OGWI's Ambassador Melanne Verveer to attend the dialogues in her official capacity as head of OGWI, in effect forcing the other country to provide a counterpart to Verveer at the same level (or to create one if not). The aim was to provide an opening to discuss women's issues (J., 2013).

The US NAP is worth examining in a bit more detail. As informed by the provisions of 1325, the US NAP identifies five primary areas of concern: national integration and institutionalization of a gender-responsive approach to diplomacy, development, and defense; strengthening women's participation in peace processes and decision-making; protecting women from sexual and gender-based violence; the promotion of women's role in conflict prevention; and gender-sensitive access to relief in the case of humanitarian crisis.

The NAP is important because it does not simply talk of objectives; rather, it outlines specific outcomes associated with each and then assigns specific executive branch agencies as accountable for the achievement of those outcomes. Thus, the expansion of human rights catalysed by 1325 is taken up formally by the state, and made part of its processes and its self-evaluation. For example, one stipulated outcome is for the Department of Defense to "incorporate modules on protection, rights, and specific needs of women in conflict into training provided to partner militaries and security personnel." Another – tasked to USAID – is to "implement the USAID Counter Trafficking Code of Conduct holding personnel, contractors, sub-contractors, and grantees to the highest ethical standards with regard to trafficking, and to develop a new Trafficking in Persons Policy with a focus on increasing anti-trafficking initiatives in conflict-affected areas." The US NAP specifies approximately 80 such outcomes.

Monitoring US progress on the implementation of its NAP is thus a much more concrete exercise than it otherwise would be. The White House National Security Staff (NSS) established the Women, Peace and Security Interagency Policy Committee (WPS IPC) to oversee and coordinate NAP efforts. Using indicators chosen by the WPS IPC, agencies report their progress to this body, which in turn reports to the National Security Council Deputies Committee, which then produces an annual report that it presents to the president. In addition to internal monitoring, this process allows monitoring by external groups, whether civil society organizations or the UN.

In addition to the NAP, another very important change was in governmental monitoring and evaluation. Nine new gender indicators designed to meet Guidance requirements were added to the Master Indicator List (MIL) used by the government – including the Office of Management and Budget (OMB), Congress, and State itself – to assess State and USAID. For example, the monitoring bureau in State, "F," has begun to formally evaluate whether its programs are producing improvement in indicators such as "the number of local women participating in a substantive role or position in a peace-building process supported with US government assistance" (USAID, 2013, p. 21).

Moreover, it wasn't just about policies, it was also about people. To change state focus, you must change state process – and the key to changing process is to change those at the table. As Donald Steinberg, former deputy director of USAID notes, the first incarnation of the Hillary Doctrine consciously assembled a "dream team." With Hillary Clinton at the helm and Melanne Verveer at OGWI, recruiting the top talent in gender analysis was easy. Steinberg (2013b) comments on the ambience thus created;

> You knew you had a receptive audience for anything you could do [for women]. There was a presupposition that women needed to be at the peace table, that women needed to be consulted. Every Monday there was a staff meeting with the Assistant Secretaries, and we'd go around the table and felt empowered to speak of these things, and if we didn't, we felt we were not discussing the important issues. The atmospherics has changed. [Clinton] approved us doing very expensive programs to address women's empowerment. Her speeches were touted by people in the field and *believed* so you took action based on those principles . . . The practical impact of Hillary Clinton was that gender issues moved up the agenda and you *had* to get to them.

AND YET: THE PITFALLS OF STATE PROMOTION OF RIGHTS EXPANSION

The programs, the benchmarks, the training, the rhetoric, the commitments, the personnel, and the organizational structure were all in place under Secretary Clinton. I would argue these in themselves constituted significant accomplishments in terms of expanding human rights through 1325 translation. And certainly in terms of inputs and indicators such as funds spent on gender programming in diplomacy and development, State under Clinton was light years ahead of any previous American administration.

One of the most important things that the United States did while Hillary Clinton was Secretary of State was to bolster the voice of women worldwide. In pursuing a feminist foreign policy, the United States incurs a special responsibility to speak out for women precisely because it is the current "hegemon," with all the militarism that term implies. Shelby Quast (2013) of Equality Now put it this way: "We need the US to say these things at the highest levels out loud. The US is the biggest funder of the UN; it's one of the P-5. We do have the responsibility to push the 1325's, the 1888's, etc." While the Russians and the Chinese seem indifferent or actually opposed to elements of the Women, Peace, and Security agenda, Anne-Marie Goetz (2013) of UNWomen noted that when Clinton spoke to the Security Council, these other nations were deferential because "they did not want to look churlish. She raised the level of discussion."

Michelle Barsa (2013) of the Institute for Inclusive Security adds, "Women come in to [negotiations] with no power network. Men come in with massive networks – arms, narcotics, etc. The US can become part of the women's power network. We can get women on delegations. Behind the scenes, there can be arm-twisting." Because of its power in the international system, the United States can – when it so chooses – be a great equalizer for women in their dealings with powerful men in their societies.

And yet . . . there were problems. Indeed, given the state's top-down nature, there will probably always be problems with utilizing the state to expand and secure human rights. Understanding the nature and source of the problems faced in this case is instructive, so they are worth categorizing: (1) moral quandaries, (2) state inconsistency, (3) insincere genuflection, or "the pet rock" problem, which ties into (4) the "who's really at the table" problem, and (5) perverse incentives and the for-profit contractor problem.

Moral and Ideological Quandaries

One of the most wrenching aspects of pursuing any rights-based foreign policy is the inevitable moral quandaries faced when states are the implementers of rights expansion. For example, Clinton was castigated for not openly confronting the Saudis on their treatment of women. However, her position was probably justified: those waiting in the wings to overthrow the Saudi royal family would arguably be a hundred times worse for women. Why, then, undermine a regime that has steadily worked to improve women's situation, though perhaps not at the pace desired? And yet, the Saudis finance the spread of Wahhabism throughout the Islamic world, which has a very atavistic stance on women. Islamic cultures that have a more tolerant view of women's rights, such as in Indonesia, have seen that tolerance profoundly undermined by Saudi-financed preachers. This is a real moral quandary.

Adding to the issue is the perception that security and human rights interests contradict each other in this case, and that when push comes to shove, human rights is what should be shoved. The moral quandary also becomes an ideological quandary. As stated in the introduction to this chapter, I do not see security and human rights as being contradictory, but many actors in government clearly do. This perception created tension within the state's bureaucracy on just such issues as the US-Saudi alliance.

Another quandary is that US state support for women in other countries can leave those women much more vulnerable. When the Taliban briefly seized Kunduz in October 2015, they reportedly had lists of women activists and working women who were targeted for summary execution (Hackel, 2015). When I visited UNWomen in spring 2013, I was taken aback to hear that some at that organization felt Hillary Clinton would have "blood on her hands," meaning that Clinton had encouraged Afghan women to stand up, and as they did, they would surely be killed. The Kunduz episode demonstrated these concerns were not fantastical. Even when the threat is not execution, accepting money from – or even just being publically praised by – a foreign state power may open women to charges of treason and subversion. Those working for an FFSP must face these types of moral quandaries.

It must also be mentioned that R2P (responsibility to protect) does not logically entail R2PW (responsibility to protect women). That is, "humanitarian military intervention" by states, if that is not an oxymoron, always produces grave consequences for women. The Libyan R2P action has hurt women, with many women activists assassinated and women sidelined in the current political chaos. The Syrian civil war, which gained assent from the West as an R2P-like process designed to oust a brutal dictator, has destroyed women's prospects in that country. Iraqi women were set back a century in terms of security by the American invasion to neutralize Saddam Hussein. The Arab "Spring" itself, meant to overthrow sclerotic autocrats in favor of nascent democracy, was surely an Arab

Winter for women. The use of military force – whether by the state or by revolutionary groups – typically results in a real regress for women. The R2P versus R2PW contradiction is thus also a persistent quandary for an FFSP.

The state's preferred instruments may undermine its objectives, and certainly did so in the cases of Iraq and Libya, leading to a "two steps back" phenomenon as adumbrated in the chapter by Stohl and Stohl (this volume). Furthermore, state use of force – ostensibly in the name of human rights – may wind up coopting feminist civil society groups in support of such action, for which they will later surely have deep regrets. These are clear pitfalls for utilizing the state in expansion of human rights.

State Inconsistency

The problem of state inconsistency is a chronic one for the United States; it may be less of a problem for other countries, such as Sweden and Norway. By state inconsistency is meant that the state's ability to mount an FFSP may be hampered by its failure to support its own women. The United States, for example, is only one of three countries in the world with no state-mandated paid maternity leave. The United States has refused to ratify the Convention on the Elimination of All Forms of Discrimination Against Women (CEDAW). Infant mortality rates in the United States are the highest in the developed world. It's difficult to put forward an FFSP when one's own house is not in order, even *pace* American exceptionalism.

And yet even countries committed to gender equality may open themselves to charges of state inconsistency. For example, Olsson and Teipar (2009, p. 29) found that the Norwegian Provincial Reconstruction Team in Afghanistan was one of the least attuned to the gender dimensions of its work in that country, despite that fact that Norway was one of the very first countries to adopt a National Action Plan on Women, Peace, and Security:

> The [Norwegian] PRT did not make any distinction between the security situation of men and women. One of the interviewees states that the PRT was probably not very conscious of any such difference in its military analysis and planning, as there had been no discussion of, or reflection on, the fact that women and men may have differing security needs. Accordingly, no gender focus was incorporated into either the planning or implementation of stabilization and security operations. Instead, women were described as being almost invisible . . . No one [interviewed] reported any discussions about the position and role of women in Afghan society that had resulted in a change in the PRT's work.

Sweden itself has come under criticism for the heavy influence of its arms manufacturers on foreign policy issues, as displayed in the diplomatic row with Saudi Arabia in spring 2015 (Carlqvist and Hegedaard, 2015; Sorene, 2015) as well as its neglect of the implications for Swedish women of the recent migration wave from the Middle East and North Africa (Hudson, 2016). State inconsistency, then, can be a problem even for nations with the strongest commitments to gender equality.

Pet Rocks, Who's Really at the Table, and the For-profit Contractor Problem

Let's discuss these final three problems together, for they are integrally interconnected, and highlight the process challenges faced in state promulgation of human rights expansion. The "pet rock" problem alludes to the infamous 2011 statement by an anonymous US senior official quoted in the *Washington Post* about the situation in Afghanistan: "Gender issues are going to have to take a back seat to other priorities. There's no way we can be successful if we maintain every special interest and pet project. All those pet rocks in our rucksack were taking us down" (Chandrasekaran, 2011). Women – fully half the population of Afghanistan – were a *pet rock* to senior US officials in the Obama Administration.

This type of attitude was very prevalent during Clinton's tenure. Genuflection to the idea that women were important in US foreign policy was commonplace, no doubt in part due to Clinton's stature; however, "when push came to shove," commitments to women's empowerment and security evaporated. In 2010, Clinton promised, "We will not abandon you, we will stand with you always . . . it is essential that women's rights and women's opportunities are not sacrificed or trampled on in the reconciliation process" (quoted in *Ms. Magazine*, 2010). But where was the United States when no Afghan women were sent to the sputtering peace talks in 2015 (Hickson, 2016)?

Political will from more than just the Secretary of State is needed, and it is arguable that was absent during the two terms of the Obama Administration. As former Ambassador to Afghanistan Ryan Crocker (2012) put it, "No one is going to be dumb enough to say, 'Oh, forget the women. That's not important.' But the extent to which you have the commitment, you know, to actually get things done, is a little harder to gauge." Grassroots advocate Sanam Anderlini (2013) concurs: "[Clinton's] president [wa]sn't behind her. You're raising expectations of the women, you're making it part of the American agenda, and then your own guys don't follow thorough. They're the first ones to sell you down the river. One US official told me, 'The issue of Afghan women is not our issue.' They didn't take it seriously, they were late to it . . . Don't just talk about it and then behind the scenes let it all go."

There are two tables, then, to be concerned about. Does the United States insist that women be meaningfully represented at any talks to which its nation is a party? And second, does the United States have its own women at the important tables, including the White House Situation Room? In a sense, it's clear that the answer to the second question also helps explain the answer to the first. Unfortunately, in both cases the answer is a disappointing "not so much." As the Afghan and Syrian cases show, the United States does not insist on hard targets for women's participation in delegations from other countries – and as Micah Zenko (2011) indicates, this may be because of the US own lack of women at the table:

> I looked at the gender breakdown at 10 prominent think tanks with a substantial foreign-policy focus. After crunching the numbers, which were culled from their publicly available rosters, I found that women constituted only 21 percent of the policy-related positions (154 of 723) and only 29 percent of the total leadership staff (250 of 874). The Center for Strategic and International Studies and Center for American Progress boasted the highest percentages of women in policy-related roles (28 percent), and the Stimson Center had the highest total percentage of women in all positions (50 percent).
>
> Given this disparity, it should come as no surprise that women are also underrepresented in the halls of power. The Pentagon's "Senior Defense Officials" website lists 129 positions, of which 21 (16 percent) are filled by women. John M. Robinson, the State Department's chief diversity officer, recently wrote that "Twenty-two percent of senior leaders at the Department of State are women." Of the 171 chiefs of mission at U.S. embassies, 50 are women (29 percent). Data for top staffers at the U.S. Agency for International Development (USAID) is less readily available, but a Women in International Security (WIIS) study found that, in 2007 "women only held 29 percent of the Senior Foreign Service positions [at USAID]."

There's a lack of will at the top, lack of will in the bureaucracy, and there's also a lack of will among implementers on the ground. The very nature of state organization may undermine the state's ability to be an effective actor in the expansion of human rights. Once a Hillary Clinton departs from her position as Secretary of State, what happens to political will?

Besides the very highest position, those who are actually there on the ground in lower-ranking positions are also key. And to understand who is there, we have to understand that much of the programming carried out under US government auspices is performed by for-profit contractors, which, while their headquarters may be based in the United States, use a series of sub- and sub-sub-contractors to actually carry out the work. Heads of projects (COPs) may be Americans, but generally the staff may be sub-contractors from countries such as India or Pakistan where the culture of gender equality is underdeveloped – and virtually all of these sub-contractors are male. And if the COP isn't thinking about gender, you can be sure the sub-contractors are not either. One of our interviewees put it this way: "It seems like a lot of COPs are selected because they have grey hair and a penis. It doesn't seem like they are vetted for quality, development skills or a sound development philosophy. I don't think they even think about women enough to have some kind of hard line position against women. They are dealing with their political world, because there are no women, women are kind of a non-entity. It just doesn't even enter their universe" (Government Offices of Sweden, 2015). Or, alternatively, women enter their universe in unintended ways at the ground level: the problem of contractor and sub-contractor purchase of commercial sex has dogged US programming in the field. Even though all federal employees, contractors and even sub-contractors are prohibited from purchasing sex acts 24/7, incidents are all too common. All this adds up to is a deep disconnect between the rhetoric of an FFSP and what actually transpires on the ground where the programming actually does – or does not – make a difference.

CONCLUSION

When the Foreign Minister of Sweden, Margot Wallström, announced in spring of 2015 that Sweden would have a "feminist foreign policy," those who had been involved in the Women, Peace, and Security agenda cheered. In Wallström's own words (Government Offices of Sweden, 2015), "A feminist foreign policy is now being formulated, the purpose of which is to combat discrimination against women, improve conditions for women and contribute to peace and development. Women's participation in decision-making must be strengthened in countries at peace, countries in conflict and countries in which reconstruction is under way. This will also strengthen the sustainability of our societies . . . A feminist foreign policy will be an integral part of activities throughout the Swedish Foreign Service, and aims to strengthen women's rights, improve women's access to resources and increase women's representation."

But as we have seen, the road to an FFSP is a rocky one: the state is a challenging mechanism through which to expand human rights. Not even a society as committed to gender equality as Sweden has been spared difficulty along the way. While the emergence of the concept of an FFSP is in itself a step forward, and while commitments have been created through mechanisms such as National Action Plans, the concept remains underdeveloped. As seen in the US case, lack of political will at both high and low levels, coupled with paralysing moral and ideological quandaries, have greatly hindered effective FFSP development. Even so, all those interested in expanding the human rights agenda will want to track this new state-focused mechanism of feminist foreign/security policy as it evolves in the next decades.

ACKNOWLEDGEMENT

Some material in this chapter is excerpted from Valerie M. Hudson and Patricial Leidl, *The Hillary Doctrine: Sex and American Foreign Policy*, New York: Columbia University Press, 2015, and used with permission.

REFERENCES

Anderlini, Sanam (2013), Telephone interview by Valerie M. Hudson, 21 November.

Barsa, Michelle (2013), Interview by Valerie M. Hudson, 21 May, Washington, DC.

Carlqvist, Ingrid and Lars Hegedaard (2015), "Sweden Surrenders to Saudi Arabia," Gatestone Institute, 9 April, accessed 3 February 2016 at http://www.gatestoneinstitute.org/5503/sweden-saudi-arabia.

Chandrasekaran, Rajiv (2011), "In Afghanistan, U.S. Shifts Strategy on Women's Rights as it Eyes Wider Priorities," *Washington Post*, 5 March, accessed 22 July 2013 at http://articles.washingtonpost.com/2011-03-05/world/35208059_1_afghan-women-afghan-government-land-rights.

Crocker, Ryan (2012), "Women, War and Peace: Lessons from Afghanistan," Council on Foreign Relations, interview with Gayle T. Lemmon 17 December, accessed 15 September 2013 at http://www.cfr.org/afghanistan/women-war-peace-lessons-afghanistan/p29684.

Feminist Wire Newsbriefs (2010), "Clinton Pledges to Not Abandon Afghan Women," *Ms. Magazine*, 14 May, accessed 29 October 2013 at http://www.msmagazine.com/news/uswirestory.asp?id=12399.

Ferraro, Geraldine (1993), "Human Rights for Women," *New York Times*, 10 June, accessed 15 September 2013 at http://www.nytimes.com/1993/06/10/opinion/human-rights-for-women.html.

Garner, Karen (2013), *Gender & Foreign Policy*, Colorado: First Forum Press.

Goetz, Anne Marie (2013), Interview by Valerie M. Hudson, 14 May, New York City.

Government Offices of Sweden (2015), *Statement of Foreign Policy 2015*, 11 February, accessed 3 February 2016 at http://www.government.se/government-policy/feminist-foreign-policy/.

Grant, Kate (2013), "20 Minutes that Changed the World: Hillary Clinton in Beijing," *Huffington Post*, 4 February, accessed 15 September 2013 at http://www.huffingtonpost.com/kate-grant/hillary-clinton_b_2603159.html.

Hackel, Joyce (2015), "The Taliban Had a Hit List of Working Women

When They Took Over Kunduz," Public Radio International, 15 October, accessed 3 February 2016 at http://www.pri.org/stories/2015-10-15/taliban-had-hit-list-working-women-when-they-took-over-kunduz.

Hickson, Ally (2016), "Why are Women Missing From These Crucial Talks?," Refinery29, 11 January, accessed 3 February 2016 at http://www.refinery29.com/2016/01/100770/afghanistan-peace-talks-women?utm_campaign=naytev&utm_content=569026f9e4b0db19b06119ae.

Hudson, Valerie M. (2016), "Abnorma Antalet Unga Män Ett Problem For Sverige," *Göteborgs-Posten*, 19 January, accessed 3 February 2016 at http://m.gp.se/nyheter/debatt/1.2961141-abnorma-antalet-unga-man-ett-problem-for-sverige?utm_source=dagenssamhalle.se&utm_medium=referral&utm_campaign=redirect.

J. (2013), Interview conducted in confidentiality by Valerie M. Hudson, Summer, Washington, DC.

Klein, Jen (2013), Interview by Valerie M. Hudson, 20 May, Washington, DC.

Meger, Sara (2012), "The Problematic Evolution of UN Resolutions on Women, Peace and Security," *E-International Relations*, 1 November, accessed 15 September 2013 at http://www.e-ir.info/2012/11/01/the-problematic-evolution-of-un-resolutions-on-women-peace-and-security/.

Olsson, Louise and Johen Teipar (eds) (2009), *Operational Effectiveness and UN Resolution 1325 – Practices and Lessons from Afghanistan*, May, Stockholm FOI, Report part of the project NATO in Afghanistan: Resolution 1325 as a Tool for Enhanced Effectiveness, accessed 14 November 2013 at http://www.peacewomen.org/portal_resources_resource.php?id=87.

Quast, Shelby (2013), Interview with Valerie M. Hudson, 21 May, Washington, DC.

Riding, Alan (1993), "Rights Forum Ends in Call for a Greater Role by U.N.," *New York Times*, 26 June, accessed 15 September 2013 at http://www.nytimes.com/1993/06/26/world/rights-forum-ends-in-call-for-a-greater role-by-un.html.

Sorene, Paul (2015), "Je Suis Margot Wallström: the Silence Over Saudi Arabia's Hatred of Women and Free Speech is Deafening," *Anorak*, 30 September, accessed 3 February 2016 at http://www.anorak.co.uk/424152/politicians/je-suis-margot-wallstrom-the-silence-over-saudi-arabias-hatred-of-women-and-free-speech-is-deafening.html/.

Steinberg, Donald (2013a), Telephone interview by Valerie M. Hudson, 12 July.

Steinberg, Donald (2013b), "USAID's Steinberg on Empowering Women Globally," Speech at USAID, 28 January, Washington, DC, accessed 15 September 2013 at http://iipdigital.usembassy.gov/st/english/texttrans/2013/01/20130123141334.html#ixzz2jDpF0pnj.

United Nations DPKO/DFS (2014), *Gender Forward Looking Strategy 2014–2018*, accessed 3 February 2016 at http://www.un.org/en/peacekeeping/documents/DPKO-DFS-Gender-Strategy.pdf.

United Nations Security Council (2000), *Resolution 1325*, 31 October, accessed 15 September 2013 at http://daccess-dds-ny.un.org/doc/UNDOC/GEN/N00/720/18/PDF/N0072018.pdf.

UNWomen (2015), *Preventing Conflict Transforming Justice Securing the Peace: A Global Study on the Implementation of United Nations Security Council Resolution 1325*, accessed 3 February 2016 at http://wps.unwomen.org/~/media/files/un%20women/wps/highlights/unw-global-study-1325-2015.pdf.

US Agency for International Development (2013), *Integrating Gender Equality and Female Empowerment in USAID's Program Cycle*, July, Washington, DC, accessed 15 September 2013 at http://www.usaid.gov/sites/default/files/documents/1870/205.pdf.

US Department of State (2010), *The First Quadrennial Diplomacy and Development Review*, accessed 15 September 2013 at http://www.state.gov/documents/organization/153108.pdf.

US Department of State Office of Global Women's Issues (2012), *Fact Sheet: Promoting Gender Equality to Achieve Our National Security and Foreign Policy Objectives*, 27 March, accessed 15 September 2013 at http://www.state.gov/s/gwi/rls/other/2012/187001.htm.

Wikipedia, s.v. (2013), "Vienna Declaration and Programme of Action," last modified 2 September 2013, accessed at http://en.wikipedia.org/wiki/Vienna_Declaration_and_Programme_of_Action.

Zenko, Micah (2011), "City of Men," *Foreign Policy*, 14 July, accessed 16 November 2013 at http://www.foreignpolicy.com/articles/2011/07/14/city_of_men.

PART V

Expanding responsibilities

11. Janus-faced: rebel groups and human rights responsibility*

Hyeran Jo and Joshua Alley

Rebel groups are now significant players in world politics. Since 1945, about 500 rebel groups in various parts of the world have fought national governments. These wars have produced tremendous human suffering. Another parallel trend in world politics is "expanding" human rights, as the theme of this edited volume suggests. What is the link between these two parallel trends? Do rebel groups understand and care about human rights? Is the norm of human rights "expanding" to rebel groups as well?

At face value, rebel groups are stereotyped as perpetrators of human rights abuse. Rebel groups often evoke images of violence against the central notions of human dignity via summary killing, torture, slavery, and other gross human rights violations. In this regard, we are reminded of amputations of children by the Revolutionary United Front in Sierra Leone (Scheffer, 2013) or modern-day slavery by the Islamic State in Syria.[1] Protection and preservation of human rights seems to be excluded from the dictionary of rebels, as these incidents show.

While some rebel groups are well-known violators of human rights, it is less well known that some strive to respect human rights, or at least claim to do so. Rebel groups are political military organizations that fight against national governments for their own human rights – rights to political, social, economic, or religious freedom. During that armed struggle, to defeat government forces that often overmatch them, rebel groups may violate the rights of other people, such as ordinary civilians or government

* Part of Hyeran Jo's research effort was supported by the National Science Foundation (SES No. 1260218). The views of this chapter, however, are the authors only. The authors thank Yvette Isidori, Grant Schauer, and Haley Wilburn for research assistance. And special thanks to Soren Jordan for his help on the text analysis.

[1] UN HRC report of the independent international commission of inquiry on the Syrian Arab Republic, November 2011–February 2012. Also see Weiss and Hassan (2015).

sympathizers. But recently, as this chapter will demonstrate, rebels claim to accept the central tenets of human rights or abide by international humanitarian rules. Some even comply with international humanitarian rules in waging their armed struggles against the government (Jo, 2015).

The puzzle is why some rebel groups care about human rights at all. We argue in this chapter that some rebel groups have inherent interests to care about human rights and are capable of expressing their intent. In support for our argument, we show that some rebel groups have a certain level of understanding of human rights by unearthing the patterns of human rights/humanitarian commitments in the Rebel Groups and International Law (RGIL) database.[2] We demonstrate that willing and capable rebel groups – with political autonomy aims, with military and internal control capabilities – subscribe to human rights and humanitarian norms. Rebel groups that seek autonomy are more willing to subscribe to the norm of human rights because they have deep roots with local civilians and reach out to international audiences with the aim of gaining political independence. This does not necessarily mean that this class of autonomy-seeking rebel groups is rights-seeking, but they are more susceptible to human rights discourse. Capability is also important as rebel groups have to get the word out to express their human rights intentions. The empirical evidence will show rebel groups expanding human rights based on these two hypotheses.

The inquiry into rebel groups and human rights matters for several reasons. The most obvious is for human security reasons. If rebel groups show respect for human rights, that will benefit the population in conflict-ridden areas. Second, from a scholarly perspective, the connection between rebel groups and human rights will aid our understanding of how norms develop over time. We show how human rights norms expand in the case of rebel groups – where we least expect the notions of human rights to operate – given the criminality of many rebel groups.

Rebel groups' adoption of human rights illustrates the themes of this edited volume – expanding mobilization, claims/frames, institutions, and responsibilities. Rebel groups' claims for rights are expanding from national liberation movements in the 1970s to civilian protection language in recent times. Rebel groups framed the narratives such that they can declare goals of achieving their own civil and political rights and more recently, framing their activities as consistent with human rights standards. Rebel groups themselves are mobilizers for human rights, and this chapter will analyse the conditions for such mobilization. Specifically,

2 The database is featured at http://hyeranjo.wix.com/compliantrebels.

some rebel groups socialize with international organizations and conduct their own diplomacy vis-à-vis international actors during the mobilization process. Although rebel groups operate in a less institutional environment compared to state actors, they create some mechanisms for fulfillment of human rights – for example, internal codes of conduct.

With those themes against the backdrop, the chapter proceeds as follows. We first define the key terms – "rebel groups" and "human rights" and then set the background for understanding the status of legal and political norms regarding rebel groups. We next propose our argument that some rebel groups *do* know human rights and *do* speak human rights. We present evidence that some rebel groups express "their" understanding of human rights vis-à-vis multiple audiences and potential constituencies – civilians, governments, and international actors. Although rebel groups' understandings about human rights might be slightly different from general understanding of human rights, we show that contemporary rebel groups *are* within the bounds of the human rights regime. We conclude with some implications for scholarship and policy.

BACKGROUND

"Rebel groups" are military organizations that fight against national governments with political aims. This definition excludes some sets of armed groups: (1) domestic terrorist groups that do not engage in military battles; (2) criminal organizations that focus on illicit economic activities without political goals; and (3) warlords without a certain level of organization. By nature, rebel groups will engage in actions that may violate fundamental human rights such as "right to life" in their armed struggles against existing political orders. This will create a theoretical puzzle as to why rebel groups would care about human rights at all.

Also note that we are analysing rebel "groups." The unit of analysis at the group level means that the spread and acceptance of norms might not be uniform throughout the ranks within a rebel organization. It is plausible to think that rank-and-file rebel soldiers might have different conceptions of human rights from their leadership. But our analysis will primarily focus on what is represented at the group level, with empirical referents such as documents released by rebel leadership (for example, military commanders or rebel spokesman).

"Human rights" are fundamental commitments to preserve dignity for all persons. Examples include political rights, economic rights, social and cultural rights (Alston and Goodman, 2013). The question of whose human rights is important for the purpose of the subsequent discussion related to rebel groups. Rebel groups might have different understandings of their human rights relative to those of others. Sometimes, rebel groups create a negative-sum game where the advancement of rebel groups' own human rights hurt other societal and political actors' human rights, as the parameters of human dignity are sharply curtailed in wartime.

The term "human rights" exhibited different meanings to rebel groups at different times. To rebel groups in the 1970s and 1980s, "human rights" meant specific civil and political rights. During the negotiation of the Additional Protocol I to the Geneva Conventions, a dozen liberation movements participated as observers (with "voice but no vote") (Provost, 2012). To those liberation movements, human rights meant self-determination and freedom of political action outside colonial-era structures. Now, the meaning of human rights is diverse across many rebel groups, as well as expansive, partly due to the broad normative development of human rights. To contemporary rebel groups, human rights include the right to life of civilians, political rights and freedom of actions, as well as economic and social rights, women's rights, and children's rights.[3] Rebel groups nowadays not only engage in advocacy of their political rights but also promote economic and social rights in the territory they govern (Arjona et al., 2015). Recent research finds that rebel groups that value gender equality are likely to have female combatants in their ranks (Thomas and Wood, 2015). The trend from the 1970s on shows that human rights are expanding from primarily rebels' "own" political rights (1970s) to civilians and "others" civil, political, economic, and cultural rights (2010s).

Depending on the type of human rights, rebel groups have taken different roles. For political and civil rights, rebel groups are advocates. They challenge governments ostensibly to improve their political and civil rights. Rebel groups often advocate minority rights (against discrimination) and recently address the questions of women's and children's rights. They also oppose torture and repression by the state, and often engage in wars of words with the government. When they are engaged in armed conflicts, they often violate the norms of human rights through the acts of killing, pillaging, rape, and so on to advance their own human rights. This advocate-violator Janus-face dimension of rebel groups is the starting point of our analysis.

The normative environment surrounding rebel groups and human rights is growing and expanding. Traditionally, human rights have been the obligations of states – as exemplified in the key legal documents such

---

[3] The Moro Islamic Liberation Front (MILF), for example, had announced the straight-18 norm will be observed within their ranks.

as the International Covenant on Civil and Political Rights (ICCPR) or International Covenant on Economic, Social, and Cultural Rights (ICESCR). Humanitarian rules are pertinent to the discussion of rebel groups and human rights.[4] Rebel groups operate during peacetime and armed conflicts, which put them in the normative environments governed by international humanitarian law (IHL) as well as international human rights law (IHRL). Although IHRL is usually applicable during peacetime and IHL during wartime, substantial overlap exists (Andreopoulos, 2006). The two normative fields are merging, especially for the regions of protracted low-level armed conflicts. The foundational notions of respect for life and human dignity are at the center of IHRL and IHL. For example, the right to life is the first article in ICCPR and civilian protection is embodied in the principle of distinction between combatants and non-combatants in IHL.

Despite the growth, the normative environment is uncertain. International law presents some prescriptions and proscriptions for rebel groups with respect to wartime behavior and post-conflict behaviors. Wartime behaviors are regulated by international humanitarian law (commonly known as the laws of war); and post-conflict conditions stipulate some boundaries, usually via peace agreements. Within the bounds of human rights norms, rebels' human rights obligations are not certain either, let alone their rights (Clapham, 2006). This situation is unlike states, the traditional rights-bears of human rights obligations.[5] Unless rebels acquire substantial governance functions and territorial control, they do not assume as many human rights obligations as states do.[6]

Despite this uncertainty, rebel groups do have legal responsibilities under international law. Most of them are under international humanitarian law – including respect for civilian life, humane treatment of prisoners, and protection of humanitarian workers. The criminal law regime established the International Criminal Court based on the Rome Statute. Consequently, the reach of criminal responsibility to rebel groups in the areas of crimes against humanity, war crimes, and genocide appears to be weak, but present (Jo and Simmons, 2016). Rebel groups are part of the pattern in

[4] In particular, Geneva Convention Common Article 3 as well as Additional Protocols.

[5] The United States and European Union (EU) opposed the language "gross violation of human rights perpetrated by terrorist groups" in the UN resolution because they did not want to equate terrorists with states (Alston and Goodman, 2013, p. 1503).

[6] See the discussion in Roberts and Sivakumaran (2012, pp. 87–100). Also see Rodenhäuser (2015) for the specific situation in Syria.

"justice cascade" (Sikkink, 2011) but the regime is in its infancy. Local norms also matter just as much as international laws. The Taliban's Code of Conduct (*Layeha*), for instance, lays out rules for local courts (Johnson and DuPee, 2012; Nagamine, 2015), catering to the right to justice.

Currently, rebels are part of the expanding human rights regime. About 50 rebel groups have signed the Deed of Commitment to ban the use of anti-personnel mines, with the Geneva Call organization. A dozen rebel groups have signed United Nations (UN) action plans to stop the use of child soldiers. Various non-governmental organizations (NGOs) have engaged local communities and rebel soldiers to reduce the incidences of sexual violence in the Democratic Republic of Congo (Lake, 2014). Many rebel groups now participate in peace negotiations that include human rights clauses (Bell, 2000; Nilsson, 2012). Some rebel group leadership follow the Facebook page of the UN Human Rights Committee. Recognition of human rights and partnership with intergovernmental organizations (IGOs) or NGOs are all signs of "expanding" human rights on the part of rebel groups.

A THEORY OF REBELS' HUMAN RIGHTS COMMITMENT

The core puzzle of this chapter concerns why rebel groups commit to human rights. Our explanation hinges on the credible commitment mechanism (North, 1993) – how rebel groups can commit credibly facing their key audiences. The explanation starts with the assumption that rebel groups are political organizations that communicate with political audiences and constituencies, both domestic and international. Domestic audiences include the civilian population and the national government forces. International audiences include external supporters (state sponsors or private charities), and international/non-governmental organizations. Rebels must address or satisfy each of these audiences to some degree.

In considering these political audiences and thinking about generating political messages, rebel groups will realize that human rights talk can be cheap – expressions of commitment have few costs given a paucity of enforcement mechanisms. The International Criminal Court has its reach but in a limited manner (Jo and Simmons, 2016). Also, rebel commitments are not legally binding in a strict sense. Rebel expressions or bilateral agreements are not binding documents and often are regarded as expressions of rebel policy at best. The violations of those commitments are rarely monitored, enforced, or punished. On the other hand, these public relations exercises can be potentially rewarding to rebels themselves, debasing the government and bolstering rebels' political agenda. If properly framed, these rebel commitments can attract human rights conscious audiences that can provide some support, if not recognition. Thus, human rights talk can enhance rebels' image and political legitimacy with liberal audiences. Violations, especially by groups that pledged to support human rights, might have the opposite impact and reduce liberal support.

Given these benefits and costs of human rights talk, the key question is how some motivated rebel groups can credibly commit without the institutional devices that national governments have at their disposal, such as ratification, laws, and enforcement power. Without those institutional mechanisms for tying hands, rebel groups commit when they are willing and when they are able to do so.

First, willingness matters. Rebel groups that seek political autonomy may commit to human rights in the hope that messages advance their political agenda. Recent studies show rebel diplomacy is prominent in the case of secessionist groups, and the promotion of human rights can be part of these diplomatic efforts (Coggins, 2014; Fazal, 2016; Huang, 2016).

Second, capacity matters in producing expressions of human rights. Rebel groups that have strong command and control, for example, can credibly commit because they can better signal that orders higher up would be respected throughout the organization. Also, rebel groups with strong military capability are likely to commit to human rights, given their associated public relations capabilities and fighting capacity. Although the talk can be cheap and not followed through later on, militarily strong groups also have strong motivations to debase governments' legitimacy and might want to commit. Moreover, militarily strong groups may feel less pressure to use whatever tactics necessary to achieve victory.

Rebels' social environment is also important. One of the ways to maintain contact with the local population is to have a political wing of some kind. Rebel political wings are associated with occasional elections, local bureaus to advance their political goals, and organized representatives to connect to the local population. Also, one of the interactions with international organizations or NGOs can be to receive sponsorship from states with a well-developed civil society. If a rebel group is sponsored by or gets funds from such states, it is likely that civic organizations are going to interact with rebel groups, which might increase the chance that rebel groups express their commitments to human rights. We call these conjectures related to rebel network structures the "social rebel hypothesis" (Staniland, 2014). Social rebels are the ones that build special relationships with their domestic constituencies via political wings; they are the ones that interact with human rights actors on the international level. The networks built by rebel groups can provide groups with incentives to respect human rights.

Willingness, capability, and social environment comprise a theory of "credible commitment in an institution-light environment." Rebel groups can craft their own commitment devices, internally and externally. The internal device includes streamlining as well as a command and control structure. The external device includes garnering help and assistance from local population or human rights/humanitarian international organizations or NGOs.

Collecting the above considerations for rebels' willingness, capability, and social environment, we present three empirically testable hypotheses with regard to rebel groups and human rights.

Willingness Hypothesis:

H1: Rebel groups with autonomy aims are more likely to commit to human rights than those without autonomy aims.

Capability Hypotheses:

H2: Rebel groups with strong command and control are more likely to commit to human rights than those with weak command and control.

H3: Rebel groups with strong military capabilities are more likely to commit to human rights than those with weaker capabilities.

Social Rebel Hypotheses:

H4: Rebel groups with political wings are more likely to commit to human rights than those without political wings.

H5: Rebel groups with sponsorship from states with civil society are more likely to commit to human rights than those without such sponsorship.

Before we move on to the statistical analysis, the case of the Moro Islamic Liberation Front (MILF) helps explain these hypotheses (Jo, 2015). The MILF is a rebel group that has been seeking autonomy of the Mindanao region in the southern Philippines with a secular Islamic agenda. The group has committed to various human rights related documents concerning the ban on anti-personnel mines and the ban on child soldiering. The group subsequently went through the revision of its internal code of conduct to streamline their policies to reflect these changes. Although these higher-order messages did not perfectly trickle down to lower-ranking cadres, the rebel group behaved significantly less violently over time. The main driver of these changes was the political committee of the MILF and its deep ties with the local population. Such connections provided incentives for the group to be more appealing to civilians during intense political and military competition with the government over three decades of struggle.

The MILF's human rights talk and its change in behavior stand in sharp relief to those of Abu Sayyaf, the more extremist spin-off from the MILF. That group was designated as a terrorist organization by the Philippines government and the US State Department. We do not find human rights related commitments by this group. The statistical test that follows examines whether the behavior of the MILF is common across a larger sample of rebel groups.

STATISTICAL ANALYSIS

The goal of this section is to present a test of our theory of rebel group human rights commitment. In order to do so, we first present the measurement of our key variables, report the patterns of Rebel Commitment Database, and present logit analysis of rebel commitment. Our primary focus will be to test the conditions under which rebel groups commit to human rights.

Data and Variables

The unit of analysis is the rebel-year. The dataset records 266 rebel groups with average longevity of three years for each group. The treatment of rebel-year means we count the same groups several times, but we think this is reflective of the amount of commitment. We try to deal with dependencies by employing robust standard errors in the logit analysis.

We measure our dependent variable of "rebel human rights commitment" as a binary outcome, with 0 indicating no commitment on an issue in a given year, and 1 indicating some commitment. The source is the TheirWords project conducted by the Geneva Call, a NGO that focuses on humanitarian issues.[7] TheirWords is a directory of armed non-state actor humanitarian commitments, but the database also includes documents created by rebel groups related to general human rights under

[7] http://theirwords.org/. We note some selectivity in this list. Many groups are heavily drawn from the interactions with the Geneva Call. Some weak groups might not be represented in this list, so we might not have the "voice" of the weak and small rebel groups.

Geneva Call's expansive definition of humanitarian commitments. Most documents are unilateral declarations, bilateral agreements with international organizations or NGOs, or peace agreements with governments that contain human rights related clauses.

In our subsequent analysis, the "human rights" category includes many subjects related to political, social, and economic rights. Political rights include freedom to organize, freedom of expression, freedom of assembly, free and fair elections, right to vote, many of which are found in the ICCPR. As most rebel groups fight for political rights, this emphasis is unsurprising. Ethnic and religious minorities are especially well represented in this category. Human rights against repression are also expressed. The mentions of personal liberty, prohibition on slavery, torture or cruel, inhumane or degrading treatment appear in this human rights category. Other social rights include freedom of movement, rights of children, and equal rights of men and women.

We want to note several things about the measurement of our dependent variable. First, it is perfectly feasible that some rebel groups might not express their views via these documents. Thus, the measure purports to be comprehensive but might miss some human rights commitments by obscure groups. Second, we also want to note that the legal force of these general human rights commitments is disputed (Roberts and Sivakumaran, 2012). Some would even argue whether some documents are really commitments or not, since there is no binding force on rebel groups. We take the position that these are "expressions" of commitment, which are not analogous to treaty commitments of states.

In Table 11.1, we list additional types of rebel documents, such as the ones that deal with the issue of child protection, anti-personnel mines, civilian protection, child soldiers, and peace agreements. The table is provided to show how they compare to general human rights related documents we coded and analysed in this chapter. Some issue areas such as child protection or civilian protection could be considered as broadly human rights issues but we leave those specific areas to future research.

Figure 11.1 tracks the incidence of the three most common human rights/humanitarian commitments by rebels. Broad human rights commitments occur in small numbers prior to the 1990s. The occurrence of these commitments becomes substantial after 1990. Human rights commitments have varied heavily from year to year, which raises the question of what explains the variation.

Whose human rights? Most of the human rights language found here concerns rebels' own political, civil, economic, and social rights. Political and civil rights include rights to vote and organize; economic and social rights involve the division of natural resources or cultural rights. What human

Table 11.1 Composition of Rebel Commitment Database

Issue Area	Number of Documents	Example
Human Rights	208	2011: ELN "Comunicado Público: Desmentido del Frente de Guerra Nororiental"
Anti-Personnel Mines	91	2005: POLISARIO "Deed of Commitment under Geneva Call"
Child Protection	46	1997: Pridnestrovian Moldavian Republic (PMR) "Law on the Rights of the Child"
Civilian Protection	77	1982: National Resistance Army (Uganda) "Code of Conduct"
Peace Agreement	113	2011: Karen National Union "KNU to Observe One-Day Ceasefire on International Day of Peace"
Action Plan to Ban Child Soldiering	39	2006: MILF "Order Promulgating a Code of Conduct Regulating the Affairs of the Bangsamoro Islamic Armed Forces, Prescribing its Powers, Duties and Functions and Other Related Purposes"
	Total 574	

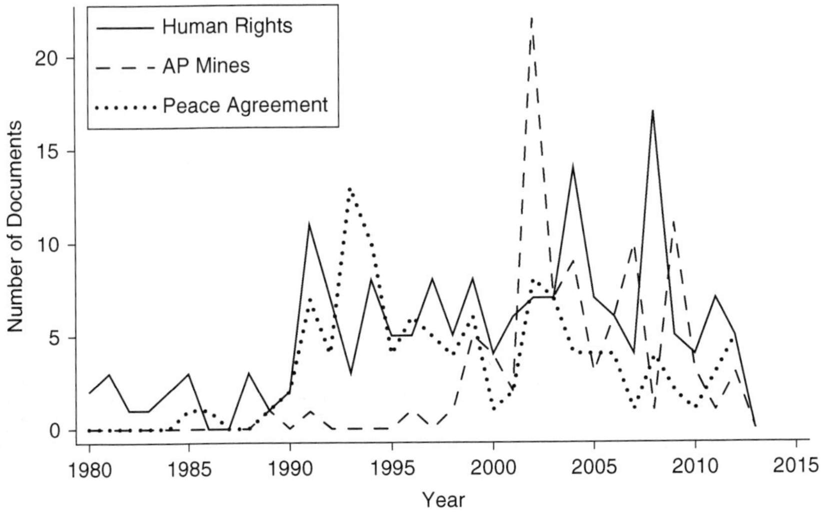

Figure 11.1 Issue commitments over time

Figure 11.2 Human rights language of rebel groups

rights? The right to life and self-determination are often expressed. This is not surprising, because rebellion usually starts with a sense of political exclusion.

We further explore these issues by drawing up a word cloud from the text data. Figure 11.2 presents the word cloud of human rights talk by rebel groups. We collected the text data of human rights related documents issued by rebel groups and selected frequently used words to make the word cloud. We want to emphasize human rights related words, from general to specific.[8] General words include "human," "right," or "respect." Specific words include those related to political rights ("elect," "govern"), economic rights ("development"), as well as conflict related words ("war," "militaries," "force," "peace"). The word cloud demonstrates that rebels also do rights talk. There is also a time trend: rebel groups talk a lot about their own political rights, civil and political, and now we see the words related to civilian protection and socio-economic rights (Simmons and Jo, 2016).

Now we turn to a discussion on the measurement of the independent variables. *Autonomy Aim* is the binary variable for secessionist groups

---

[8] Note that some words are "stemmed" in making the word cloud. For example, "forc" is a stem word for "force" or "forces."

or groups that seek political autonomy. Secessionist groups usually seek territorial as well as political autonomy, but there are other groups that seek political autonomy, shy of territorial ambitions.[9] This measure is the recoded version of conflict type in the Non-State Actor dataset. *Strength of Central Command and Control* is the variable that measures the capacity of a rebel group, as well as *Rebel Strength* variable. Both are from the Non-State Actor dataset. *Strength of Central Command and Control* is an ordinal variable ranging from low (1), medium (2), to high (3). *Rebel Strength* is an ordinal variable that measures the rebel military strength relative to the opposing government, with five scales, from much weaker (1), weaker (2), parity (3), stronger (4), and much stronger (5). *Rebel Political Wing* is the degree of links to political wing of a rebel group in four levels, no (1), alleged link (2), acknowledged link (3), and explicit link (4). *Human Rights Sponsorship* measures the number of human rights groups in the rebel group's state sponsor and ranges from 0 to 71.[10]

Statistical Analysis of Rebel Commitment

Table 11.2 presents the results from a multivariate logit analysis of human rights commitments. The dependent variable is whether a rebel group expressed their human rights intent in a document, as described in the previous section. The first three models test the hypotheses outlined in the theory section sequentially.

Model 1 tests whether willingness of a rebel group, in the form of autonomy aim, affects the commitment to human rights. We see support for the hypothesis: rebel groups with autonomy aims are more likely to commit to human rights in some form. These may be advocating for their own human rights or for other civilian rights as they are deeply rooted in the social environment in their respective regions.

Model 2 tests whether rebel capability, in the form of command and control or military strength, affects the commitment to human rights. The capability hypothesis also garners some empirical support. Capable rebels – with strong central command and control and/or with military strength – are more likely to commit. We interpret this as evidence that rebels with internal controls are more likely to be able to credibly

[9] MILF is one example. The group wanted to get political autonomy, disenchanted by the previous MNLF's cooptation with the government on the autonomous region.

[10] More details on these variables can be found in Jo (2015) and Cunningham and Lemke (2014).

Table 11.2 Logit models of rebel group commitment to human rights

	Model 1 Willingness Hypothesis	Model 2 Capability Hypothesis	Model 3 Social Rebel Hypothesis	Model 4 Additional Factors
Autonomy Aim	0.246**			0.735***
	(0.122)			(0.160)
Command and Control		0.212**		0.286**
		(0.108)		(0.131)
Military Strength		0.569***		0.939***
		(0.102)		(0.149)
Rebel Political Wing			−0.051	−0.203***
			(0.049)	(0.063)
Human Rights Sponsorship			−0.002	−0.018
			(0.011)	(0.012)
Terrorist Organization				1.491***
				(0.252)
Territorial Control				0.632***
				(0.186)
Post-9/11				0.165
				(0.159)
Observations	1165	1066	907	571

Note: Robust standard errors in parentheses. *** $p < 0.01$, ** $p < 0.05$, * $p < 0.1$; constants suppressed to save space.

commit; also, that military strength is translated into public relations capability, including commitment to human rights.

Model 3 looks at the social rebel hypothesis – rebel groups' links with human rights based state sponsors or the presence of rebel political wings – influence their human rights commitment behaviors. There is no support for this hypothesis. There does not seem to be a relationship between increasing links to rebel political wings and commitment to human rights.

Model 4 tests out additional factors that might explain rebel commitment. September 11th was the watershed event in responses to terrorism. Since some rebel groups are classified as terrorist organizations, the year 2001 might be thought as an inflection point for rebel groups' human rights commitment, as rebels sought to avoid the ire of the United States by professing respect for human rights. We test this fulcrum point idea with a dummy variable that marks pre and post-9/11,

Table 11.3 Predicted probabilities for rebel commitment to human rights

Scenario 1	Scenario 2	Difference
Without autonomy aim 0.3260 [0.2795, 0.3725]	With autonomy aim 0.4829 [0.4317, 0.5340]	16%
Command and control, low strength 0.3032 [0.2369, 0.3695]	Command and control, high strength 0.4916 [0.4223, 0.5608]	19%
Much weaker rebel groups 0.3091 [0.2654, 0.3529]	Much stronger rebel groups 0.8361 [0.7148, 0.9574]	53%

as well as a binary variable that denotes a rebel terrorist organization.[11] There is no specific significance to the proposition, although surprisingly, terrorist rebels are more likely to engage in human rights talk than non-terrorist rebel groups. Also, rebel groups that control territory are more likely to commit to human rights.[12] This finding is consistent with our theoretical claim that the close relationship with civilians that comes with territorial control may be a contributing factor to rebel commitment.

Predicted probabilities of various scenarios can give more context to the interpretation of the results.[13] The estimation results are reported in Table 11.3. Rebel groups with the aim of autonomy are 16 percent more likely to make human rights commitments. Those rebels with strong command and control capabilities are 19 percent more likely to commit to human rights related documents. Lastly, rebel groups that are much stronger than the state are 53 percent more likely than much weaker rebels to undertake a commitment to human rights. The numbers indicate further support for our willingness and capability hypotheses.

11 This variable follows the classification of conflict types in Cunningham and Lemke (2014). Of course, the designation of terrorist groups is a controversial one, as various classifications exist (for example, see Jones and Libicki, 2008 as well as the list of Foreign Terrorist Organization by the US State Department).

12 Rebel territorial control is a binary variable in Cunningham and Lemke (2014).

13 All the predicted probabilities were calculated based on Model 4, using – prvalue-command from Long's SPost suite in STATA.

FINDINGS AND IMPLICATIONS

Conventional wisdom is that rebel groups are human rights violators. We find that the picture is more nuanced and that rebel groups are Janus-faced on the issue of human rights. They are human rights advocates as well as perpetrators of human rights violations. Our research demonstrates that many rebel groups are strong advocates of their own human rights, and in some cases, rebel groups care about the general population's human rights.

The phenomenon of expanding human rights in the case of rebel groups has several implications. Our work shows that rebel groups do not live outside the realm of human rights politics. They can no longer ignore expanding human rights norms. But the incentive to violate human rights is generally strong in fighting against governments. But we also have to note that some rebel groups are willing to express their human rights credentials and are capable of doing so.

Next, the question is "how to bind the players [rebel groups] to agreements across space and time" (North, 1993, p. 11). We focused on the rebel groups' understanding and expression of human rights. But the natural next step question is whether rebel groups follow through their promises and expressive signals. Are the signals ultimately credible and effective to advance human rights? How different are rebel behaviors across issue areas, such as in the case of anti-personnel mines issue, the issue of sexual violence, or the problem of child soldiering? While some case studies suggest a positive trend, more systematic future research is needed to tackle these important questions that turn rights into responsibilities.

REFERENCES

Alston, Philip and Ryan Goodman (2013), *International Human Rights*, New York: Oxford University Press.

Andreopoulos, George (2006), "On the Accountability of Non-state Armed Groups," in Zehra F. Kabasakal Arat, George Andreopoulos, and Peter Juviler (eds), *Non-state Actors in the Human Rights Universe*, New York: Kumarian Press, pp. 141–63.

Arjona, Ana, Nelson Kasfir, and Zachariah Mampilly (eds) (2015), *Rebel Governance in Civil War*. New York: Cambridge University Press.

Bell, Christine (2000), *Peace Agreements and Human Rights*, New York: Oxford University Press.

Clapham, A. (2006), "Human Rights Obligations of Non-state Actors in Conflict Situations," *International Review of the Red Cross*, **88**(863), 491–523.

Coggins, Bridget (2014), *Power Politics and State Formation in the*

Twentieth Century: The Dynamics of Recognition, New York: Cambridge University Press.

Cunningham, D.E. and D. Lemke (2014), "Beyond Civil War: A Quantitative Examination of Causes of Violence within Countries," *Civil Wars*, **16**(3), 328–45.

Fazal, T. (2016), "Rebellion, War Aims, and the Laws of War," *Dædalus*, forthcoming.

Gal-Or, Naomi, Cedric Ryngaert, and Math Noortmann (eds) (2015), *Responsibilities of the Non-state Actor in Armed Conflict and the Market Place*, Boston, MA: Brill Nijhoff.

Huang, R. (2016), "Rebel Diplomacy in Civil War," *International Security*, **40**(4), 89–126.

Jo, Hyeran (2015), *Compliant Rebels: Rebel Groups and International Law in World Politics*, Cambridge: Cambridge University Press.

Jo, H. and B. Simmons (2016), "Can the International Criminal Court Deter Atrocity?," *International Organization*, **40**(3), 443–75.

Johnson, T. and M. DuPee (2012), "Analyzing the New Taliban Code of Conduct (Layeha): An Assessment of Changing Perspectives and Strategies of the Afghan Taliban," *Central Asian Survey*, **31**(1), 77–91.

Jones, Seth and Martin Libicki (2008), "How Terrorist Groups End," Rand Corporation.

Lake, M. (2014), "Organizing Hypocrisy: Providing Legal Accountability for Human Rights Violations in Areas of Limited Statehood," *International Studies Quarterly*, **58**(3), 515–26.

Nagamine, Yoshinobu (2015), *The Legitimization Strategy of the Taliban's Code of Conduct. Through the One-way Mirror*, New York: Palgrave Macmillan.

Nilsson, D. (2012), "Anchoring the Peace: Civil Society Actors in Peace Accords and Durable Peace," *International Interactions*, **38**(2), 243–66.

North, D. (1993), "Institutions and Credible Commitment," *Journal of Institutional and Theoretical Economics* (JITE), **149**(1), 11–23.

Provost, Rene (2012), "Asymmetrical Reciprocity and Compliance with the Laws of War," in Benjamin Perrin (ed.), *Modern Warfare: Armed Groups, Private Militaries, Humanitarian Organizations, and the Law*, Vancouver, CA: UBC Press, pp. 17–41.

Roberts, A. and S. Sivakumaran (2012), "Lawmaking by Non-state Actors: Engaging Armed Groups in the Creation of International Humanitarian Law," *Yale Journal of International Law*, **37**(1), 107–52.

Rodenhäuser, T. (2015), "International Legal Obligations of Armed Opposition Groups in Syria," *International Review of Law*, **1**(2), 1–16.

Scheffer, David (2013), *All the Missing Souls: A Personal History of the War Crimes Tribunals (Human Rights and Crimes against Humanity)*, Princeton, NJ: Princeton University Press.

Sikkink, Kathryn (2011), *The Justice Cascade: How Human Rights Prosecutions are Changing World Politics*, New York: Norton.

Simmons, Beth and Hyeran Jo (2016), "Measuring Norms and Normative Contestation: The Case of International Criminal Law," Paper presented at the International Studies Association Annual Meeting, Atlanta, GA, 17–19 March.

Staniland, Paul (2014), *Networks of Rebellion: Explaining Insurgent Cohesion and Collapse*, Ithaca, NY: Cornell University Press.

Thomas, J. and R. Wood (2015), "The Social Origins of Female Fighters," Paper presented at the Annual Meeting of the American Political Science Association, San Francisco, CA.

Weiss, Michael and Hassan Hassan (2015), *ISIS: Inside the Army of Terror*, New York: Regan Arts Publishers.

12. Expanding responsibilities: the consequences of World Bank and IMF policies on child welfare

Clair Apodaca

The child's right to life is a human right guaranteed by Articles 3 of the Universal Declaration of Human Rights, Article 6 of the Convention on the Rights of the Child (CRC), Article 6 of the International Covenant on Civil and Political Rights, and Article 12, regarding the right to health, of the International Covenant on Economic, Social and Cultural Rights (ICESCR). Yet, the World Health Organization (2015) estimates that worldwide there were a total of 6.3 million deaths of children under the age of five in 2013. The number of children dying before their fifth birthday, for the 161 countries included in this study, was 74.4 deaths per 1000 live births in 1996. Encouragingly, the child mortality rate dropped to 39.7 in 1000 in 2013, a reduction of nearly 47 percent. However, this impressive figure obscures the reality that the weight of child mortality is increasingly being concentrated in the underdeveloped regions of sub-Saharan Africa and South Asia (O'Hare et al., 2013). A human rights approach to the child's right of survival calls on the binding obligation or duty of the states and other duty-bearers to promote, protect, and fulfill the right holders' entitlements. As a human right, the child's right to life entails a claim on both domestic and international resources, imposing duties on states and international actors.

The World Health Organization (2015) reports that the underlying cause of the majority of these deaths is poverty: living in squalid housing conditions without access to clean water and sanitation facilities, lack of nutritious food, and limited health care. The key to improving child survival rates is to eliminate extreme poverty. The World Bank and International Monetary Fund (IMF) are international financial institutions (IFI) whose stated mission is economic development and poverty eradication. Both the Bank and the IMF have endorsed the Millennium Development Goals of reducing by two-thirds the mortality rate among children under five (Goal 4). The lending decisions of the Bank and IMF can greatly influence, directly or indirectly, the realization of the child's right of survival. Yet, IFI loans come with conditions that can interfere with the ability of the recipient state to fulfill its human rights obligations to the child. IFIs exercise considerable influence on the economic and social environments within recipient countries through the conditions placed into loan agreements. Conditionality is a mechanism used by the IMF and the World Bank whereby money is made available to nations that restructure their economies to eliminate economic inefficiencies, mismanagement, and spendthrift programs (Apodaca, 2010). Conditionalities are intended to restore macroeconomic stability and solve the balance of payment problems to ensure that the loan recipient can repay the lending institution. However, many analysts believe that conditionalities increase poverty and worsen income distribution, at least in the short term (Oberdabernig, 2013). The requirements that recipient countries reduce government expenditures by making cuts to their social welfare spending (including medical and nutrition programs) along with the introduction of user fees in health sectors degrade the wellbeing of children when their parents cannot afford to seek medical treatment for ill children or to seek preventive care for healthy children. Low levels of government investment in social welfare sectors contribute to an increase in child mortality in the developing countries. Yet, a reduction in government expenditures is a requirement of most IFI loans.

IFI OBLIGATIONS

The Bank and the IMF have claimed that they are exempt from obligations emanating from human rights treaties, including the Convention on the Rights of the Child, because of the political neutrality clauses found in their respective Articles of Agreement. Yet, there is a growing awareness among academics, international lawyers, and United Nations (UN) human rights agencies that IFIs do have an obligation to protect and promote human rights. IFIs are theoretically subject to human rights obligations on several fronts:

1. The Bank and IMF are specialized agencies of the UN family. With the conclusion of the Relationship of Agreement, the IMF and the Bank are "formally part of the family of the UN and have to co-ordinate their activities with the main bodies of the UN active in the field on international social and economic co-operation" (Gómez Isa, 2008, p. 11). As members of the UN family of specialized agencies, they are bound by the UN Charter and are required to uphold the

mission and purpose of the UN.[1] Mac Darrow, in his influential 2006 book *Between Light and Shadow: The World Bank, the International Monetary Fund and International Human Rights*, believes that the UN Charter is an important source of human rights obligations for the IFIs. Chief among the goals of the UN is to "achieve international co-operation in solving international problems of an economic, social, cultural, or humanitarian character, and in promoting and encouraging respect for human rights and for fundamental freedoms for all without distinction as to race, sex, language, or religion" (1945, Article 1(3)). UN agencies cannot ignore nor negate the purposes of the UN Charter, which expressly and unconditionally promotes human rights, including the rights of children. Human rights law, therefore, binds IFIs.

2. Both IFIs have an international legal personality and are autonomous subjects of international law with rights and duties (Gómez Isa, 2008). Consequently, they are bound by the general principles of international law, peremptory norms, and norms derived from customary law, including the Universal Declaration of Human Rights. Van Genugten, a renowned professor of international law, writes that "as subjects of international law and as international legal personalities, the WBG and the IMF are capable of possessing rights and duties under their constituent instruments, general rules of international law, and the treaties to which they have acceded" (2015, p. 9). Thus, Van Genugten (2015) concludes that the IFIs have obligations for human rights that must be satisfied either separately from or jointly with their member states.
3. The Bank and IMF are bound by the obligations of their constituent member states. Although the Bank and IMF are not parties to international treaties, they are bound indirectly since the IFIs are composed of states that are bound by the treaties they have ratified. Article 103 of the UN Charter prioritizes the legal obligations originating from the Charter over other treaty obligations. IFI loan agreements are international treaties (Van Genugten, 2015). Article 103 states:

> in the event of a conflict between the obligations of the Members of the United Nations under the present Charter and their obligations under any other international agreement, their obligations under the present Charter shall prevail.

Thus, the loan agreements negotiated between states and the IFIs are subordinate to the principles and purposes of the UN Charter. The Bank and IMF are compelled to respect the treaty provisions and human rights obligations of their member states, and they have a duty to help the states fulfill their obligations. The Bank acknowledges that human rights are "actionable legal obligations . . . as they are enshrined in national laws, where the Bank's role is to support its members to fulfill those obligations where they relate to World Bank projects and policies" (World Bank website, www.worldbank.org). Darrow (2006) states that the IFIs have, as a minimum obligation, to respect and not violate the human rights responsibilities of their members. States maintain their human rights obligations as members of an international organization. In the respected opinion of Byrnes, "States must conduct themselves consistently with those obligations when they participate in the activities of the organisation and must endeavour to ensure that the actions and consequences of the actions taken by those organisations do not involve violations of rights guaranteed by human rights treaties and customary international law" (2011, p. 11).

4. The IFIs play a leading role in shaping international and domestic development policy-making and as such are subjects of the right to development. At the domestic level, economic and social policy is influenced and constrained by the conditionalities attached to IFI loans. IFIs can require reforms of economic policies and institutions within recipient states by placing conditionalities in loan and credit agreements, which are binding under the international law of treaties (Boisson de Chazournes, 2000). As the primary creditors to developing states, the IFIs possess considerable power in the decision-making process within member states. Abouharb et al. conclude that "The IMF and the World Bank have enacted a broad set of policies designed to carefully regulate the behavior of borrower states. These policies are incorporated into loan agreements" (2015, p. 38). Developing states in need of funds must modify their domestic economic and social policies in order to satisfy the IFIs' preconditions for the receipt of aid. Thus, to expand Howard-Hassmann's argument (Chapter 13, this volume), IFIs, along with states, can de-develop economies. IFIs have significant leverage to enforce development policies that actually result in de-development. Furthermore, like other agents of de-development, the IFIs escape their responsibilities to citizens and deprive children of the right of survival. A major shortcoming of the programs initiated by the IFIs is that they focus on development as state economic growth rather than on human development and poverty alleviation.

EVOLUTION OF THE BANK

The initial purpose of the World Bank was to promote economic development, while the IMF function was to foster monetary cooperation and maintain currency stability. This division of labor, in the words of Darrow, "is one of the principal reasons why human rights have not made it onto the Fund's radar" (2006, p. 51). The Bank has over time become more willing to accept its responsibility for human welfare. Ravallion writes: "Over its history, the Bank has made many efforts to adapt, re-invent and rationalize its role . . . [with the] Bank adopting a broader social welfare objective, emphasizing poverty reduction through equitable economic growth and delivering social services to poor people" (2015, p. 4). The Bank has endorsed the Millennium Development Goals, joined the Child Survival Partnership, and the Partnership for Maternal, Newborn and Child Health, and it also funds development and health projects needed to eradicate poverty and reduce child mortality.

In the early years, the Bank lent money with the myopic aim of promoting economic growth with little attention to the social repercussions of its projects. In the early1980s, the Bank introduced non-project funding, in the form of structural adjustment lending (SAL), now renamed Development Policy Loans (DPL), to support policy reform in recipient countries. SAL loans provided conditional funding for economic stabilization and balance of payment distortions. Due to strong criticism from non-governmental organizations (NGOs), human rights advocates, and poverty reduction activists, the Bank put more emphasis on protecting the poor from the adverse effects of these programs during the 1990s. As criticism continued to mount and human rights gained support, the Bank's rhetoric evolved to reflect a broader understanding of what the concept of development means. No longer is development measured simply in economic terms. Development now includes social elements. The Bank has stated that "creating the conditions for the attainment of human rights is a central and irreducible goal of development" (World Bank, 1998, p. 2). Bank rhetoric reflects a growing awareness that child welfare is both a development and a rights issue. As a result, the Bank reports that it has positioned health at the core of its lending programs in poor countries, emphasizing a reduction in child mortality. The Bank increased its health program budget through funding from the International Bank for Reconstruction and Development (IBRD) and the International Development Association (IDA) from $1.78 billion in 2000 to $2.19 billion in 2012, an increase of 46 percent, with the majority (44 percent) disbursed through IBRD (Díaz-Martínez, 2013).

Nevertheless, the extent to which human rights have become part of the culture of the Bank is uncertain. Sarfaty writes: "Despite the Bank's rhetoric that protecting human rights is critical for development, its employees do not systematically incorporate human rights concerns into their everyday decision making or consistently take them into consideration in lending" (2012, p. 2). In Sarfaty's opinion, the Bank has not yet fully adopted a human rights policy or agenda despite outside pressure and its own human rights rhetoric. Although the Bank recognizes the importance of creating the conditions for the realization of rights, it has, along with the IMF, fervently resisted any responsibility for assuring or guaranteeing rights (Taillant, 2002).

CONSTANCY OF THE IMF

The IMF, on the other hand, has been steadfast in its conviction that it is not "bound by various human rights declarations and conventions" (Capdevila, 2001). The Fund's General Counsel, François Gianviti (1987–2004), argued strongly that the Fund is not subject to international human rights law. Human rights considerations are only relevant for the IMF "to the extent that major violations of economic and social human rights would trigger civil unrest or a lack of foreign financing" (Gianviti, 2002, p. 40, para. 51). Neglecting the opinions of legal scholars and even the UN Human Rights Committee, the Fund has continued to act in accordance with its own interpretation of its Articles of Agreement. In conjunction with the Bank, the IMF instituted structural adjustment loans in the 1980s. In the 1980s, when developed countries were able to access private capital flows, IMF's clientele became developing and transitional economies almost exclusively. With the shift in borrowing countries and the IMF's overriding interest in maintaining financial and monetary stability, concern increased that IMF conditional lending worsened the situation of the poor (Lundberg and Squire, 2003). Under severe criticism, the IMF reluctantly included poverty alleviation in its lending considerations. For example, the IMF dutifully changed the names of its lending facilities from the vilified term "structural adjustment" to the pro-poor sounding concept of "poverty reduction." In 1986, the IMF launched the Structural Adjustment Facility (SAF), which became the Enhanced Structural Adjustment Facility (ESAF) in 1989, and later was renamed the Poverty Reduction and Growth Facility (PRGF) in 1999. The Extended Credit Facility (ECF) is presently the latest reincarnation of the PRGF. Although the names have changed, critics maintain that the loan conditions remain the same (Cunningham and Lavalette, 2014).

IMF conditionalities have remained a controversial issue because they require the state to take corrective measures consistent with the Fund's provisions and policies and with little consideration for their socioeconomic consequences. The IMF reasons that market-friendly structural reforms, no matter how painful, are necessary for rapid and sustainable economic growth, which is a precondition for poverty reduction (Blackmon, 2008; Darrow, 2006). Thus, in the IMF's opinion, structural adjustment policies (SAPs) will indirectly help realize the rights under the CRC and ICESCR. Critics, in contrast, believe that government spending cuts required by the SAPs target social programs (such as health, nutrition, and sanitation) essential for the reduction of child mortality. An IMF review of its own procedures in 2012 found that although conditionalties were "broadly appropriate" (effective, streamlined, and utilizing IMF expertise), macro-social issues (jobs and growth) and social protections needed to be preserved during economic crises (IMF website, www.imf.org). The IMF believes that its programs "help governments to protect and even increase social spending, including social assistance" in order to mitigate the impact of lending programs and to protect the most vulnerable people in society (IMF website).

ECONOMIC REPERCUSSION OF CHILD MORTALITY

Child mortality ought to be of grave concern for the IFIs due to mortality's impact on economic development. Kirigial et al. contend that child mortality

> increase[s] health expenditure, cause attrition of future labour and productivity, and erode investments in human and physical capital formation . . . Child deaths reduce future spending on goods and services; future labour force; future household savings, and hence investments; the number of future tax payers, and hence future tax revenues; and the number of future exports producers, bleeding future exports earnings. (2015, p. 1107)

Using a cost-of-illness model,[2] Kirigial et al. (2015) determine that the non-health gross domestic product (GDP) future loss due to Africa's 2.96 million child deaths in 2013 was $150.3 billion. Indeed, Soares (2005) found that larger investments in children increase productivity and growth. Declines in child mortality rates are associated with increased parental investment in the health and education of their children, which will have large beneficial effects on children's physical and cognitive development (Canning and Schultz, 2012). The rise in human capital accumulation and improved worker performance will have positive outcomes for economic growth and development. Thus, there are sound economic reasons for improving child welfare. Countries with low-income levels have high child mortality rates while high child mortality reduces economic growth. Therefore, lending for programs to reduce child mortality can promote economic development – the stated goals of IFI lending. Certainly, the impact of child mortality on current or future rates of economic growth and development would constitute an "economic consideration" under the Articles of Agreement. Yet, work by Hoddie and Hartzell (2014) found that IMF lending exposes the recipient government's population to adverse health outcomes both in the short and the longer terms.

RESEARCH DESIGN AND METHODS

In order to explore the human rights impact and responsibility of IFIs, this study attempts to initiate an investigation of the effects of IFI lending on child mortality rates. The study uses an unbalanced panel of observations from 161 developing countries, covering the years 1996–2013 for an n = 2857 (list of countries included in the study available on request).

The models are estimated using a cross-sectional time series with country fixed effects with robust standard errors. The cross-sectional time series allows the researcher to pool the data, taking advantage of both the spatial (cross-sectional units of observation reflected in the differences between cases) and temporal (observations over a particular time span or within-subject information reflected in the changes within cases over time) dimensions of the data set. Fixed effects regression is the appropriate model to use to control for omitted variables or unobservable variables that may affect both lending and child mortality and that differ between cases but are constant over time (Princeton University Data and Statistical Service). The fixed effects estimator corrects for selection bias in panel data.[3] This estimation method assumes that there exist time-invariant and country-specific unobservable characteristics that differentiate IFI recipient from non-recipient countries. The equation for the fixed effects model becomes:

$$Y_{it} = \beta_1 X_{it} + \alpha_i + u_{it} \qquad 12.1$$

Where αi_i (I = 1. . ..n) is the unknown intercept for each country (n case-specific intercepts); Y_{it} is the dependent variable (DV) where i = country and t = time; X_{it} represents one independent variable (IV); β_1 is the coefficient for that IV; u_{it} is the error term.

To minimize the problems of heteroskedasticity associated with using data with a large range of distributions, data are logged where appropriate. Unless otherwise noted the data used in this study were obtained from the Bank's World Development Indicators online database (http://databank.worldbank.org). Table 12A.1 in the Appendix presents the descriptive statistics of the dependent and independent variables used in this study.

The dependent variable is child mortality rates. Child mortality is defined as the probability of a child dying between birth and the age of five, expressed per 1000 live births. The Bank concludes that child mortality rates "are among the indicators most frequently used to compare socioeconomic development across countries" (World Development Indicators (WDI) online, www.data.worldbank.org).

The independent variables of interest are IFI lending and debt forgiveness. The Bank has two major lending agencies.[4] The International Bank for Reconstruction and Development (IBRD) is a branch of the Bank that lends money at market rates to middle-income and creditworthy low-income countries displaying principles of good governance but which have only sporadic access to private market capital. The mandate of IBRD is to assist member states to develop economically, thus raising "the standard of living and conditions of labor" (Article 1). The International Development Association (IDA) provides loans (credits) and grants to the poorest countries at concessional rates.[5] IDA's Articles of Agreement list its purpose as to "promote economic development, increase productivity and thus raise standards of living in the less-developed areas of the world . . . thereby furthering the developmental objectives of the International Bank for Reconstruction and Development" (Article 1). IDA loans money for poverty reduction and human development projects such as primary education, health services, and water and sanitation facilities.

The IMF has a dizzying array of lending instruments, known as facilities, that apply to different countries. Concessional lending to low-income countries is provided through the Extended Credit Facility (ECF), the Standby Credit Facility (SCF), and the Rapid Credit Facility (RCF). Non-concessional lending is available to all members through the Stand-By Arrangements (SBA), the Flexible Credit Line (FCL), the Precautionary and Liquidity Line (PLL), the Extended Fund Facility (EFF), and the Rapid Financing Instrument (RFI). The majority of non-concessional IMF lending is channeled through the SBA, while the ECF is the Fund's main tool for providing medium-term support to low-income countries (IMF website). IMF lending always carries structural adjustment requirements as a condition of the loan. In this study, IMF lending is broken down as concessionary programs and non-concessionary programs in order to allow the programs to have separate effects.

Proponents of debt cancellation policies believe that poverty alleviation is hindered by demands on the economy and on government resources from a heavy debt burden. Social and health services, needed to increase the survival of children, are cut because the scarce resources of developing countries must be diverted to pay creditors first. The Highly Indebted Poor Country Initiative (HIPC) was launched in order to provide debt relief to the world's poorest countries under the guidance of the IMF and Bank. The primary purpose of debt forgiveness was to redirect resources that had previously gone to servicing a country's debt, and to use the freed-up funds for specific poverty reduction programs primarily aimed at social services, such as health care and education (World Bank, 2005, p. xii). Consequently, debt reduction ought to be associated with a decrease in child mortality rates.

It is unlikely that IFI loans or debt relief would have an immediate effect on child survival rates, so the IFI variables and debt forgiveness are lagged one, three, five, and seven time periods so that both the short- and medium-term effects of IFI loans on the dependent variables can be tested. Also included are four control variables – economic development, health expenditures, military expenditures, and level of democracy – commonly found in recent cross-national research on child mortality.

Prior research consistently shows a beneficial relationship between child mortality rates and levels of economic development (Frey and Field, 2000; Jorgenson and Rice, 2010).[6] Countries that have higher levels of economic development, as measured by GDP per capital, enjoy higher standards of living, better medical care, improved water and sanitation, and lower fertility rates. Higher income levels also enable the fulfillment of other basic needs such as food and housing (Houweling et al., 2005; McGuire, 2006).

Democracy helps to make the government accountable and responsive to the needs of citizens since leaders must court the vote of a large segment of the population to win elections. Voters can influence governmental leaders, which may translate into better health programs and stronger social safety nets. When leaders must win contested elections to gain or remain in power, they provide public goods for the general welfare. Kudamatsu (2007), using a subsample of 28 sub-Saharan African countries, investigated whether democratization reduced infant mortality. He found that greater levels of democracy reduced infant mortality by 1.8 percentage points. Equally important is the fact that the reduction in mortality was higher for babies born to uneducated mothers from marginalized ethnicities.

Because private health care will not provide adequate access to life-saving medical assistance to poor children, government spending is required for the reduction of child mortality. Bokhari et al. (2007)

found that increases in domestic health expenditures are responsible for a decrease in child mortality rates. They determined that a 10 percent increase in health expenditures results in a 2.5 to 4 percent decrease in child death rates. Higher levels of government expenditures on health translate into greater public access to health care, family planning, nutrition counseling, prenatal care, and births attended by trained personnel (Houweling et al., 2005).

Military expenditures can crowd out public spending for basic social services too (Mehrotra and Delamonic, 2002). Regimes that are engaged in extravagant defense spending divert government resources away from the provision of social services and toward the acquisition of expensive, and often repressive, military armaments. In poor states, the result can be the denial of basic health, nutrition, and educational services to the poor. The amount of resources committed to defense indicates the priority the state places on the military over the needs of the population.

FINDINGS

This research utilizes a fixed effects model to investigate the impact of IFI lending, as well as macroeconomic and governance variables, on child mortality rates. The results are presented in Table 12.1. The control variables behaved as predicted and support previous research on their effects.

This research differentiates between IBRD and IDA lending because IDA is concessional with a specific focus on poverty reduction and human development. As a non-self-sustaining agency, the IDA is particularly open to fulfilling the human rights obligations of member states. IDA funds must be replenished by state contributions every three years. This makes the IDA "particularly exposed to shifts in the political climate" and responsive to reforms explicitly linking replenishment to poverty reduction and human rights improvements (Darrow, 2006, p. 12).

Table 12.1 indicates that IBRD lending (at t−3 and t−5) increases child mortality while IDA lending decreases child mortality (at t−1, t−3, and t−5). Child welfare and survival have not yet entered the mainstream of IBRD operations.[7] IBRD's focus of lending is on middle-income creditworthy countries with some access to private market capital. Therefore, the emphasis is on increasing GDP, investment, and exports while reducing inflation rates. McPake's (1994) early review of the use of user fees in health service holds IBRD responsible for their introduction. The institution of user fees for health and educational services is to compensate for the IFI-imposed reduction of government funding. User fees result in a decline in the use of health services among the poor, which

Table 12.1 Fixed effects regression of World Bank lending on child mortality using panel data

	Model 1: Lendings effects on child mortality with a 1 year lag (t−1) Coef (se)	Model 2: Lendings effects on child mortality with a 3 year lag (t−3) Coef (se)	Model 3: Lendings effects on child mortality with a 5 year lag (t−5) Coef (se)	Model 4: Lendings effects on child mortality with a 7 year lag (t−7) Coef (se)
IBRD	0.0027	0.0046*	0.0042#	0.0015
	(0.0020)	(0.0020)	(0.002)	(0.0012)
IDA	−0.0056*	−0.0086**	−0.0088***	−0.0018
	(0.0025)	(0.0025)	(0.0024)	(0.0012)
IMF	0.00003	−0.0007	0.0001	0.0013**
Concessional	(0.0005)	(0.0004)	(0.0004)	(0.0004)
IMF	0.0001	−0.0003	−0.0012**	−0.0003
Non-Consessional	(0.0004)	(0.0004)	(0.0004)	(0.0004)
Debt Forgiveness	−0.0005	−0.0002	−0.0004	−0.0002
	(0.0008)	(0.0010)	(0.0010)	(0.0008)
GDP pc	−0.3841***	−0.3800***	−0.3771***	−0.3840***
	(0.0202)	(0.0204)	(0.0205)	(0.0222)
Health	−0.1412***	−0.1303**	−0.1321**	−0.1375**
Expenditures	(0.0413)	(0.0407)	(0.0402)	(0.0387)

Military Expenditures	0.0670**	0.0650**	0.0681**	0.0696**
	(0.0241)	(0.0238)	(0.0236)	(0.0231)
Democracy	−0.0060*	−0.0053#	−0.0048#	−0.0060#
	(0.0030)	(0.0029)	(0.0030)	(0.0031)
Constant	6.645***	6.623***	6.596***	6.602***
	(0.1565)	(0.1558)	(0.1567)	(0.1617)
Overall R^2	0.708	0.692	0.691	0.717
Within R^2	0.709	0.715	0.718	0.718
N	2157	2157	2157	2157
Average N per group	16.2	16.2	16.2	16.2

Note: $^*p < 0.05$, $^{**}p < 0.01$, $^{***}p < 0.001$.

can help account for the increase in child mortality rates due to IBRD lending three and five years out. Moreover, Kaja and Werker (2010) determined that membership on IBRD's Executive Board resulted in approximately double the IBRD funding compared to countries that were not on the board. Favoritism rather than poverty reduction controlled IBRD lending. Similar research has shown that IBRD loans are heavily influenced by a recipient government's temporary seat on the UN Security Council (Dreher et al., 2009; Kuziemko and Werker, 2006).

However, Kaja and Werker (2010) also found that membership on IDA's Board had no influence on IDA's lending decisions.[8] Morrison (2013) reports that the IDA had instituted procedures to reflect its development agenda. Morrison writes:

> One of the norms that has evolved over time in IDA is that member countries should receive more money if, all else equal, they have greater promise for development because of the policies and institutions they have in place. This norm has been institutionalized in a rating system, which Bank staff use to evaluate every country each year. According to historical accounts, this rating has become increasingly important in determining the allocation of lending from IDA. (2013, p. 292)

IDA is less political, with established criteria to lend to poverty-stricken countries with development policies in place. The analysis supports conventional wisdom that politically motivated aid is less effective in promoting positive developmental goals. IDA loans money for poverty reduction and human development projects such as primary education, health services, and water and sanitation facilities. IDA-financed investments reduce the incidence of child mortality. The results also indicate that recipient states are using the funds in ways that are beneficial to their citizens. Babb (2005) reports that the World Bank has mandated that the most impoverished borrowers, those that are IDA eligible, reserve a fixed percentage of their expenditures for pro-poor spending. Yet, the encouraging results of the quantitative analyses for IDA lending must be tempered by the fact that the coefficients are so small.

This research also separates IMF concessional and non-concessional lending in order to determine whether non-concessional lending to low-income countries (countries that exhibit the greatest levels of human deprivation) benefits child survival. Overall, whatever benefits a country may receive from restructuring its economy to meet the requirements of IMF's imposed conditions is offset by the harm done by these reforms. IMF non-concessional lending reaches statistical significance (at the $p > 0.01$ level) in Model 3. Proponents of IMF loans acknowledge that although conditionalities may produce adverse outcomes in the short term, they will generate beneficial developmental effects in the long term. Here, this study finds that IMF non-concessional loans have a small beneficial effect on child mortality rates. Five years after a country receives a non-concessional loan, there is a reduction in child deaths. The inclusion of poverty alleviation policies in IMF lending may have some desired effects (Oberdabernig, 2013). The International Monetary Fund (2000) suggests that the social benefits of its lending programs could be greater if it was not hindered by weak administrative capacity in the recipient country. IMF maintains that market-friendly reforms and macroeconomic stability are pro-poor poverty reduction strategies. IMF loans are intended to stabilize a country's economy and foster economic growth. However, IMF economic development strategies and the resultant reduction in poverty take time. Many countries simply failed to comply, and the programs collapsed or were interrupted (Clements, 2013). Clements et al. (2013) found that IMF lending has a positive and significant effect on social spending, specifically education and health care. SBA, the IMF's workhorse for non-concessional lending, is open to all member countries but is used most often by middle-income countries since low-income countries have a number of concessional loan options. The beneficial impact of IMF non-concessional loan is short-lived as the coefficient is statistically insignificant seven years after the loan initiation.

According to the IMF website, IMF concessional loans are "medium-term" facilities with a time horizon of a five and a half year grace period and a final maturity of ten years (the SCF has a four year grace period and an eight year maturity). Concessional loans are only statistically significant at the seven year lag. Clements et al. (2013) found that IMF-supported programs increase education and health spending in low-income countries compared to non-program countries or during non-funded time periods. We see that at seven years post-loan, there is an increase in child mortality rates. Once the conditions are lifted and the low-income country is no longer bound by the requirements of the concessional loan, child mortality rates increase.[9] Rickard and Caraway (2014) conclude that governments tend to comply with conditionalities in the short run in order to receive subsequent disbursements of loan funds. But as public discontent grows and interim reviews lift conditionalities, the government reverts to pre-loan spending. Returning to pre-loan budgetary behaviors has an adverse impact on child mortality rates.

Debt service has no direct effect on child mortality rates in any of the models. The resources freed up by the cancellation of the debt have not been used to reduce child mortality. Once the debt is cancelled, the government may or may not follow through on its promise to fund the programs listed in the Poverty Reduction Strategy Papers (PRSPs). In addition, the elimination of bad debts allows poor nations to apply for new loans, thus creating a new unending cycle of dependency. Countries continue to borrow money and are now, again, in severe debt.

CONCLUSION

The IFIs associated with the UN have a shared responsibility to uphold the core mission of the UN. Thus, it is reasonable to expect that these specialized agencies will refrain from conducting themselves in a manner that increases child mortality rates. IFIs have at minimum a duty to respect and protect the right of the child to survival. Yet, in contrast to the IFI's explicit reference to poverty reduction in many of their documents and papers, the statistical analysis performed here shows mixed results. The IBRD lending arm of the Bank is falling short of fulfilling its human rights obligations, and millions of children are continuing to die as a result. IBRD lending subjects children to conditions that increase their risk of death. IDA lending, on the other hand, benefits child survival, but the coefficients are small. IMF concessional lending, lending to low-income countries, is statistically insignificant in reducing child mortality until the year in which the program expires (seven year lag), at which time child mortality increases. IMF non-concessional lending has no effect on child mortality, although in the medium term, five years after the IMF loan, it reduces mortality. This supports the view that monetary stability is beneficial in the medium term for child survival. However, even for those lending programs that do improve the child mortality rates, more could be done as indicated by the small effects lending has on improving child survival. Ultimately, one can conclude that powerful international financial actors have been allowed to escape their human rights obligations as autonomous subjects of international law and as UN affiliates. IFIs have been allowed to dictate the economic policies of developing states with little or no regard to consequences in terms of human rights. It is vitally important that IFIs be held accountable for the human rights consequences of their directives. The welfare of millions of children depends on the legal and moral accountability of these actors.

NOTES

1. Specialized agencies are required to adhere to the provisions of the UN Charter. The UN Charter (Article 57), in accordance with the provisions of Article 63, established

a collaborative relationship with the UN's specialized agencies with a view to creating international economic and social cooperation.
2. A cost-of-illness model measures the economic burden of disease and estimates the amount of money that can be saved or gained if the illness was eradicated.
3. The Hausman specification test substantiated that the correct model is a fixed effects model.
4. The Bank also includes an agency that provides loans to private institutions, the International Finance Corporation (IFC). This is an agency that provides insurance and credit guarantees for private investors, the Multilateral Investment Guarantee Agency (MIGA), and the International Centre for Settlement of Investment Disputes (ICSID) used for conciliation and arbitration.
5. Concessional loans have a low or zero interest rate while non-concessional loans are subject to market related interest rates (called rates of charge).
6. Several risk factors known for influencing deaths in children are not included due to their high correlation with GDP pc. For example, access to improved water and sanitation facilities, age dependency ratios, births attended by trained personal, and fertility rates.
7. Safeguard policies are designed to avoid or mitigate detrimental impacts of Bank-funded infrastructure projects on the environment, natural habitats, pest management, forests, cultural property, projects in disputed areas, projects on international waterways, and safety of dams, and on specific groups of people, indigenous groups or those facing involuntary resettlement. The Bank developed safeguard policies to deflect criticism from its lending projects. It is easy to see the deleterious impact of a Bank-funded dam project on the environment and the forceful involuntary resettlement of communities. But it is far more difficult to locate culpability for an increase in child mortality.
8. This finding is particularly striking since the IDA and the IBRD share many of the same board members.
9. The IMF conducts interim reviews of its loans and may remove or modify a conditionality. A review occurs when IMF Staff periodically visit a country to monitor whether policy conditions are being met.

REFERENCES

Abouharb, Rodwan, David Cingranelli, and Mikhail Filippov (2015) "Do Non-human Rights Regimes Undermine the Achievement of Economic and Social Rights?," in LaDawn Haglund and Robin Stryker (eds), *Closing the Rights Gap: From Human Rights to Social Transformation*, Berkeley, CA: University of California Press, pp. 29–48.

Apodaca, Clair (2010) *Child Hunger and Human Rights: International Governance*, London: Routledge Research in Human Rights.

Babb, Sarah (2005) "The Social Consequences of Structural Adjustment: Recent Evidence and Current Debates," *Annual Review of Sociology*, **31**, 199–222.

Blackmon, Pamela (2008) "Rethinking Poverty through the Eyes of the International Monetary Fund and the World Bank," *International Studies Review*, **10**, 179–202.

Boisson de Chazournes, Laurence (2000) "Policy Guidance and Compliance: The World Bank Operational Standards," in Dinah Shelton (ed.), *Commitment and Compliance: The Role of Non-binding Norms in the International Legal System*, Oxford and New York: Oxford University Press, pp. 281–303.

Bokhari, Farasat, Yunwei Gai, and Pablo Gottret (2007) "Government Health Expenditures and Health Outcomes," *Health Economics*, **16**, 257–73.

Byrnes, Andrew (2011) "The Asian Development Bank and the Role of Human

Rights in the Pursuit of Just and Sustainable Development in the Asia-Pacific Region: An Advocacy Role for Australia?" *Australian International Law Journal*, **18**, 1–21.

Canning, David and T. Paul Schultz (2012) "The Economic Consequences of Reproductive Health and Family Planning," accessed 14 December 2015 at http://www.mamaye.org/sites/default/files/evidence/The%20economic%20consequences%20of%20reproductive%20health%20and%20family%20planning.pdf.

Capdevila, Gustavo (2001) "IMF Not Taking into Account Human Rights Issues," Global Policy Forum, accessed 24 December 2015 at http://www.globalpolicy.org/component/content/article /209/42944.html.

Clements, Benedict, Sanjeev Gupta, and Masahiro Nozaki (2013) "What Happens to Social Spending in IMF-supported Programmes?" *Applied Economics*, **45**,≈4022–33.

Clements, Paul (2013) "Multilateral Development Banks and the International Monetary Fund," in John Linarelli (ed.), *Research Handbook on Global Justice and International Economic Law*, Cheltenham, UK and Northampton, MA, USA: Edward Elgar, pp. 121–45.

Cunningham, Steve and Michael Lavalette (2014) "Children's Rights or Employers' Rights," in Stephen Wagg and Jane Pilcher (eds), *Thatcher's Grandchildren: Politics and Childhood in the Twenty-first Century*, New York: Palgrave, pp. 275–300.

Darrow, Mac (2006) *Between Light and Shadow: The World Bank, the International Monetary Fund and International Human Rights*, Portland, OR: Hart Publishing.

Díaz-Martínez, Elisa (2013) "The Questionable Power of the Millennium Development Goal to Reduce Child Mortality," accessed 17 October 2016 at https://cdn2.sph.harvard.edu/wp-content/uploads/sites/5/2013/09/The-Questionable-Power-WP-92413.pdf.

Dreher, Axel, Jan-Egbert Sturm, and James Vreeland (2009) "Development Aid and International Politics: Does Membership on the UN Security Council Influence World Bank Decisions?" *Journal of Development Economics*, **88**, 1–18.

Frey, R. Scott and Carolyn Field (2000) "The Determinants of Infant Mortality in Less Developed Countries: A Cross-national Test of Five Theories," *Social Indicators Research*, **52**(3), 215–34.

Gianviti, François (2002) *Economic, Social and Cultural Rights and the International Monetary Fund*, Washington, DC: International Monetary Fund.

Gómez Isa, Felipe (2008) *Mainstreaming Human Rights in the International Financial and Trade Institutions: Achievements and Prospects*, Bilbao: Alboan.

Hoddie, Mathew and Caroline Hartzell (2014) "Short-term Pain, Long-term Gain? The Effects of IMF Economic Reform Programs on Public Health Performance," *Social Science Quarterly*, **95**(4), 1022–42.

Houweling, Tanja, Anton Kunst, Caspar Looman, and Johan Mackenbach (2005) "Determinants of Under-5 Mortality Among the Poor and the Rich: A Cross-national Analysis of 43 Developing Countries," *International Journal of Epidemiology*, **34**, 1257–65.

International Monetary Fund (2000) *Social Policy Issues in IMF-supported Programs: Follow-up on the 1995 World Summit for Social Development*, accessed 17 October 2016 at http://www.imf.org/external/np/fad/wldsum/.

Jorgenson, Andrew and James Rice (2010) "Urban Slum Growth and Human

Health: A Panel Study of Infant and Child Mortality in Less-developed Countries, 1990–2005," *Journal of Poverty*, **14**(4), 382–402.

Kaja, Ashwin and Eric Werker (2010) "Corporate Governance at the World Bank and the Dilemma of Global Governance," *World Bank Economic Review*, **24**(2), 171–98.

Kirigial, Joses, Rosenabi Karimi Muthuri, Juliet Nabyonga-Orem, and Doris Gatwiri Kirigia (2015) "Counting the Cost of Child Mortality in the World Health Organization African Region," *BMC Public Health*, **15**(3), 1103–16.

Kudamatsu, Masayuki (2007) "Has Democratization Reduced Infant Mortality in Sub-Saharan Africa? Evidence from Micro Data," ISER Discussion Paper, Institute of Social and Economic Research, Osaka University, No. 685, accessed 4 January 2016 at http://www.econstor.eu/bitstream/10419/92566/1/537563822.pdf.

Kuziemko, Ilyana and Eric Werker (2006) "How Much is a Seat on the Security Council Worth? Foreign Aid and Bribery at the United Nations," *Journal of Political Economy*, **114**(5), 905–30.

Lundberg, Mattias and Lyn Squire (2003) "The Simultaneous Evolution of Growth and Inequality," *Economic Journal*, **113**(487), 326–44.

McGuire, James (2006) "Basic Health Care Provision and Under Five Mortality: A Cross-national Study of Developing Countries," *World Development*, **34**, 405–25.

McPake Barbara (1994) "User Charges for Health Services in Developing Countries: A Review of the Economic Literature," *Social Science Medicine*, **39**, 1189–201.

Mehrotra, Santosh and Enrique Delamonic (2002) "Public Spending for Children: An Empirical Note," *Journal of International Development*, **14**, 1105–16.

Morrison, Kevin (2013) "Membership No Longer has its Privileges: The Declining Informal Influence of Board Members on IDA Lending," *The Review of International Organizations*, **8**(2), 291–312.

Oberdabernig, Doris (2013) "Revisiting the Effects of IMF Programs on Poverty and Inequality," *World Development*, **46**, 113–42.

O'Hare, Bernadette, Innocent Makuta, Levison Chiwaula, and Naor Bar-Zeev (2013) "Income and Child Mortality in Developing Countries: A Systematic Review and Meta-analysis," *Journal of the Royal Society of Medicine*, **106**(10), 408–14.

Ravallion, Martin (2015) "World Bank: Why it is Still Needed and Why it Still Disappoints," CGD Working Paper 400, Center for Global Development, Washington, DC, accessed 24 December 2015 at http://www.cgdev.org/publication/world-bank-why-it-still-needed-and-why-it-still-disappoints-working-paper-400.

Rickard, Stephanie and Teri Caraway (2014) "The International Politics of Austerity: The Puzzling Case of Public Sector Reforms," accessed 17 October 2016 at http://wp.peio.me/wp-content/uploads/2014/04/Conf7_Rickard-Caraway-1.1.2014.pdf.

Sarfaty, Galit (2012) *Values in Transition: Human Rights and the Culture of the World Bank*, Stanford, CA: Stanford University Press.

Soares, Rodrigo (2005) "Mortality Reductions, Educational Attainment, and Fertility Choice," *American Economic Review*, **95**(3), 580–601.

Taillant, Jorge (2002) "Human Rights and the International Financial Institutions,"

Paper prepared for Sustainable Justice 2002: Implementing International Sustainable Development Law, Montreal, Canada, 13–15 June.

Van Genugten, Willem (2015) *The World Bank Group, the IMF and Human Rights*, Cambridge: Intersentia.

World Bank (1998) *Development and Human Rights: The Role of the World Bank*, Washington, DC: World Bank.

World Bank (2005) *Introduction to Poverty Analysis*, Washington, DC: World Bank, accessed 17 October 2016 at http://siteresources.worldbank.org/PGLP/Resources/PovertyManual.pdf.

World Health Organization (2015) *World Health Statistics 2015*, Geneva: WHO.

APPENDIX

Table 12A.1 Variable summary table

	Obs	Mean	SD	Min	Max
Child Mortality (log)	2851	3.58	1.01	1.03	5.59
IRBD $_{t-1}$ (log)	2857	8.39	9.62	0	23.41
IDA $_{t-1}$ (log)	2857	11.70	9.53	0	24.00
IRBD $_{t-3}$ (log)	2857	8.17	9.56	0	23.35
IDA $_{t-3}$ (log)	2857	11.59	9.51	0	23.98
IRBD $_{t-5}$ (log)	2857	8.22	9.57	0	23.35
IDA $_{t-5}$ (log)	2857	11.37	9.52	0	23.96
IRBD $_{t-7}$ (log)	2857	6.20	9.04	0	23.25
IDA $_{t-7}$ (log)	2857	8.18	9.57	0	23.92
IMF Concessional $_{t-1}$ (log)	2857	0.417	9.14	−21.27	20.95
IMF Non-Concessional $_{t-1}$ (log)	2857	−1.43	8.76	−23.89	23.22
IMF Concessional $_{t-3}$ (log)	2857	0.473	8.97	−21.27	20.95
IMF Non-Concessional $_{t-3}$ (log)	2857	−1.47	9.13	−23.89	23.22
IMF Concessional $_{t-5}$ (log)	2857	0.396	8.72	−21.27	20.98
IMF Non-Concessional $_{t-5}$ (log)	2857	−1.95	9.36	−23.89	23.22
IMF Concessional $_{t-7}$ (log)	2857	0.590	8.47	−21.27	20.98
IMF Non-Concessional $_{t-7}$ (log)	2857	−1.79	9.16	−23.89	23.22
GDP per capita (log)	2780	7.64	1.37	4.28	11.48
Health Expenditures (log)	2791	0.954	0.624	−4.70	2.99
Military Expenditures (log)	2275	0.597	0.741	−2.29	3.68
Polity IV	2506	2.31	6.42	−10	10
Debt Forgiveness $_{t-1}$ (log)	2856	−4.57	7.52	−23.11	0
Debt Forgiveness $_{t-3}$ (log)	2857	−4.72	7.64	−23.11	0
Debt Forgiveness $_{t-5}$ (log)	2857	−4.84	7.71	−23.11	0
Debt Forgiveness $_{t-7}$ (log)	2857	−4.78	7.70	−23.11	0

13. Human rights contraction: sovereignty and denial of the right to food

Rhoda E. Howard-Hassmann

THE FULL-BELLY THESIS REVISITED

While most of the chapters in this volume consider human rights expansion, this chapter notes that sovereign states can either completely deny human rights or can significantly contract them. State sovereignty remains the single most significant barrier to fulfilment of human rights.

I discuss how three states, or rather the politicians and elites who control them, namely, North Korea, Zimbabwe, and Venezuela, deny their citizens the right to food. They do so by denying civil and political rights and by rejecting or ignoring international mechanisms that could alleviate the rights violations endured by their citizens. This denial is a matter of political will, not state incapacity; these are three states whose leaders make deliberate choices in their own interests as individuals to institute policies that deny their citizens access to food and/or the means to produce or procure it. These leaders exercise a "bastardized sovereignty"[1] for their own benefit, instead of for the benefit of their citizens, and completely neglect the state's duty to respect, protect, and fulfill the right to food. Not only do they not attempt to distribute food to citizens who do not have access to it, they also remove food from those who previously had had such access. Even when motivated to do so, the international community cannot protect citizens against these privileges of sovereignty because its mechanisms are too weak, are not resorted to, or do not address violations of economic human rights.

In 1983 I published an article entitled "The Full-Belly Thesis" in which I argued against the then-influential proposition that until a man's belly was full, he did not need freedom. That article was based on research on nine English-speaking sub-Saharan African countries: Ghana, Nigeria, Gambia, and Sierra Leone in West Africa and Kenya, Uganda, Malawi, Tanzania, and Zambia in East and Central Africa (Howard, 1983).

Perhaps it was too soon to write such an article, since the earliest date of independence for any of those countries was 1957 (Ghana). Nevertheless, some trends were already appearing. The first of these was "development" policies that actually resulted in de-development. By de-development, I mean policies that reduce production of food or that undermine activities producing foreign exchange that can be used to buy food.

Colonial rule, it was plausibly argued, had resulted in underdevelopment; at the time of independence, colonized countries may well have been less developed than they would have been had they never been colonized. However, even if one accepts that colonialism had caused underdevelopment, the rulers of newly independent countries began to de-develop their economies. In Tanzania, for example, the government had to divert foreign exchange to import food after it instituted a resettlement program in the mid 1970s that removed peasants from the fertile land they cultivated and sent them to infertile areas. In Ghana, cocoa farmers were underpaid by a state monopsony (monopoly of purchases) that sold cocoa on the world market but retained profits for the government to buy off urban voters; paid so little for their cocoa, the farmers did not have enough money to buy food (Howard, 1983, pp. 471–3).

All over sub-Saharan Africa, corruption was a huge problem, as predatory states arose based on personalist and nepotistic rule. The formal democracies set up at independence soon deteriorated into autocracies or were overthrown by military dictators. Governments undermined judicial independence and restricted freedom of speech, assembly, and press, so that when they introduced policies that restricted access to food citizens could not protest.

Thus, the proximate cause of de-development in many African countries from the 1960s to the 1990s was public policies instituted by governments that were either incapable of organizing efficient economies or uninterested in or unwilling to do so. Leaders of underdeveloped countries are capable of moral (or immoral) agency. For reasons of profit, greed, power, or ethnic affiliation they may very well replicate undemocratic colonial rule. Without collective and communal constraints, without an independent judiciary, and without any commitment to civil and political rights they often become authoritarian dictators.

Sadly, the sovereign rights of states to de-develop their economies and deny civil and political rights continue to the present. The same policies that undermined the right to food in the nine countries I wrote about in the 1980s continue in the 21st century, as I have shown in recent research on North Korea, Zimbabwe, and Venezuela (Howard-Hassmann, 2016).

THE SOVEREIGN RIGHT TO VIOLATE THE RIGHT TO FOOD

The right to food is not a new claim. It is included in the 1948 Universal Declaration of Human Rights (UDHR), Article 25, 1, which states that "Everyone has the right to a standard of living adequate for the health and well-being of himself and of his family, including food." The 1976 International Covenant on Economic, Social and Cultural Rights (ICESCR) mentions the rights to adequate food (Article 11, 1) and freedom from hunger (Article 11, 2). One cannot analyse the right to food, however, without reference both to states' economic ("development") policies and violations of civil and political rights in countries where the right to food is at risk. This section reviews international development standards, while the next discusses internal violations of civil and political rights.

For several decades the international process of standard-setting ignored internal policy decisions, instead focusing on international obligations and the apparent inequities of the world market. Yet states' sovereign legal right to violate human rights is a major cause of violations of the right to food and supersedes universal, individual human rights. It is, moreover, buttressed in the human rights discourse by the collective right to self-determination, protected in Article 1,1 of both the 1976 International Covenant on Civil and Political Rights (ICCPR) and the ICESCR. Self-determination was originally included in the Covenants as an anti-colonial measure (Burke, 2010) and most recently has been used to buttress the collective rights of indigenous people, as Gómez Isa discusses in this volume. However, it has often been used by states as an excuse to ignore international pressures to protect the rights of their inhabitants. But self-determination is a right of peoples, not states; it is especially not the right of elites that claim to represent their citizens but do not.

Two sets of international human rights standards are pertinent to this discussion: the right to development and the actual right to food. Until the late 1990s neither set insisted on states' responsibilities to respect, protect, and fulfill their citizens' right to food. Instead, both portrayed development as a politically neutral process, and/or blamed underdevelopment on colonialism and the international market rather than the policies of independent states. These policies included authoritarianism, brutal dictatorship, corruption, outright theft of national resources, and ideologically driven attempts at third world socialism. "Development" and economic human rights were de-politicized, while states insisted above all on protection of their right to sovereignty.

Under these circumstances, it is not surprising that the right to food was compromised. During the period when many African governments were consolidating their authoritarian and corrupt economic policies, the United Nations General Assembly (UNGA) voted in 1974 for a Declaration on a New International Economic Order (NIEO). This document advocated reorganization of world trade to remedy what it considered to be mechanisms unfair to less developed countries. For example, it called for a "just and equitable relationship" between the prices of exports and imports of developing countries to rectify their unbalanced terms of trade (United Nations General Assembly, 1974b, Article 4, j). An Iranian expert hired to write the first draft of the NIEO focused not only on international exchange but also on states' internal responsibilities, but by his second draft these latter responsibilities had disappeared (Whelan, 2015, pp. 8–12). States' sovereign rights to make their own economic policies (United Nations General Assembly, 1974b, Article 4, d) superseded any responsibility they had to ensure that those policies benefitted their citizens.

The Charter of Economic Rights and Duties of States (CERDS), also passed by the UNGA in 1974, contained a nod to "respect for human rights and fundamental freedoms," and noted that "the responsibility for the development of every country rests primarily upon itself" (United Nations General Assembly, 1974a, chapter I, k, and preambular par. 10). Yet, like the NIEO, the CERDS insisted on state sovereignty, especially states' sovereign right to choose their own economic systems, albeit "in accordance with the will of [their] people" (United Nations General Assembly, 1974a, chapter II, 1), even if systems such as command economies that eliminated markets and the right to own property (Article 17 of the UDHR) effectively de-developed their countries and even if the people had not been consulted.

By 1986, the NIEO and the CERDS had morphed into a right to development (R2D) but by this time the abuses committed by developmental (actually de-developmental) dictatorships were well known. Thus, the actual right R2D was now defined, rather redundantly, as "an inalienable human right by virtue of which every human person and all peoples are entitled to participate in, contribute to, and enjoy economic, social, cultural, and political development, in which all human rights and fundamental freedoms can be fully realized" (United Nations General Assembly, 1986, Article 1, 1). But like its predecessors, the R2D did not refer to states' internal responsibilities: rather, under the rubric of sovereignty the R2D permitted states to promote "development" in any way they wished. Thus, the NIEO, the CERDS, and R2D all protected states' sovereign right to de-develop their economies.

The evolution of the right to food parallels that of the R2D. The Universal Declaration on the Eradication of Hunger and Malnutrition

(UDEHM) was adopted by the World Food Conference and endorsed by the UNGA in 1974. Just as the NIEO does not attribute any responsibility to states for de-developing their countries, so the UDEHM does not attribute to them any responsibility for depriving their citizens of the right to food. Rather, it refers to colonialism, apartheid, and the market economy as causes of food deprivation (World Food Conference, 1974, paras. c and d). Moreover, while the UDEHM criticized the world economy, it did not acknowledge that functioning market economies are often essential to the right to food. It also ignored citizens' need to exercise their civil and political rights in order to protect their right to food. Rather, like the NIEO and the CERDS, it stresses national sovereignty and non-interference in the internal affairs of states (World Food Conference, 1974, para. h).

By 1999, the international community had begun to acknowledge that the right to food could not be separated from civil and political rights. In that year the United Nations Committee on Economic, Social and Cultural Rights issued its General Comment 12. The Comment condemned "the use of food as a political weapon," and noted that "Violations of the right to food can occur through the direct action of States" (Committee on Economic, Social and Cultural Rights, 1999, Articles 5 and 19). In 2005, the Food and Agriculture Organization (FAO) adopted voluntary guidelines on food security. These guidelines were modeled on General Comment 12 and noted the importance of civil and political rights to the economic human right to food. Guideline 1, 2 focused on democracy, good governance, human rights, and the rule of law, and specifically mentioned freedom of opinion, expression, information, press, and assembly/association. It further stated that "Food should not be used as a tool for political and economic pressure" (Food and Agriculture Organization, 2005).

Thus, by the 2000s the international human rights regime recognized the indivisibility and interdependence of civil and political and economic human rights. The 1993 United Nations conference on human rights in Vienna had proclaimed that "All human rights are universal, indivisible and interdependent and interrelated" (United Nations, 1993, Article 5). It was now fully acknowledged that to satisfy their economic human right to food, people must also enjoy their civil and political human rights. Nevertheless, for almost half a century international standards on development and the right to food were characterized by colossal cynicism and resort to state sovereignty as a cover for, at best, government mismanagement of entire economies and, at worst, elite theft of resources needed to promote the right to food. This undermined serious attention to the real requirements for development and concomitant protection of the right to food, especially civil and political rights.

CIVIL AND POLITICAL RIGHTS: PREREQUISITES TO THE RIGHT TO FOOD

The right to food is neither a mere matter of devising the right economic policies, although such policies are its necessary prerequisite, nor is it a matter of legal standard-setting, although such standards might assist critics of states that deny their citizens access to food. The right to food depends on enjoyment of civil and political rights, which many government leaders deny to their citizens. Some people starve so that other people can enrich themselves or maintain themselves in power.

Regime type is a significant factor determining whether citizens enjoy their right to food. Personalist dictatorships such as existed in sub-Saharan Africa in the 1980s, totalitarian governments such as North Korea, and authoritarian quasi-democracies such as Zimbabwe and Venezuela all deny their citizens the rule of law and other civil and political rights, thus also rendering civil society organization in defense of rights either completely impossible or extremely difficult. Totalitarian and authoritarian regimes also routinely ban or undermine official political opposition. There is, however, some space in authoritarian regimes for political opposition and civil society organizations, compared to none in totalitarian regimes.

In this chapter I refer to "citizens" of the three contemporary states under discussion, but such terminology is accurate only in a passive, legal sense. Active citizenship depends upon "the right to have rights," the right to act upon one's rights in the public sphere, and the consequent capacity to influence government policies (Arendt, 1951 [1973], p. 296). Citizenship in this sense is not merely a formal legal status, it is "that set of practices (juridical, political, economic, and cultural) which define a person as a competent member of society, and which as a consequence shape the flow of resources to persons and social groups" (Turner, 1993, p. 2). Yet totalitarian regimes such as North Korea turn their citizens into mere inhabitants of the state, absolutely rightless in all respects.[2] As mere inhabitants, they depend upon a capricious state to provide or deny them food, without remedy if the food is insufficient or nonexistent. Authoritarian regimes such as Zimbabwe and Venezuela impose severe constraints upon citizenship, as the net tightens around political opponents and civil society activists.

Civil and political rights are key mechanisms that force the state to implement policies that protect the right to food. They are not only the rights to freedom of the press, free elections, and the existence of a genuine political opposition mentioned by Amartya Sen in his influential argument that there are no famines in functioning democracies (Sen, 1999, pp. 178–86). In my research on state food crimes in North Korea, Zimbabwe, and Venezuela from 1990 to 2015 I concluded that citizenship rights, mobility rights, the right to own property, and the right to work are also key to the right to food.

Since its creation in 1948, North Korea has been ruled by a dynastic dictatorship of the Kim family; grandfather, father, and son. This family's economic policies are based on the Soviet Union's model of collectivized agriculture and abolition of private property and markets. Without private plots of land, without a market economy, without investment in agriculture, and without the fuel, fertilizer, and food previously provided by the Soviet Union and China, North Koreans suffered a famine in the 1990s and severe malnutrition in the 21st century. They had no rights as citizens, rather being mere inhabitants of their own country. They had no mobility rights, risking imprisonment if they dared to travel in search of food, either within North Korea or abroad as refugees. They were not permitted to own property in land or other productive goods with which they could grow food or earn money to purchase it. While they were provided with work – or in many case, make-work – they were paid very little and the majority were dependent for food on minimal rations provided by the state (Howard-Hassmann, 2012b). The Kims were not simply making policy errors; rather, they used food as a weapon against their citizens, forcing them to rely completely on the state for all their needs.

Zimbabweans endured severe malnutrition after 2000 as a result of a government policy of "invasion" of large commercial farms owned mainly by whites, some of them Zimbabwean citizens: the land invasions constituted arbitrary deprivation of property, prohibited by Article 17, 2 of the UDHR. These farms had produced food for both the internal and export markets; they were ostensibly to be redistributed to landless peasants, many of whom were descendants of black Africans whose land had earlier been stolen by white settlers. However, many farms were instead given to the family and cronies of Robert Mugabe, the President of Zimbabwe since its independence in 1980, and in many cases the new owners did not farm the land at all.

The result of the takeovers was a drastic reduction in the country's food supply. Moreover, many black farm laborers were left without employment and thus without income to buy food. Simultaneously, a massive expulsion of Zimbabweans from the cities in 2005 deprived them of their livelihoods, including their capacity to produce or buy food. Thus, white Zimbabweans were deprived of property rights, although they did not suffer malnutrition or starvation. Black Zimbabweans retained citizenship but were deprived of mobility rights (the right to stay put as well as the right to move). Workers expelled from the white-owned farms and urban expellees were also effectively deprived of their right to work; without work they could not buy food. At the same time all civil and political rights were undermined, and the political opposition suffered mass violence, torture, and rape, especially but not only during the 2008 elections (Howard-Hassmann, 2010b).

Venezuela was ruled by Hugo Chávez from 1999 until his death in 2013, and thereafter by Nicolás Maduro. Both were populist leaders who manipulated the market and political system in attempts to provide food to the poor, but their policies actually resulted in severe reduction in its supply. They undermined the right to own property by expropriating large ranches and farms, as well as some wholesalers. They instituted controls that forced retailers to sell food at such low prices that it was easier to simply go out of business; this also deprived some Venezuelans of the right to work. Chávez and Maduro progressively undermined the independent judiciary and freedom of the press and association; periodic elections were marred by manipulation of citizenship rolls, political violence, and threats of civil war. However, no one was deprived of legal (as opposed to effective) citizenship or mobility rights (Howard-Hassmann, 2015). Nevertheless, by 2015 reports of child malnutrition and even starvation surfaced, as citizens had to spend more and more of their time searching for less and less food (The Economist, 2015).

These three cases demonstrate the importance of effective, active citizenship utilizing civil and political rights to protect the right to food. Yet in all three, either the citizens never enjoyed civil and political rights, as in North Korea, or they were progressively deprived of those rights as their access to food declined, as in Zimbabwe and Venezuela. None of the three countries had an independent judiciary that could protect citizens from their governments. Such a judiciary had never existed in North Korea, while in Zimbabwe and Venezuela governments packed courts with their supporters and used intimidation and threats to undermine the independent judiciary that had been present when they took power.

Political opposition never existed in North Korea and was progressively curtailed and intimidated in Zimbabwe and Venezuela. Nevertheless, there remains a difference between totalitarian and authoritarian regimes. In Venezuela, political opposition groups continued to function despite threats, torture, imprisonment, and some assassinations, and indeed won the 2015 congressional elections, although Maduro continued as president. The opposition also continued to function in Zimbabwe despite massive violence, rapes, and torture.

Civil society was completely prohibited in North Korea but had a limited presence in the other two countries. Unlike in democracies such as India where, as Hertel discusses in this volume, there is active "bottom-up" advocacy for the right to food, in totalitarian and authoritarian regimes there is no or very little room for civil society actors, unless they are willing to risk imprisonment, if not death. External civil society actors also have limited capacity to aid victims of violation of the right to food. Christian activists try to distribute food in North Korea. They also assist refugees in north-east China to escape detection by Chinese officials, who return them to face torture, imprisonment, and execution in North Korea. But these activists run severe risks of arrest in both countries. In any event, these external civil society actors cannot assist North Koreans to realize their civil and political rights so that they can act in their own interests. In contrast to North Korea's totalitarian control on civil society actors, there is some room for independent civil society groups such as churches in Zimbabwe. Others, such as women's groups, operate but run risks of arrest and worse.

Just as the sub-Saharan countries that I discussed in 1983 showed that there can be no separation of the economic human right to food from civil and political rights, so these three contemporary cases also demonstrate this principle. The most that people who do not enjoy civil and political rights can hope for is that they will live under a relatively benign dictator or regime that, for reasons of ideology or self-interest, will distribute food to its citizens. But even benign intentions to distribute food can be easily undermined without civil and political rights and sensible economic policies, as Venezuela shows. An effective claim for the economic human right to food requires intensified and expanded exercise of civil and political rights. Without these rights, citizens are obliged to rely on international mechanisms to pressure their governments to ensure their access to food.

INTERNATIONAL MECHANISMS TO PROTECT THE RIGHT TO FOOD

Several international mechanisms might be considered available to remedy sovereign state violations of the right to food: these include international law, international standard-setting, sanctions and foreign aid, and non-law international organizations. Unfortunately, none has proved successful regarding North Korea, Zimbabwe, or Venezuela. While the institutional infrastructure exists for some weak enforcement of human rights by the international community, states can reject, ignore, or sidestep pressures.

The 1948 Convention on the Prevention and Punishment of the Crime of Genocide condemns the practice of "deliberately inflicting on the group conditions of life calculated to bring about its physical destruction in whole or in part," but this convention applies only to people selected because of their membership in particular national, racial, ethnic, or religious groups (United Nations General Assembly, 1948, Article 2). It does not, therefore, apply to what might be considered genocide by state-induced famine in North Korea, where the people who starved to death were, for the most part, of the same "racial"/ethnic, national, and religious background as their oppressors.

The International Criminal Court (ICC) can try individuals for genocide, crimes against humanity, and war crimes. One aspect of crimes against humanity is "extermination," including deprivation of access to food (International Criminal Court, 1998, Article 7, 2, b). In 2014 a Commission of Inquiry established by the United Nations Human Rights Council recommended referring the situation in North Korea to the ICC for consideration of possible crimes against humanity, including denial of access to food (COI: United Nations General Assembly, 2014). It might be of some value if the ICC were indeed to indict North Korean leaders for the crime of extermination, as the Commission suggested. However, the international community must also negotiate with and/or sanction North Korea because of its ongoing program to develop nuclear weapons. This program could affect the lives and security of many tens of millions of people not only in the Koreas but also in the surrounding region; concern to stop it often takes precedence over the international community's desire to assist starving North Koreans.

As Sandholtz discusses in this volume, some meso-level regional courts, especially the European and Inter-American Courts of Human Rights, have the capacity to bring states to account, but only if states submit to their authority. Venezuela withdrew from the Inter-American Commission of Human Rights in 2012 (Kornblith, 2013, p. 52) and in general ignored criticism by the Organization of American States. This criticism pinpointed violation of civil and political rights rather than the right to food, but as discussed above, civil and political rights are required so that citizens can act in defense of other rights.

The African Union (AU), a regional inter-governmental body, might have persuaded Mugabe to mitigate his violations of human rights in Zimbabwe, but instead it supported him as one of the "grand old men" of the liberation struggle against colonialism. The AU blocked any referral of Mugabe or other Zimbabweans to the ICC for the crime of extermination, claiming that the Court was a creation of Western imperialists (Magliveras and Naldi, 2013). The Southern African Development Community (SADC) is a sub-regional African organization. A SADC Tribunal ruled in 2008 that Zimbabwe had violated the rights of white farmers by denying them access to Zimbabwean courts and engaging in racial discrimination; in response, the SADC heads of states suspended the Tribunal. Thus, African and especially SADC heads of states might be considered enablers of Mugabe's violations of the right to food.

Sanctions also proved to be a weak mechanism to protect the right to food. Since 2009 the United Nations Security Council (UNSC) has imposed sanctions on North Korea, not as punishment for its food policies but for its threatened development of nuclear weapons. These are "smart sanctions," designed not to harm the general population but to punish specific individuals via travel bans and bans on imports of luxury goods to North Korea; arms bans are also in place. In 2016, after a fourth nuclear test, the UNSC reinforced and extended these sanctions (United Nations Security Council, 2016). China supported the new sanctions, suggesting that its previous tolerance of North Korea as a client state was wearing thin and that its role as an enabler of human rights violations was weakening.

The international community's attempts to sanction Mugabe failed. He ignored expulsions from international organizations such as the Commonwealth; he also used the sanctions on individuals imposed by the Commonwealth, the European Union, and the United States (including travel bans on and freezing of assets of key officials) as propaganda tools to argue that sanctions were the cause of Zimbabwe's economic chaos. As for Venezuela, very little could be done by the international community to protect its inhabitants' right to food. Chávez's and Maduro's policies did not reach the level of crimes against humanity, nor was the intent to starve Venezuelans; indeed, the original intent was to fulfill their need for food. Venezuela's undermining of the right to food and its violations of civil and political rights were well within the norm for the many rights-violating states that still existed in 2016.

Sanctions are a "stick" approach to countries that violate human rights, while food aid is a "carrot" approach. North Korea used its nuclear policy to manipulate donor nations such as the United States, South Korea, and Japan into providing food aid. The aid provided budgetary support to North Korea, which could then divert other funds to its nuclear program. It seemed also that food aid meant for civilians was diverted to the military and that some regions were less likely to receive it than others, depending on their perceived political reliability. Zimbabwe also manipulated food aid, distributing it to Mugabe's supporters and denying it to supporters of the opposition, even to their children. As of 2015, Maduro's policy in Venezuela was to import more and more food, rather than call for food aid.

Finally, there is the problem of the sovereign right to de-development. Above I discussed the 20th-century hypocrisy in evolving standards for the right to development and the right to food that ignored the responsibilities of states. The term "gatekeeper" refers to "entities at the core of the human rights movement, whose support for a claim can boost it substantially" (Bob, 2009, p. 6). To date, no human rights gatekeepers have taken up the problem of the sovereign right to de-development. Rather, the international check on policies of de-development lies with the International Monetary Fund (IMF) and the World Bank (WB). In return for loans, the IMF can require changes in internal economic policies, but as Apodaca points out in this volume, the IMF has weak, if any, obligations regarding human rights. While one might argue that it has those obligations as an organ of society (as in preambular para. 8 of the UDHR), it is reluctant to accept them. Nevertheless, since the human rights catastrophes of its structural adjustment policies became known (Abouharb and Cingranelli, 2007), the IMF has accepted that poverty reduction strategies should go hand in hand with monetary stabilization. The WB accepts stronger human rights obligations and accepts that economic human rights are intertwined with civil and political rights. (On the IMF and WB, see Howard-Hassmann, 2010a, pp. 93–8.) But no sovereign government is obliged to accept the IMF's advice or accept development aid from the WB. Governments can simply ignore these organizations, as they can ignore international laws and norms, with almost complete impunity.

EFFECTIVE STATE IMPUNITY

The "new" claim to the right to food is in fact an old one. The claim has always been there, hidden under standards that until the 1990s exculpated states and the elites that control them from the responsibility to honor it, while simultaneously undermining the very mechanisms that would actually protect it. The cynical manipulation of the false debate on the relative importance and merits of civil and political and economic, social and cultural rights is one mechanism by which states avoid their responsibilities to protect the right to food. Another mechanism is manipulation of the claim to sovereignty to avoid criticism by outside states or actors such as civil society groups. Sovereignty over economic policy, combined with the sovereign right to violate human rights and the impunity that permits these violations, makes it easy – and often personally worthwhile – for state elites to undermine the right to food.

Despite the existence of an international legal regime supposedly protecting all human rights, very little can be done by the international community to protect citizens from governments that violate them, even when such violations reach the level of crimes against humanity. States are only marginally more likely to be punished for undermining the right to food in 2016 than they were in 1983. All three countries discussed in this chapter violated all human rights with almost complete impunity.

How then, if at all, can the right to food be protected within sovereign states that are totalitarian or authoritarian, where so-called citizens are actually mere inhabitants of their states, and where it is almost impossible for the political opposition and civil society to organize? Strengthening of the normative value of economic human rights might be of some value. At the moment, despite the fact that as of March 2016 there were 164 parties to the ICESCR, much international opinion still considers them to be "soft" rights, perhaps somewhat stronger than mere aspirations but not strong enough to be rigorously enforced in law.

A strengthened normative commitment to economic human rights would not, however, permit international intervention in countries that violate their citizens' right to food via irrational economic policies and suppression of civil and political rights, as in Venezuela and Zimbabwe. The IMF and WB gatekeepers on economic policy have only weak, if any, human rights obligations. The IMF and the WB are organizations of states, however, and it is ultimately states' obligation to change their policies (Gibney, 2016, p. 50).

As for violations of those civil and political rights necessary for the right to food, no international human rights court exists in which the leaders of states that intentionally and systematically violate human rights can be tried. In any event, states would be able to ignore the rulings of such a court, just as some do the rulings of the International Court of Justice. Meanwhile, weak protective mechanisms such as monitoring and shaming have little or no effect on the most rights-abusive leaders. Totalitarian states are almost completely immune to shaming, but sometimes authoritarian ones are susceptible to condemnatory international opinion, and sometimes certain sectors within them, such as judges, seek respect from their counterparts elsewhere.

Despite this pessimistic assessment of enduring state impunity, a contrast with the situation that existed in 1983 shows some legal and normative development over the past 33 years.

The ICC did not exist in 1983; the Rome Statute that established it was not negotiated until 1998 and the Court did not come into effect until 2002. Twelve years later, a Commission established by the Human Rights Council did recommend that some unnamed North Korean individuals be referred to it for crimes against humanity, including the crime of extermination via deprivation of food. As for normative if not yet legal change, the concept of rights-based development entered the lexicon of development agencies in the late 1990s (Nelson and Dorsey, 2008, pp. 19–22). Earlier, strong feminist advocacy had already forced development agencies to consider the role of women in development, especially as rural food producers (Howard, 1993); this concern was reflected in Article 14 of the 1979 Convention against All Forms of Discrimination against Women. Many international documents, such as the 1989 Convention on the Rights of the Child (Article 24, 1, c) specifically mention the right to food, thus further strengthening international normative concern (Apodaca, 2014; Niada, 2006–07).

There is not yet an international law specifically prohibiting denial of the right to food, although some international lawyers have called for one (Marcus, 2003). In any event, there is much debate about the conditions, if any, under which a state's ratification of international human rights law actually improves its performance (Hathaway, 2002; Simmons, 2009); thus, there is no guarantee that such a new law would have any concrete effect. It might, however, serve as a benchmark against which both local and international civil society groups could measure the performance of individual states.

Perhaps the right to food is not the best frame for addressing food deprivation, as it implies judicialization of what may fundamentally be problems of economic and political policies. Some newer frameworks for the right to food might be more effective. One is food security, part of the human security agenda promoted actively within the United Nations and by some states since the mid 1990s. This agenda implies that states are responsible in some instances for the security of people living outside their borders, thus breaking down strict notions of sovereignty (Howard-Hassmann, 2012a). Using this frame, one might argue that state-induced starvation is a reason to invoke the doctrine of the responsibility to protect, which so far is confined to protection against large-scale loss of life through such practices as genocide and ethnic cleansing (International Commission on Intervention and State Sovereignty, 2001).

Another alternative framework is food sovereignty, promoted by international and local civil society groups, especially Via Campesina, a peasants' movement originally started in South America (Patel, 2009). Via Campesina is now a world-wide social movement that seeks to protect peasants' rights and in general advocates protectionist stances by states against the global food market (Haugen, 2009). This movement is not concerned with my own focus in this chapter; that is, states that deliberately, as a matter of policy, deprive their citizens of food. Nevertheless, it reinforces the relatively new claim to the right to food.

Thus, it is perhaps too strong to argue that states possess complete impunity when they violate the right to food. Silence is no longer a frame for this right.

NOTES

1. I owe this term to a comment by George Lopez at the workshop organized by our editor, Alison Brysk, at University of California Santa Barbara, 25–27 February 2016.
2. I owe this terminology to a comment by George Lopez.

REFERENCES

Abouharb, M.R. and D. Cingranelli (2007). *Human Rights and Structural Adjustment*. New York: Cambridge University Press.

Apodaca, C. (2014). "The Right to Food." In T. Cushman (ed.), *Handbook of Human Rights*. New York: Routledge, pp. 349–58.

Arendt, H. (1951). *The Origins of Totalitarianism*. Reprinted in 1973. New York: Harcourt Brace Jovanovich.

Bob, C. (2009). "Introduction: Fighting for New Rights." In C. Bob (ed.), *The International Struggle for New Human Rights*. Philadelphia, PA: University of Pennsylvania Press, pp. 1–13.

Burke, R. (2010). *Decolonization and the Evolution of International Human Rights*. Philadelphia, PA: University of Pennsylvania Press.

COI: United Nations General Assembly (2014, 7 February). *Report of the Detailed Findings of the Commission of Inquiry on Human Rights in the Democratic People's Republic of Korea*. Human Rights Council. A/HRC/25/CRP.1.

Committee on Economic, Social and Cultural Rights (1999). General Comment No. 12: The Right to Adequate Food. Economic and Social Council, United Nations, Geneva.

Food and Agriculture Organization (2005). Voluntary Guidelines to support the progressive realization of the right to adequate food in the context of national food security. Food and Agriculture Organization, Rome.

Gibney, M. (2016). *International Human Rights Law: Returning to Universal Principles*, 2nd edn. New York: Rowman and Littlefield.

Hathaway, O.A. (2002). "Do Human Rights Treaties Make a Difference?" *The Yale Law Journal* **111**(8), 1935–2042.

Haugen, H.M. (2009). "Food Sovereignty – An Appropriate Approach to Ensure the Right to Food?" *Nordic Journal of International Law* **78**, 263–93.

Howard, R. (1983). "The Full-Belly Thesis: Should Economic Rights Take Priority Over Civil and Political Rights? Evidence from Sub-Saharan Africa." *Human Rights Quarterly* **5**(4), 467–90.

Howard, R.E. (1993). "Women's Rights and the Right to Development." In R. Cohen, G. Hyden, and W.P. Nagan (eds), *Human Rights and Governance in Africa*. Gainesville, FL: University Press of Florida, pp. 111–38.

Howard-Hassmann, R.E. (2010a). *Can Globalization Promote Human Rights?* University Park, PA: Pennsylvania State University Press.

Howard-Hassmann, R.E. (2010b). "Mugabe's Zimbabwe 2000–2009: Massive

Human Rights Violations and the Failure to Protect." *Human Rights Quarterly* **32**(4), 898–920.

Howard-Hassmann, R.E. (2012a). "Human Security: Undermining Human Rights?" *Human Rights Quarterly* **34**(1), 88–112.

Howard-Hassmann, R.E. (2012b). "State-induced Famine and Penal Starvation in North Korea." *Genocide Studies and Prevention* **7**(2/3), 147–65.

Howard-Hassmann, R.E. (2015). "The Right to Food Under Hugo Chavez." *Human Rights Quarterly* **37**(4), 1024–45.

Howard-Hassmann, R.E. (2016). *State Food Crimes*. New York: Cambridge University Press.

International Commission on Intervention and State Sovereignty (2001). *The Responsibility to Protect*. Ottawa: International Development Research Centre.

International Criminal Court (1998). Rome Statute of the International Criminal Court.

Kornblith, M. (2013). "Chavismo After Chavez?" *Journal of Democracy* **24**(3), 47–61.

Magliveras, K.D. and G.J. Naldi (2013). "The International Criminal Court's Involvement with Africa: Evaluation of a Fractious Relationship." *Nordic Journal of International Law* **82**, 417–46.

Marcus, D. (2003). "Famine Crimes in International Law." *American Journal of International Law* **97**(2), 245–81.

Nelson, P.J. and E. Dorsey (2008). *New Rights Advocacy: Changing Strategies of Development and Human Rights NGOs*. Washington, DC: Georgetown University Press.

Niada, L. (2006–07). "Hunger and International Law: The Far-reaching Scope of the Human Right to Food." *Connecticut Journal of International Law* **22**, 131–201.

Patel, R. (2009). "What Does Food Sovereignty Look Like?" *Journal of Peasant Studies* **36**(3), 663–706.

Sen, A. (1999). *Development as Freedom*. New York: Alfred A. Knopf.

Simmons, B.A. (2009). *Mobilizing for Human Rights: International Law in Domestic Politics*. New York: Cambridge University Press.

The Economist (2015, 20 June). "Food and Venezuela: Let Them Eat Chavismo." *The Economist*, 36.

Turner, B.S. (1993). "Contemporary Problems in the Theory of Citizenship." In B.S. Turner (ed.), *Citizenship and Social Theory*. London: Sage, pp. 1–18.

United Nations (1993, 12 July). World Conference on Human Rights: Vienna Declaration and Program of Action. United Nations.

United Nations General Assembly (1948, 9 December). Convention on the Prevention and Punishment of the Crime of Genocide.

United Nations General Assembly (1974a). Charter of Economic Rights and Duties of States.

United Nations General Assembly (1974b). Declaration on the Establishment of a New International Economic Order.

United Nations General Assembly (1986). Declaration on the Right to Development.

United Nations Security Council (2016, 2 March). Security Council Imposes Fresh Sanctions on Democratic People's Republic of Korea, Unanimously Adopting Resolution 2270 (2016).

Whelan, D.J. (2015, June). "'Flammis Acribus Addictis': Requiem for the Right to Development." ISA Human Rights Joint Conference. Hague Institute for Global Justice, The Hague.

World Food Conference (1974, 17 December). Universal Declaration on the Eradication of Hunger and Malnutrition. United Nations General Assembly, New York.

PART VI

Conclusion

14. Conclusions on norms, institutions and processes

Michael Stohl

As this volume was going to press, the International Criminal Court (ICC) sentenced Jean-Pierre Bemba, a Congolese military commander and current vice president, to 18 years in prison for the crimes of his subordinates and for using sexual violence as a weapon of war. Jurists, human rights activists and some governments as well as the United Nations (UN) High Commissioner for Human Rights hailed the decision. For example, the United States – although not a signatory to the ICC – stated the conviction "is a significant victory for international justice and a major advancement in the fight against impunity for crimes of sexual violence" (Power, 2016). On the other hand, most African governments and the Organisation of African Unity (OAU) were either silent or indicated their displeasure with the targeting of African leaders by the ICC and indicated that they thought the conviction was "political." (See http://www.ijmonitor.org/2016/03/reactions-to-bembas-conviction/.) An exception was Botswana, a signatory, which praised the decision.

The recognition that sexual violence is a weapon of war and a clear violation of human rights illustrates the arguments we have made throughout this volume that the mobilization of new actors, new rights claims, new institutions and channels of leverage, and new modes of accountability continue to lead to the identification of new standards, new norms and new institutions for the development and protection of human rights. And while activists rightly think that this particular right took far too long to recognize, the challenges they raised and the process of reframing rape as a war crime and transferring the framing of the crime from the private, personal sphere to the public was at the core of what led to the successful court decision (see Brysk, this volume for a discussion of the process).

As we have seen throughout in the contributions to this volume, new mechanisms for enforcing existing rights and new strategies for claiming rights for new populations and processes continue to emerge. Contributors have noted the potential and limitations of these expansions of the horizon of human rights and highlighted how an expanded notion of human rights can lead to new possibilities for reform, but noted where expectations and aspirations still fall short. As Baer (this volume) in her discussion of water rights notes, "Human rights have become a modern lingua franca – a frame that provides an 'emancipatory script' that resonates with powerful global actors (Brysk, 2013, p. 32). However, there is also resistance to expanding the human rights repertoire, and particularly strong resistance to empowering and legitimizing ESCR (economic, social, and cultural) rights claims in a human rights regime that focuses primarily on civil/political rights." Before considering some general conclusions, let us turn to some of the major insights from the contributors.

Ayoub emphasizes the importance of transnational resources – social spaces and organizational capacity – that were scarce in Poland and readily available in Berlin. These resources served as mobilizing structures for activism, bringing together cross-border networks of distinct actors who were connected by common identities. Tactical outcomes in Poland included gaining the support of some political elites, police protection for protestors, media visibility and international attention. However, the expansion of human rights to include LGBT people has happened in a contested terrain, and backlash and resistance to such claims and mobilization is common, if not expected – and Ayoub recounts the steps by which the LGBT/human rights debate was altered in Poland. The 2015 Polish election, which returned a nationalist and socially conservative government whose outspoken opposition to gender and sexual rights is counterproductive to the movement in the long run remains unclear, but activists of various liberal social justice groups have taken to the street in the thousands to denounce the politics of the new government. In sum, the fluidity of LGBT identities – ones that can benefit them in human rights discourses – has also made them particularly threatening to national identities, which are usually more fixed, provoking opposition. Ayoub demonstrates how the expansion of rights is a dynamic process.

Tsutsui reinforces Ayoub's insights. He traces the case of the Japanese Burakumin. The Burakumin sought help at the UN to overcome social discrimination within their own setting in Japan. They challenged the discrimination accorded them within the Japanese social and political structure in the global forum. As they worked for recognition and remedies for their own human rights deprivations within the UN, their perspective on their problem was globalized and they reframed the problem in more general terms and eventually became activists on behalf of other groups across the globe. They not only established a non-governmental organization (NGO) that was accorded consultative status but were able to move past their own particular discrimination challenge and establish discrimination based on work and descent as a new global category of human right.

Baer, as did Brysk in her discussion of women's rights, demonstrates how expanding rights may require reframing an old problem in new terms. She demonstrates how reframing water as a human right rather than an economic good transformed the debate about the right to water. Baer (as does Hertel discussed below) finds that much of this reframing and subsequent debate occurred outside the traditional human rights regime and was led by NGOs that were not traditional human rights organizations. Baer shows how champions within the International Governmental sphere included governments in the global south and global north (which also had significant opposing governments) while traditional human rights organizations who often act as key gatekeepers in the debates about the expansion of rights such as Amnesty International and Human Rights Watch did not begin to champion water rights until 2010 and 2013, respectively.

Baer also, as we see also in the chapter by Gómez Isa, finds that moving the issue of enforcement and implementation forward is key to the expansion of rights. The success in securing UN General Assembly (UNGA) and Human Rights Council (HRC) Resolutions has not led to implementation of the human right to water and sanitation (HRtWS). However, as Gómez Isa argues in the case of the United Nations Declaration on the Rights of Indigenous Peoples (UNDRIP), the resolutions create the basis for the standards that may shape international, regional and national level changes that can be developed for implementation by providing benchmarks for continued advocacy efforts that over time should lead to the development of the principles as a norm. Indeed, Gómez Isa demonstrates how indigenous peoples moved from being considered as populations that required protection to peoples having rights that should be recognized and secured both domestically and internationally. He examines how indigenous peoples used the UN as a mobilizing structure to increase visibility of their marginalized position and to pursue some strategic goals in terms of recognition and protection. The adoption of the UNDRIP, in spite of the opposition of some key member states, led in a short time to its acceptance as both a standard and norm among member states. Further, the movement to norm was followed at both the regional and national levels to its incorporation into existing law. At the regional level, both the Inter-American Court of Human Rights and the African Commission on Human and Peoples' Rights are using the UNDRIP as one of the legal bases for their findings and decisions and the UNDRIP has provided the basis for national courts to also import these rights into legal decisions.

Hertel offers a different path forward to the expansion of rights in her examination of the Right to Food (RTF) campaign. Indian activists developed a hybrid approach that simultaneously demanded prevention of hunger deaths (that is, guarantee of the right to life) and progressive implementation of economic rights (that is, improved food distribution through ongoing reform of public feeding programs). Hertel argues that "[T]he RTF campaign's main contribution to broader economic rights discourse has been this creative melding of non-derogable and progressively realized rights demands (Hertel, 2015, p. 76)."

Hertel forces us to consider how we might rethink norms evolution and advocacy strategies given that national institutions in countries outside the West in some instances have stronger track records on economic rights interpretation and implementation than do governments or institutions in industrialized countries. Hertel rightly directs attention to the important role of economic rights advocates who have, in this case, been much more than translators and acted as creators of new frames and discourses by which to expand the approach and campaign to extending human rights.

Sandholtz in his examination of the regional human rights courts concludes that these courts act as protagonists in the struggle over defining and fulfilling rights. He argues that the courts provide an institutional arena in which new kinds of claims can be advanced and recognized, that they can empower previously marginalized persons and that they contributed not only to consolidating the regional human rights regimes but also to developing human rights law. Sandholtz highlights the political context for the rights process and the role of the courts in balancing their desire to expand the scope of human rights norms with the necessity of maintaining acceptance and support among their compliance constituencies. He highlights the difference in strategy that flows from the differing political context in which the two courts operate. While the European Court of Human Rights' (ECtHR) main strategy for expanding rights has been steadily to reduce the scope allowed to states to restrict individual rights for the sake of public purposes, the Inter-American Court's most consistent approach has been to expand rights by establishing positive duties for states to ensure respect for rights, prevent violations and investigate and prosecute serious abuses. While both courts have confronted resistance to their decisions and worry about backlash and even non-compliance by states with their decisions, Sandholtz argues that this resistance and backlash has not yet reduced the Court's formal authority and that therefore the regional human rights courts are likely to continue as important sources of rights innovation and expansion.

Stohl and Stohl explore the development of new conceptions of corporate social responsibility (CSR) as an expansion of the concept of human rights. They highlight the tension between those that view CSR as voluntary and private and those who approach the question in terms of business and human rights through compulsory actions. They argue that while CSR and its connection to human rights still remain highly contested concepts, there have nonetheless been advances in the development of not only voluntary actions but international regulation and compliance. To illustrate they focus especially on corporate behaviors with respect to emergent social media and communication rights. The chapter highlights the interplay of NGOs, states and corporations in the development of CSR as both a norm of global behavior and an arena for expanding conceptions of human rights. Stohl and Stohl argue that while the UN Guiding Principles on Business and Human Rights has boosted the standard-setting, promotion and protection mechanisms that foster successful regimes and that another step has been taken on the path to securing the legitimacy and institutionalization of the CSR, it has also provided the focus for resistance to CSR as an approach to human rights.

Apodaca explores the record of the international financial institutions (IFIs) associated with the UN. Apodaca argues that IFIs have at a minimum a duty to respect and protect the right of the child to survival. Yet the International Bank for Reconstruction and Development (IBRD) lending arm of the World Bank is falling short of fulfilling its human rights obligations, and millions of children are continuing to die as a result. On the other hand, International Development Association (IDA) lending benefits child survival, but the coefficients are small. Even more discouraging, International Monetary Fund (IMF) concessional lending to low-income countries is statistically insignificant in reducing child mortality until the year in which the program expires (seven-year lag), at which time child mortality increases. IMF non-concessional lending has no effect on child mortality, although in the medium term, five years after the IMF loan, it reduces mortality, supporting the argument that monetary stability is beneficial in the medium term for child survival. Apodaca argues for a clear expansion of IFI human rights duties, providing evidence for activists to employ and argues that IFIs should be held accountable for the human rights consequences of their policies, lending and directives.

Jo and Alley argue that the conventional wisdom that rebel groups are human rights violators is complicated by the fact that rebel groups are Janus-faced on the issue of human rights. Rebel groups often act as human rights advocates as well as perpetrators of human rights violations. And in some cases, rebel groups advocate on behalf of not only their own but also the population's human rights. The clear establishment of human rights particularly physical integrity rights as a norm of international behavior means that rebel groups cannot live outside the realm of human rights politics. They can no longer ignore expanding human rights norms. Although the incentive to violate human rights is generally strong in fighting against governments, we also have to note that some rebel groups are willing to express their human rights credentials and are capable of doing so.

However, as Howard-Hassmann demonstrates, there are still very important gaps and impediments that give pause to the celebration of the expansion of rights that we have witnessed throughout much of the volume. "Despite the existence of an international legal regime supposedly protecting all human rights, very little can be done by the international community to protect citizens from governments that violate them, even when such violations reach the level of crimes against humanity." State sovereignty and the willingness of authoritarian regimes to ignore the shaming that is directed toward them remain key impediments. This is no less the case for Howard-Hassmann's analysis of the right to food than is the case of the condemnation of the behavior of the Syrian regime over the past five years by much of the world community (with clearly some notable exceptions such as Russia). A global human rights regime that ultimately relies on the state for much of the implementation, protection and enforcement of rights in a world of state sovereignty over peoples and territory will continue to contain this important impediment to fulfillment. However, as we have also seen, the development of new standards, norms and the growth of international law have also continued to chip away at the abilities of states to ignore human rights challenges.

This is further illustrated by the examination by Hudson of the consequences for human rights of a state-initiated feminist foreign policy embracing the idea that human rights and national security can coexist and understanding that women's empowerment, women's voice and women's security are the key to implementation. Hudson traces the development of the rights focus, highlighting the June 1993 UN World Conference on Human Rights in Vienna, the role of Hillary Clinton at the Beijing World Conference on Women in 1995 where she proclaimed "Women's rights are human rights and human rights are women's rights" and the October 2000 UN Security Council Resolution 1325 which defined women not only as passive recipients of aid or justice, but also as *agents* integral to peace, stability and security.

Hudson highlights Hillary Clinton's appointment as Secretary of State in 2009 and her partnership with Barack Obama in expanding the attention to women's rights. Clinton fostered institutional changes within the State Department for addressing women's rights. These changes included expanding the role, reporting structure and securing a tenfold funding increase for OGWI, the Office of Global Women's Issues. Nonetheless, despite Clinton's achievements, which also included creating a US National Action Plan for Women Peace and Security with five primary areas of concern and corresponding specific outcome measures, Hudson closes on a much more pessimistic note, arguing that "lack of political will at both high and low levels, coupled with paralysing moral and ideological quandaries, have greatly hindered effective FFSP development," and the continuing difficulty of depending on states consistently to foster the expansion of human rights.

As each of these chapters demonstrates, the concept, challenges and implementation of human rights are expanding. The expansion is often slow, and progress toward implementation is often uneven both in scope and depth of fulfillment and with continued inadequacies and contradictions. Through the contributors' examinations of the potential, limitations and implications of the unexpected ways rights expand, human rights advocates and activists may glean some ideas for building upon some of these past successes and seize opportunities when they are presented.

Clearly, expanding rights is a dynamic process, not a static goal or model. As our investigations have shown, the process may empower new and different actors, may cumulate, complement or compete with prior practices, involve new and exciting models of mobilization, as well as new forms of backlash-or reinforce old forms. We have seen that the fulfillment of rights is much broader than compliance, and even the subset of enforcement via states and international institutions often follows an indirect path. Across cases, we have seen that the advocates for rights are not necessarily or only human rights NGOs, especially in economic, social and cultural rights (ECSR). This insight opens up new pathways for thinking about mobilization for rights expansion as at the same time it complicates our understanding of how the process for expanding rights "works." A lesson that may be drawn is that the ability of actors to create or reframe the concept of rights is often key to the mobilization of new actors and coalitions and the bridging of political conflicts.

As the contributors make clear, human rights do not exist or expand in a vacuum. The development, protection, implementation and expansion of human rights continually encounters backlash, resistance, counterframes or silences, and this is a critical determinant of the success of maintaining and expanding rights. In more successful cases, bridging frames and coalitions overcome some of the resistance (Baer, Tsutsui, Ayoub and Hudson). In others, structurally embedded challenges exert a continuing drag on rights expansion (Gómez Isa, Brysk and Howard-Hassmann). As always, we will continue to need to investigate how these new expansions both leverage and further interact with the shifting power relations of globalization and the opportunities for expansion and contraction that they create. While much is uncertain, we may be confident that our conceptions of, expectations for and movement toward expanding rights will continue unabated.

REFERENCES

Brysk, Alison (2013). *Speaking Rights to Power: Constructing Political Will.* Oxford: Oxford University Press.

Hertel, Shareen (2015). "Hungry for Justice: Social Mobilization on the Right to Food in India," *Development and Change* **46** (1), 72–94.

Power, Samantha (2016). Statement on the Conviction by the ICC of Jean-Pierre Bemba Gombo of War Crimes and Crimes Against Humanity, 21 March.

Index